Typographic Design: Form and Communication

Third Edition

"The whole duty of typography,
as with calligraphy,
is to communicate to the imagination,
without loss by the way,
the thought or image
intended to be communicated
by the Author."

Thomas James Cobden-Sanderson

Saint Barbara. Polychromed
walnut sculpture, fifteenth-
century German or French.
The Virginia Museum of
Fine Arts.

Typographic Design:
Form and Communication

Third Edition

Rob Carter

Ben Day

Philip Meggs

JOHN WILEY & SONS, INC.

For Akira Ouchi: designer, teacher, and friend

Introduction

Typography has undergone continuous change over the past four decades. It is the authors' intention to provide a concise yet comprehensive overview of the fundamental information necessary for effective typographic-design practice. A knowledge of form and communication encompasses a range of subjects, including our typographic heritage, letterform anatomy, visual organization, and the interface between form and meaning.

In addition to these fundamentals, this volume presents other topics critical to informed design practice. Recent research provides the designer with an expanded awareness of legibility factors, enabling increased communicative clarity. Technological complexity requires comprehension of earlier and current typesetting processes, for both affect the language of typography. Theoretical and structural problem-solving approaches, evolved by design educators, reveal underlying concepts. Case studies in applied problem solving demonstrate a knowledge of typographic form and communication. An understanding of typographic classification and form subtlety is gained from the study of type specimens.

Through the seven chapters of this book, the authors share a compilation of information and examples with practitioners and students. It yields both insights and inspiration, bringing order to the complex and diversified subject of typographic design.

Contents

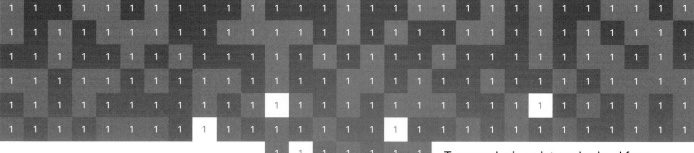

Typography is an intensely visual form of communication. Because this visible language communicates thoughts and information through human sight, its history is presented here in chronological visual form on four timelines. This evolution is shown in the context of world events, architectural development, and art history.

The first timeline predates typography. It begins with the invention of writing over five thousand years ago and ends with the invention of movable type in Europe during the middle of the fifteenth century. The second timeline covers the long era of the handpress and handset metal types. This period, from Gutenberg's invention of movable type to the end of the eighteenth century, lasted about three hundred and fifty years. In the third timeline, the Industrial Revolution and nineteenth century, are revealed as an era of technological innovation and an outpouring of new typographic forms. The fourth timeline begins with the year 1900 and covers the twentieth century, when type was shaped by the aesthetic concerns of modernism, the need for functional communication, and technological progress. In the late twentieth century, the digital revolution in typography occurred, followed by the dawning of a new century and millennium.

From the origins of writing to Gutenberg's invention of movable type: 3150 B.C.–A.D. 1450

Note: Picture credits and further descriptive information for timeline illustrations start on page 302.

1.
c. 3150 B.C.: The earliest written documents are impressed clay tablets from Sumer. The signs represent clay tokens, which were used for record keeping before the invention of writing.

2.
c. 3000 B.C.: Cuneiform, a very early writing system, consisting of wedge-shaped marks on clay tablets, was invented by the Sumerians.

2500 B.C.: Egyptians begin to make papyrus, a new writing material derived from the stems of the papyrus plant.

3.
c. 2600 B.C.: Completion of the pyramids at Giza, Egypt.

4.
c. 2400 B.C.: False-door stele inscribed with hieroglyphic writing, from Old Kingdom Egypt.

5.
c. 2100 B.C.: Cuneiform tablet listing expenditures of grain and animals.

6.
c. 1800–1400 B.C.: Stonehenge, a megalithic monument of thirty-foot-tall stones set into circular patterns.

7.
c. 1570–1349 B.C.: Polychromed wood sculpture from New Kingdom Egypt, with hieroglyphic inscriptions.

8.
c. 1450 B.C.: Detail, *The Book of the Dead* of Tuthmosis III, hieroglyphic writing on papyrus.

c. 3150 B.C.

1.

5.

7.

2.

3.

4.

6.

9.

c. 1500 B.C.: The twenty-two characters of the Phoenician alphabet.

c. 800 B.C.: Homer writes the *Iliad* and *Odyssey*.

540 B.C.: The first public library is established in Athens, Greece.

10.

389 B.C.: Inscription in the Phoenician alphabet on a fragment of a marble bowl.

11.

Fourth century B.C.: Greek manuscript writing.

12.

448–432 B.C.: The Parthenon, temple of the goddess Athena, on the Acropolis in Athens, Greece.

13.

414–413 B.C.: Fragment of a Greek record of sale, carved on stone.

c. 160 B.C.: Parchment, a new writing material made from animal skins, is developed in the Greek state of Pergamum.

44 B.C.: Julius Caesar is murdered.

14.

c. 50 B C.–A.D. 500: Roman square capitals (*capitalis quadrata*) were carefully written with a flat pen.

c. A.D. 33: Crucifixion of Christ.

15.

c. 79: Brush writing from a wall at Pompeii, preserved by the volcanic eruption of Vesuvius.

105: Ts'ai Lun invents paper in China.

150: The Roman codex, with folded pages, begins to be used alongside the rolled scroll.

16.

c. 100–600: Roman rustic writing (*capitalis rustica*) conserved space by using more condensed letters written with a flat pen held in an almost vertical position.

c. 1500 B.C.

8.

9.

JE EI PIAITENAESE
·EHBANNE⌐NΓO
AΞOYΣIMΠYPOΣ⊿EA

11.

12.

13.

MARTISQ·DOLO

14.

M·SEX·H

15.

CONNETIANTERIA
SINMANIBUSVESTRI
VLTROASIAMMAGNO

16.

10.

17.

118–25: The Pantheon, Rome.

18.

Undated: The fluid gestural quality, harmonious proportions, and beautiful forms of Roman writing are effectively translated into the permanent stone carving of monumental capitals *(capitalis monumentalis).*

19.

312–315: Arch of Constantine, Rome. Carved into marble, monumental Roman capitals survived the thousand-year Dark Ages.

325: Emperor Constantine adopts Christianity as the state religion of the Roman Empire.

c. 400–1400: During the thousand-year medieval era, knowledge and learning are kept alive in the Christian monastery, where manuscript books are lettered in the scriptoria.

452: Attila the Hun invades and ravages northern Italy.

476: Emperor Romulus Augustulus, last ruler of the western Roman Empire, is deposed by the Ostrogoths.

20.

533–49: Church of Sant' Apollinare in Classe, Ravenna.

21.

Third–sixth centuries: Uncials are rounded, freely drawn majuscule letters, first used by the Greeks as early as the third century B.C.

22.

Third–ninth centuries: Half-uncials, a lettering style of the Christian Church, introduces pronounced ascenders and descenders.

23.

Sixth–ninth centuries: Insular majuscules, a formal style with exaggerated serifs, was developed by Irish monks from the half-uncials.

A.D. 118

17.

19.

18.

20.

musadquequamuisconsci mitatisnostraetrepidatio mur·tamenfideiæstuincit
21.

mortuaut scm
22.

magnum quod erit
23.

est quiautemsuperp
27.

732: The Battle of Tours ends the Muslim advance into Europe.

800: Charlemagne is crowned emperor of the Holy Roman Empire by Pope Leo III.

24.
c. 800: Portrait of Christ from *The Book of Kells,* a Celtic manuscript.

868: The earliest extant printed manuscript, the *Diamond Sutra,* is printed in China.

25.
Tenth century: High Cross at Kells, Meath County, Ireland.

26.
c. Eleventh century: Round tower on the Rock of Cashel, Tipperary County, Ireland, a lookout and refuge against Viking invaders.

27.
Eighth–twelfth centuries: Caroline minuscules became the standard throughout Europe after Charlemagne issued his reform decree of 796, calling for a uniform writing style.

1034: Pi Sheng invents movable type in China.

1096–1099: The First Crusade.

28.
1163–1250: Construction of Notre Dame Cathedral, Paris.

29.
Eleventh–twelfth centuries: Early Gothic lettering, a transitional style between Caroline minuscules and Textura, has an increased vertical emphasis.

30.
Twelfth century: Bronze and copper crucifix from northern Italy.

1215: The Magna Carta grants constitutional liberties in England.

31.
Thirteenth–fifteenth centuries: Gothic Textura Quadrata, or Textura, the late Gothic style with rigorous verticality and compressed forms.

1347–1351: First wave of the Black Death, a plague that decimates the European population.

32.
Thirteenth century: Byzantine School, *Madonna and Child on a Curved Throne.*

A.D. 732

32.

25.

26.

nostro qui sedet super thronum et agno. Et omnes angli stabant i circuitu throni z senderunt z adora uerunt deum dicentes. amen. Benedictio z claritas z sapientia z gratiarum actio. honor z uirtus z fortitudo deo nostro in secula seculorum. amen

31.

early gothic

29.

24.

28.

30.

5

33.
Thirteenth–fifteenth centuries: Rotunda, a more rounded Gothic letter, flourished in southern Europe.

34.
Fourteenth century: Lippo Memmi, *Saint John the Baptist*.

35.
1420–36: Filippo Brunelleschi, Dome of Florence Cathedral.

36.
1431: Jeanne d'Arc is burned at the stake.

36.
Fifteenth century: First page of a block-book, *Apocalypse*. Woodblock printing probably appeared in Europe before 1400.

37.
1440–45: Fra Filippo Lippi, *Madonna and Child*.

c. 1450: Johann Gutenberg invents movable type in Mainz, Germany.

38.
c. 1450–55: Page from Gutenberg's 42-line Bible, the first European typographic book.

39.
Woodblock print of the hand-printing press, with compositors setting type from a typecase in the background.

40.
The cathedral in the medieval city of Mainz, Germany.

c. 1200

34.

37.

35.

36.

Rotunda

33.

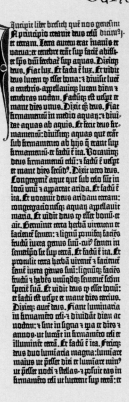

38.

39.

40.

Typography from Gutenberg to the nineteenth century: A.D. 1450–1800

The humanist philosophy that flowered during the Renaissance embraced the study of classical literature, a belief in human dignity and worth, a spirit of individualism, and a shift from religious to secular concerns.

40.
1450–1500: Books printed in the first half century of typographic printing are called Incunabula.

41.
1465: Sweynheym and Pannartz, the first type designed in Italy. It had some Roman features.

42.
1467: Sweynheym and Pannartz, the first Roman-style type, influenced by Roman inscriptional capitals and manuscripts written in Caroline minuscules.

43.
1470: Nicolas Jenson, early Venetian roman typeface.

44.
1475: William Caxton, typography from the first book printed in the English language.

45.
c. 1485: Filippino Lippi, *Portrait of a Youth*.

46.
1486: Erhard Ratdolt, the earliest known specimen sheet of printing types.

1492: Christopher Columbus lands in America.

47.
c. 1494: Scholar and printer Aldus Manutius established the Aldine Press in Venice to publish works by the great Greek and Roman thinkers.

48.
1495: Francesco Griffo (punch cutter for Aldus Manutius), roman type first used in *De aetna* by Pietro Bembo.

1450

bat ille ihesus: q quom pmu auses uocaret moises figura psentiens iussit eu
ihesum uocari: ut dux militie delectus esset aduersus amalech qui oppug-
nabant filios israhel: et aduersariu debellaret p nois figuram: et populu m

41.

esse sensum semitas queritur. tanq illi ad cogitandum rheda &
quadrigis opus eet. Democritus quasi in puteo quodam sic alto
ut fundussit nullus: ueritatem iacere demersam nimirum stulte

42.

ab omnipotenti deo missus deus uerbum quasi lucis isi
cunctis annuciat. Non hinc aut alrunde: sed undiq; cun
ad deum uerum: græcos simul et barbaros omnem sexu

43.

In the tyme of þ troublous world/ and of the
sions Beyng and reygnyng as well in the rop
englond and fraunce as in all other places vn

44.

45.

47.

46.

lud admirari ,quod uulgus solet: magnu
esse scilicet tantas flammas ,tam immen
sos ignes post hominum memoriam sem

48.

7

49.
1501: Francesco Griffo, the first italic typeface, based on chancery script handwriting.

50.
Home of Albrecht Dürer, Nuremberg, Germany.

51.
Woodblock initial by Geoffroy Tory, who returned to France from study in Italy in 1505, inspired by roman letterforms and Renaissance design ideals.

1517: Martin Luther posts his ninety-five theses on the door of Wittenberg Palace Church, launching the Reformation.

52.
1523: Lodovico Arrighi, an Italian writing master, introduces his formal chancery italic type.

53.
1525: Albrecht Dürer, construction of the letter *B*.

54.
1529: Geoffroy Tory, construction of the letter *B*.

55.
1519–47: Pierre Nepveu, Chateau of Chambord, France.

56.
c. 1480–1561: Claude Garamond, outstanding designer of Old Style typefaces during the French Renaissance.

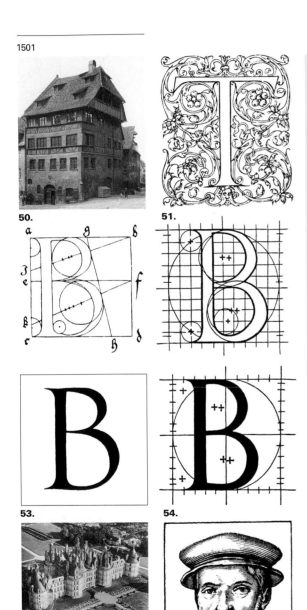

1501

50.

51.

53.

54.

55.

Claude Garamont.

56.

49.

P.O.N·IN·PRIMVM·GEORGICORVM,
ARGVMENTVM·

Quid faciat lætas segetes, quæ sydera seruet
Agricola, ut facilem terram proscindat aratris,
Semina quo iacienda modo, cultusq; locorum
E docuit, messes magno olim fœnore reddi.

P.V·M·GEORGICORVM LIBER PRI
MVS AD MOECENATEM·

Vid faciat lætas segetes, quo sydere
terram,
q   Vertere Mœcenas, ulmisq; adiun
gere uites,
Conueniat, quæ cura boum, quis
cultus habendo
Sit pecori, atq; apibus quanta experientia parcis,
Hinc canere incipiam.   Vos o clarissima mundi
Lumina, labentem cœlo quæ ducitis annum
Liber, et almâ Ceres, uestro si munere tellus
Chaoniâm pingui glandem mutauit arista,
Poculaq; inuentis Acheloia miscuit uuis,
Et uos agrestum præsentia numina Fauni,
Ferte simul, Fauniq; pedem, Dryadesq; puellæ,
Munera uestra cano, tuq; o cui prima frementem
Fudit equum magno tellus percussa tridenti
Neptune, et cultor nemorum, cui pinguia Cææ
Tercentum niuei tondent dumeta iuuenci,
Ipse nemus liquens patrium, saltusq; Licæi
c

Dele uarie sorti de littere poi, che in questo Tratta-
tello trouerai se io ti uolessi ad una per una descriuere **52.**

57.

c. 1540: Titian, *Portrait of Cardinal Pietro Bembo.*

1543: Copernicus publishes his theory of the heliocentric solar system.

58.

1544: Simone de Colines, title page with woodcut border.

59.

1546: Jacques Kerver, typography, illustration, and decorative initials, which were combined into a rare elegance during the French Renaissance.

60.

After 1577: El Greco, *Saint Martin and the Beggar.*

1582: Pope Gregory XIII initiates the Gregorian Calendar, which is still in use.

1584: Sir Walter Raleigh discovers and annexes Virginia.

61.

1595: Johann Theodor de Bry, illustrative initial *E.*

1603: Shakespeare writes *Hamlet.*

62.

1607: Carlo Maderna, facade of St. Peter's, the Vatican.

1609: Regular weekly newspapers appear in Strasbourg, Germany.

63.

1621: Jean Jannon, typefaces upon which twentieth-century Garamonds are based.

64.

1628: The Vatican Press, specimen of roman capitals.

c. 1540

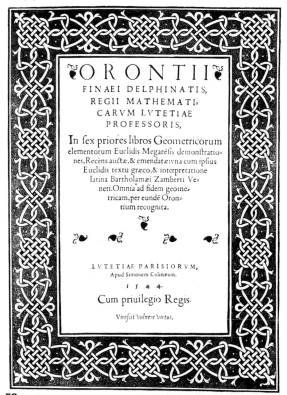

58.

60.

57.

FRANCISCVS

64.

59.

61.

62.

La crainte de l'Eternel eſt le chef de ſcience: mais les fols meſpriſent ſapiéce &

63.

65.
1632–43: The Taj Mahal, India.
66.
c. 1630: Sir Anthony van Dyck, portrait of *Henri II de Lorraine*.

1639: The first printing press in the British Colonies is established in Massachusetts.

1657: First fountain pen is manufactured, in Paris.
67.
c. 1664: Jan Vermeer, *Woman Holding a Balance*.

1666: The great fire of London.

1667: Milton publishes *Paradise Lost*.

68.
c. 1670: Christoffel van Dyck, Dutch Old Style type.

1686: Sir Isaac Newton sets forth his law of gravity.
69.
1675–1710: Sir Christopher Wren, St. Paul's Cathedral, London.

During the eighteenth century, type design went through a gradual transition from Old Style to Modern Style fonts designed late in the century.

1700: The emergence of the Rococo Style.
70.
1702: Philippe Grandjean (punch cutter), Romain du Roi, the first transitional face.

71.
1709: Matthaus Poppelmann, Zwinger Palace, Dresden.

1709: England adopts the first modern copyright law.
72.
1720: William Caslon, Caslon Old Style types, which from this date were used throughout the British Empire.

1632

Ad me profectam esse aiebant. D. quid Quæso, igitur commorabare, ubi id

68.

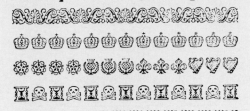
ABCDEFGHIKLMN
OPQRSTUVWXYZJ
Quousque tandem abutere, Catilina, patientia nostra? qu
Quousque tandem abutere, Catilina, patientia nostra? quam-

65.

67.

69.

This new Foundery was begun in the Year 1720, and finish'd 1763; and will (with God's leave) be carried on, improved, and inlarged, by WILLIAM CASLON and Son, Letter-Founders in LONDON.

66.

73.

72.

sa doctrine et de ses lois. Après, il nous fait voir tous les hommes renfermés en un seul homme, et sa femme même tirée de lui ; la concorde des mariages et la

70.

71.

73.
1722: Castletown, near Dublin, Ireland.

1738: First spinning machines are patented in England.

74.
1744: Benjamin Franklin, title page using Caslon type.

75.
1750: François Boucher, *The Love Letter* (detail).

76.
1750s: John Baskerville creates extraordinary transitional typefaces.

77.
1765: Thomas Cottrell introduces display types two inches tall (shown actual size).

78.
1768: Pierre Simon Fournier le Jeune, ornamented types.

79.
1773: Johann David Steingruber, letter *A* from *Architectonishes Alphabet*.

80.
1774: John Holt, broadside of the American revolutionary era, using Caslon type.

1775: James Watt constructs the first efficient steam engine.

1776: American Declaration of Independence is signed.

81.
1784: François Ambroise Didot, the first true Modern Style typeface.

1789: The fall of the Bastille launches the French Revolution.

82.
1791: Giambattista Bodoni, Modern Style typefaces of geometric construction, with hairline serifs.

1791: American Bill of Rights.

guarantees freedoms of religion, speech, and the press.

1793: French King Louis XVI and Marie Antoinette are sent to the guillotine.

1796: Aloys Senefelder invents lithography.

1799: Nicolas-Louis Robert invents the papermaking machine.

1722

M. T. CICERO's
CATO MAJOR,
OR HIS
DISCOURSE
OF
OLD-AGE:
With Explanatory NOTES.

PHILADELPHIA:
Printed and Sold by B. FRANKLIN,
MDCCXLIV.

74.

LA
DIVINA
COMMEDIA
DI
DANTE ALIGHIERI
CON
ILLUSTRAZIONI

TOMO I.

PISA
DALLA TIPOGRAFIA
DELLA SOCIETÀ LETTERARIA
MDCCCIV.

82.

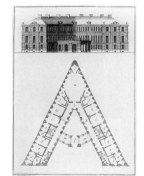
75.

76.

C

77.

HISTOIRE
DE
LOUIS DE BOURBON,
SECOND DU NOM,
*PRINCE
DE CONDÉ,*
PREMIER PRINCE DU SANG,
Surnommé *LE GRAND.*

LIVRE PREMIER.
1621-1643.

LOUIS DE BOURBON, fecond du nom, naquit à Paris 1621. le 7 Septembre 1621 ; il fut titré *Duc d'Enguien* , nom heureux qui rappelloit la mémoire du vain-

78.

79.

To the PUBLICK.
NEW-YORK, OCTOBER 5, 1774.

80.

lumes in-4° sur papier-vélin de la fabrique de messieurs Matthieu Johannot pere et fils, d'Annonai, premiers fabricants de cette sorte de papiers en

81.

The nineteenth century and the Industrial Revolution: A.D. 1800–1899

The Industrial Revolution had a dramatic impact upon typography and the graphic arts. New technology radically altered printing, and designers responded with an outpouring of new forms and images.

83.
c. 1803: Robert Thorne designs the first Fat Face.

1804: Napoleon Bonaparte crowned Emperor of France.

1808: Beethoven composes his Fifth Symphony.
84.
1812: Jacques-Louis David, *Napoleon in His Study.*

1814: Friedrich Koenig invents the steam-powered printing press.

85.
1815: Vincent Figgins shows the first Egyptian (slab-serif) typefaces.
86.
1815: Vincent Figgins shows the earliest shaded type.

87.
1816: William Caslon IV introduces the first sans serif type.
88.
1818: Page from *Manuale Tipographico,* which presented the lifework of Giambattista Bodoni.
89.
1821: Robert Thorne, Tuscan styles with splayed serifs.

1800

R. THORNE

85.

ABCDEFGHIJK

86.

ABCDEFGHIKM

87.

89.

Manchester

{ ❧ PARANGONE ❧ }

Quousque tandem abutêre, Catilina, patientiâ nostrâ? quamdiu etiam furor iste tuus nos eludet? quem ad finem sese effrenata jactabit audacia? nihilne te nocturnum præsidium Palatii, nihil urbis vigiliæ, nihil timor populi, nihil concursus bonorum omnium, nihil hic munitissimus habendi se-

MARCUS TULL. CICERO
ORATOR ATQUE PHILOSOPHUS.

CHERASCO

83.   84.   88.   90.

90.

1822: Thomas Jefferson, Rotunda of the University of Virginia in the neoclassical style based on Greek and Roman architecture.

1822: Joseph Niepce produces the first photographic printing plate.

91.

c. 1826: Bower, Bacon and Bower, early reversed type entitled White.

1826: Joseph Niepce takes the first photograph from nature.

92.

1827: Darius Wells invents the mechanical router, making the manufacture of large display wood types possible.

93.

1833: Vincent Figgins introduces outline types.

94.

1836: Davy and Berry, poster printed with wood type.

1830s–80s: Wood-type posters and broadsides flourished in America and Europe.

95.

1836: Vincent Figgins, perspective type.

96.

1837: Handbill set in Fat Face.

1837: Victoria crowned queen of England.

1822

STOCKS

91.

THEATRE-ROYAL, NORWICH.

FOR THE BENEFIT OF

R. Battley, FRUITERER.

On THURSDAY, 12th May, 1836, Will be performed the POPULAR PLAY, of The

CASTLE SPECTRE.

Earl Osmond....Mr. MADDOCKS
Reginald .....Mr. HAMERTON | Kenric....Mr. G. SMITH
Earl Percy.....Mr. NICHOLS | Saib.....Mr. HARRISON
Father Philip..Mr. GRAY | Muley....Mr. BRYAN
Motley ......Mr. GILL | Hassan....Mr. NANTZ

Angela ....Mrs. G. SMITH
Alice.....Mrs. WATKINSON | Evelina ....Miss HONEY.

END OF THE PLAY,

A COMIC SONG

BY MR. MARTIN.

To conclude with the NAUTICAL DRAMA, of The

PILOT, OR, A STORM AT SEA!

The Pilot, Mr. MADDOCKS
Barnstable, Mr. G. SMITH—Captain Boroughcliffe, (a regular Yankee), Mr. GILL
Long Tom Coffin, Mr. NANTZ
Captain of the Alacrity, Mr. HAMERTON—Colonel Howard Mr. GRAY
Lieutenant Griffith, Mr. TAYLOR—Serjeant Drill, Mr. NICHOLS.
Sailors, Soldiers, &c.
Kate Plowden, Mrs. PLUMER—Cecilia, Miss HONEY
Irish Woman, Mrs. WATKINSON.

DAVY & BERRY, PRINTERS, ALBION OFFICE.

94.

HOUSEHOLD FURNITURE, PLATE, CHINA-WARE, JEWELS, WATCHES

93.

DARIUS WELLS.

92.

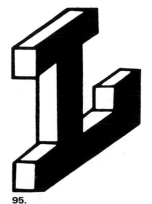

95.

96.

Working Men, Attention!!

Globe Office
Saturday, November 20. 1837

It is your imperious duty to drop your *Hammers and Sledges!* one and all, to your post repair, *THIS AFTERNOON,* at *FIVE* o'clock P. M. and attend the

GREAT MEETING

called by the papers of this morning, to be held at the CITY HALL, then and there to co-operate with such as have the GREAT GOOD OF ALL THEIR *FELLOW CITIZENS* at Heart. Your liberty! yea, your *LABOUR!!* is the subject of the call: who that values the services of HEROES of the *Revolution* whose blood achieved our Independence as a Nation, will for a moment doubt he owes a few hours this afternoon to his wife and children?

HANCOCK.

97.

c. 1840–52: Sir Charles Barry and A. W. N. Pugin, Houses of Parliament, inspiration for the Gothic Revival.

98.

c. 1841: Wood and Sharwoods, ornamental type.

During the 1840s, ornamented type becomes increasingly important.

99.

1845: Robert Besley, the first Clarendon style.

1848: The California gold rush begins.

1851: Joseph Paxton designs the Crystal Palace.

100.

1853: Handbill combining Egyptian, outline, and decorative types.

101.

1854: Broadside using elongated Fat Face fonts.

1854: The United States makes its first treaty with Japan.

1856: Sir Henry Bessemer develops process for converting iron to steel.

102.

1859: William H. Page and Company, Ornamented Clarendons.

1859: Charles Darwin publishes *Origin of Species by Means of Natural Selection.*

103.

1860: *Charleston Mercury,* broadsheet announcing the dissolution of the Union.

c. 1840

97.

ODD-FELLOWS' HALL.
On Wednesday, Feb. 16, 1853.

AN EVENING

WITH THE

CHRISTY

MINSTRELS.

MR. WARDEN

RESPECTFULLY announces a Series of his Popular Musical Entertainments at the above place.
Dispensing with the use of burnt cork, and the vulgar burlesque of Ethiopian character, (which many suppose render the music effective!) Mr. Warden will sing the Pathetic and Humorous Songs of the Christy Minstrels in a style unobjectionable and pleasing to all.

ADMITTANCE:
TWENTY-FIVE CENTS.

☞ TURN OVER.

100.

audacia tua? nihilne te noc
dium palatii, nihil urbis vigi

99.

PRES'T. MADISON'S LIBRARY,

AT AUCTION.

AT Orange Court House Virginia, on Tuesday the 27th day of June, prox., being the day after the County Court of Orange in that month, I shall sell at public auction, to the highest bidder, that part of the Library of the late James Madison, which, in a recent division of his books with the University of Virginia, fell to the share of my testator; and at the same time I will sell other books, the property of my said testator. In all there are some

SEVEN OR EIGHT HUNDRED VOLUMES,

among which are many very rare and desirable works, some in Greek, some in Latin, numerous others in French, and yet more in English, in almost all the departments of Literature; not a few of them being in this manner exposed to sale only because the University possessed already copies of the same editions. The sale beginning on the day above mentioned, will be continued from day to day till all the books shall have been sold, on the following terms:

Cash will be required of each purchaser whose aggregate purchases shall amount to no more than Five dollars; those whose purchases shall exceed that amount, will have the privilege either to pay the cash or to give bond with approved security, bearing interest from the date, and payable six months thereafter.

ELHANON ROW, Administrator,
with the will annexed of John P. Todd, dec'd.

May 30, 1854.

101.

98.

102.

1861–65: American Civil War.

1863: Abraham Lincoln signs the Emancipation Proclamation.

104.

c. 1865: Honoré Daumier: *The Third-Class Carriage*.

1866: The first successful transatlantic cable is laid.

1867: Alfred Nobel invents dynamite.

1867: Christopher Sholes constructs the first practical typewriter.

105.

1868: Currier and Ives, *American Homestead Winter*.

106.

c. 1875: J. Ottmann, chromolithographic card for Mrs. Winslow's Soothing Syrup.

1876: Alexander Graham Bell invents the telephone.

1877: Thomas Edison invents the phonograph.

1879: Thomas Edison invents the electric lightbulb.

107.

1883: The Brooklyn Bridge is opened to traffic.

1883: William Jenney designs the first skyscraper, a ten-story metal frame building in Chicago.

1885: Maverick and Wissinger, engraved business card.

109.

c. 1880s: Lettering printed by chromolithography.

110.

1886: Ottmar Mergenthaler invents the Linotype, the first keyboard typesetting machine.

1861

105.

107.

106.

109.

108.

110.

103.

104.

111.
1887: Advertisement for Estey Organs.

1887: Tolbert Lanston invents the monotype.

112.
1889: Alexandre Gustave Eiffel, the Eiffel Tower.

113.
c. 1890s: Coca-Cola syrup jug.

114.
1892: Paul Gauguin, *By the Sea.*

115.
William Morris' typeface designs: 1890, Golden; 1892, Troy; 1893, Chaucer.

116.
1891–98: William Morris' Kelmscott Press launches a revival of printing and typography.

117.
1892: William Morris, page from *News from Nowhere.*

1887

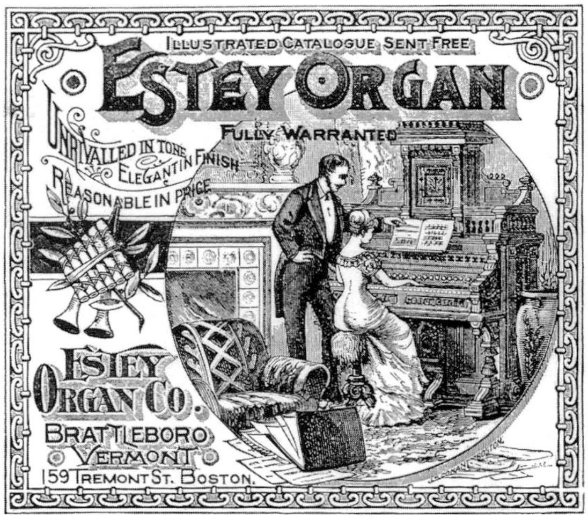

111.

112.

This is the Golden type.
This is the Troy type.
This is the Chaucer type.

115.

116.

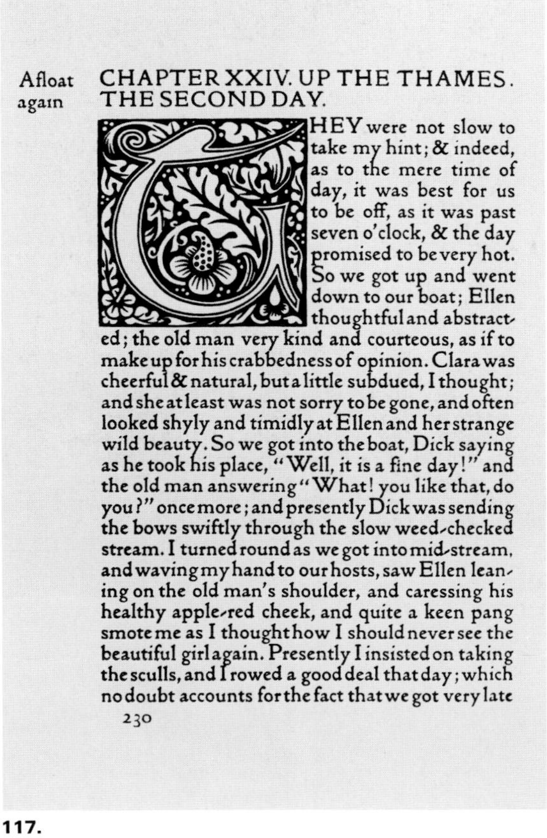

Afloat again

CHAPTER XXIV. UP THE THAMES. THE SECOND DAY.

THEY were not slow to take my hint; & indeed, as to the mere time of day, it was best for us to be off, as it was past seven o'clock, & the day promised to be very hot. So we got up and went down to our boat; Ellen thoughtful and abstracted; the old man very kind and courteous, as if to make up for his crabbedness of opinion. Clara was cheerful & natural, but a little subdued, I thought; and she at least was not sorry to be gone, and often looked shyly and timidly at Ellen and her strange wild beauty. So we got into the boat, Dick saying as he took his place, "Well, it is a fine day!" and the old man answering "What! you like that, do you?" once more; and presently Dick was sending the bows swiftly through the slow weed-checked stream. I turned round as we got into mid-stream, and waving my hand to our hosts, saw Ellen leaning on the old man's shoulder, and caressing his healthy apple-red cheek, and quite a keen pang smote me as I thought how I should never see the beautiful girl again. Presently I insisted on taking the sculls, and I rowed a good deal that day; which no doubt accounts for the fact that we got very late

230

114.

113.

117.

118.

1893: Henri van de Velde, title page for *Van Nu en Straks.*

1895: The Lumiére brothers give the first motion-picture presentation.

119.

1897: Edmond Deman, title page in the curvilinear Art Nouveau style.

120.

1890s–1940s: Inspired by Kelmscott, Americans Frederick Goudy and Bruce Rogers bring renewed excellence to book and typeface design.

121.

1897: Will Bradley, title page in his "Chap Book" style, reviving Caslon type and colonial woodcut techniques.

1898: Zeppelin invents his airship.

122.

1899: Josef Hoffmann, catalogue cover for a Vienna Secession exhibition.

123.

1898–1902: Hector Guimard, entrance to Paris Metro Station.

1893

118.

122.

FRED·W·GOUDY
DESIGNING
940 FINE ARTS BUILDING
BOOK AND CATALOGUE COVERS, BORDERS,
INITIAL LETTERS, ADVERTISEMENTS. Etc.
⚜ ⚜ ⚜ ⚜ ⚜ ⚜ F. W. GOUDY, CHICAGO

120.

119.

A LADY OF QUALITY

Being a most curious, hitherto unknown history, as related by Mr. Isaac Bickerstaff but not presented to the World of Fashion through the pages of *The Tatler*, and now for the first time written down *by* **Frances Hodgson Burnett**

New York: From the Publishing House of CHARLES SCRIBNER'S SONS, 153-157 Fifth Avenue. *MDCCCXCVII.*

121.

123.

Typography in the twentieth century: 1900–2000.

The twentieth century was a period of incredible ferment and change. Unprecedented advances in science and technology, and revolutionary developments in art and design have left their marks on typography.

124.
1900: Peter Behrens, dedication page from *Feste des Lebens und der Künst.*

1903: The Wright brothers succeed in the first powered flight.

1905: Einstein proposes his theory of relativity.

125.
1909: Filippo Marinetti founds Futurism, experimentation with typographic form and syntax.

126.
c. 1910: German sans-serif "block style."

127.
1913: Wassily Kandinsky, *Improvisation 31 (Sea Battle).*

1914–18: World War I.

c. 1915: Kasimir Malevich, Suprematist painting shown at the *0.10* group exhibition launching Suprematism.

128.
c. 1916: Bert Thomas, British war bonds poster.

1917–22: The Dada movement protests the war and conventional art.

129.
1917: John Heartfield, Dadaist advertisement.

130.
1917: Vilmos Huszar, De Stijl magazine cover.

1918: Czar Nicholas II and his family are executed.

131.
1919: Raoul Hausmann, Dada poem.

1900

124.

126.

125.

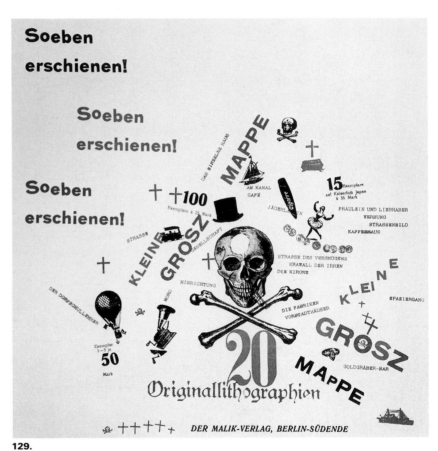

127.

129.

128.

130.

131.

1920: Women's suffrage is granted in the United States.

1920: Bolsheviks triumph in the Russian Revolution.

132.
1921–25: Piet Mondrian, *Diamond Painting in Red, Yellow, and Blue.*

133.
c. 1923: Alexander Rodchenko, Russian Constructivist poster.

1924: Surrealist manifesto.

134.
1924: Gerrit Rietveld, Schroeder house.

135.
1925: El Lissitzky, title page.

136.
1925: Herbert Bayer, universal alphabet.

137.
1925: Constantin Brancusi, *Bird in Space.*

138.
1925: Jan Tschichold, title page for his article "Elementary Typography."

139.
1926: Piet Zwart, advertisement.

1927: Charles Lindbergh makes the first solo Atlantic flight.

140.
1928: Piet Zwart, advertisement.

1920

132.

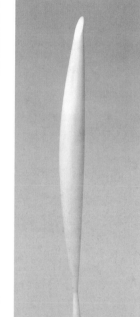

134.

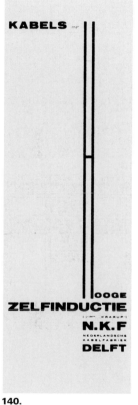

140.

133.

135.

138.

139.

bauhaus

136.

1929: The New York Stock Market collapses, and the Great Depression begins.
141.
1930: Paul Renner, prospectus for Futura.

142.
1930: Chrysler Building, an example of Art Deco decorative geometric style.
143.
1931: Max Bill, exhibition poster.
144.
c. 1932: Alexey Brodovitch, exhibition poster.

1933: Adolf Hitler becomes chancellor of Germany.
145.
1936: Walker Evans, photograph of sharecropper family.

1939: Germany invades Poland; World War II begins.
146.
1942: Jean Carlu, advertisement.
147.
1944: Max Bill, exhibition poster.

1945: Atomic bombs destroy Hiroshima and Nagasaki; World War II ends.
148.
1948: Paul Rand, title page.

1929

FUTURA
DIE
SICH DIE WELT
EROBERTE

MAPPE 2

141.

konkrete kunst

147.

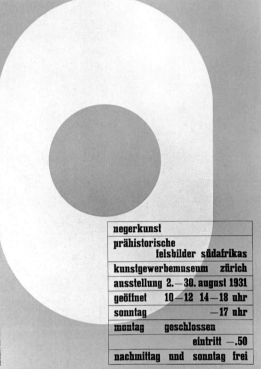

negerkunst
prähistorische felsbilder südafrikas
kunstgewerbemuseum zürich
ausstellung 2.—30. august 1931
geöffnet 10—12 14—18 uhr
sonntag —17 uhr
montag geschlossen
eintritt —.50
nachmittag und sonntag frei

143.

DESIGN FOR THE MACHINE
PENNSYLVANIA MUSEUM OF ART PHILA

144.

a
r
p

148.

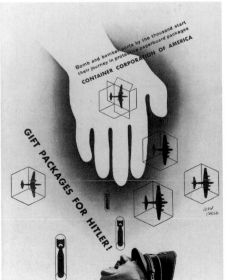
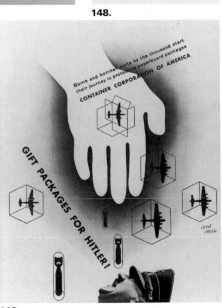

Bomb and bomber parts by the thousand start their journey in protective paperboard packages
CONTAINER CORPORATION OF AMERICA
GIFT PACKAGES FOR HITLER!

146.

145.

142.

20

149.
1948: Willem de Kooning, *Painting*.
150.
1950: Ladislav Sutnar, book cover.

1950: North Korea invades South Korea.

151.
1950–55: Le Corbusier, Notre Dame de Haut.

1952: School segregation is declared unconstitutional by the Supreme Court.

152.
1952: Henri Matisse, *Woman with Amphora and Pomegranates*.
153.
1955: Josef Muller-Brockmann, concert poster.
154.
1956: Saul Bass, advertisement.

155.
1956: Willem Sandberg, book cover.

1957: Russia launches Sputnik I, the first Earth satellite.

156.
1959: Saul Bass, film title.
157.
1959: Frank Lloyd Wright, the Guggenheim Museum, New York.
158.
1958: Carlo L. Vivarelli, magazine cover.

1948

149.

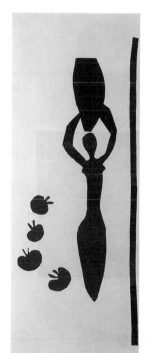

152.

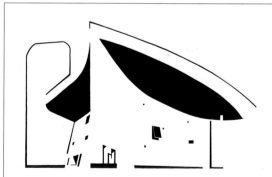

158.

151.

153.

155.

150.

157.

154.

156.

1959

159.

160.

DIVINE TO EAT, EASY TO MAKE, AND BEAUTIFUL TO LOOK ON: ELEGANT PARFAITS. THERE ARE TWO TYPES: THE FRENCH, WHICH IS A CREAMY, DELICATE, COOL (BUT NOT ICY) MIXTURE WITH A BASE OF SUGAR, EGGS, CREAM, FRUIT AND/OR FLAVORINGS; AND THE AMERICAN, MADE WITH COMMERCIAL ICE CREAMS OR SHERBETS OR BOTH WITH A SURPRISE INGREDIENT, SUCH AS FRUITS, CORDIALS, COGNAC, NUTS, SAUCES (SEE McCALL'S FINE SAUCE RECIPES ON PAGE 00). WITH AMERICAN PARFAITS, YOUR IMAGINATION CAN HAVE FREE REIN. WITH THE FRENCH, HOWEVER, YOU MUST FOLLOW RECIPE DIRECTIONS TO THE LETTER. PARFAIT MEANS, OF COURSE, PERFECT, AND WE CAN IMAGINE FEW MORE PERFECT DESSERTS, ESPECIALLY IF YOU WANT TO SHOW OFF. FOR THESE ARE TRULY SHOW-OFF RECIPES! FROM THE COOK'S STANDPOINT, THERE IS A REAL ADVANTAGE IN SERVING FROZEN DESSERTS. FOR THE OBVIOUS REASON, THEY MUST BE MADE WELL AHEAD AND REFRIGERATED. THUS, THE BIG DESSERT PROBLEM IS OUT OF THE WAY WHEN IT'S TIME TO PREPARE THE MAIN PART OF THE MEAL. AT FAR RIGHT, YOU SEE AN AMERICAN PARFAIT, VANILLA ICE CREAM LAYERED WITH PISTACHIO AND TOPPED WITH WAL-NUTS AND WHIPPED CREAM. THE STRAW-BERRY AND APRICOT PARFAITS ARE BOTH CLASSIC FRENCH. FOR THE RECIPES, TURN TO PAGE 00, WHERE YOU WILL FIND THE FRENCH AS WELL AS GOOD VARIATIONS OF THE QUICK AND POPULAR AMERICAN PARFAITS. THEN, PLAN A PARTY.

161.

ugh! 'ly?

Ugliness, like beauty, is in the eye of the beholder. It is a value imposed upon a thing which, properly used, might well be called beautiful. At S H & L we try to avoid misleading labels. Our business is to design for advertising. Typography is one of our essential tools. If what we do with it is effective, we don't care if it is called pretty, ugly, or pretty ugly. If you think as we do, we ought to get together. Call Herb Lubalin at Plaza 1-1250, where we take the ught out of ugly

ugh! 'ly?

163.

164.

165.

162.

"Oh my God
—we hit
a little girl."

The true story of M Company.
From Fort Dix to Vietnam.

167.

Filmsense

166.

168.
c. 1968: Seymour Chwast and Milton Glaser, poster.

169.
1968: R. Buckminster Fuller, American Pavilion, Montreal World's Fair.

170.
c. 1967: Symbol for the environmental movement.

171.
1969: First Moon walk.

172.
1972: Wolfgang Weingart, typographic interpretation of a poem.

173.
1974: Herb Lubalin, newspaper cover.

174.
1974: Cook and Shanosky, standard symbol signs.

1975: The Vietnam War ends.

175.
1976: American bicentennial, symbol design by Bruce Blackburn.

1968

168.

169.

170.

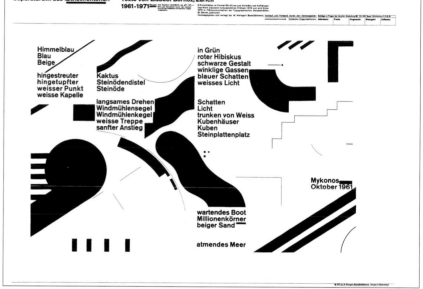

172.

171.

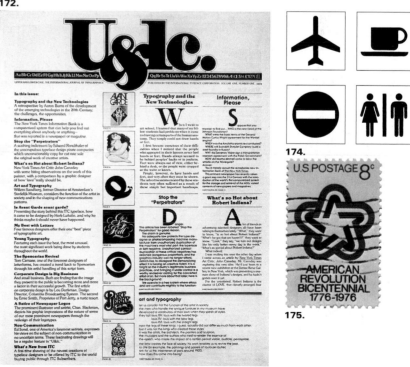

173.

174.

175.

176.
1977: Pompidou National Center of Arts and Culture, Paris.

177.
1977: Bill Bonnell, RyderTypes trademark.

178.
1978: Willi Kunz, poster design.

179.
1979: Richard Greenberg, film titles.

1979: Soviet troops invade Afganistan.

1980s: Digital typography and computer technology impact typographic design, leading to electronic page design by the end of the decade.

1981: Bitstream founded; first independent digital type foundry.

180.
Pat Gorman and Frank Olinsky, Manhattan Design, MTV logo.

181.
1983: Michael Graves, Portland, Oregon, city hall.

182.
1984: Warren Lehrer, page from *French Fries.*

1984: Apple Macintosh computer, first laser printer, and PageMaker page layout software are introduced.

183.
1985: Zuzana Licko, Emperor, early bitmapped typeface designs.

1986: Fontographer software makes possible high-resolution font design on desktop computers.

1988: Tiananmen Square massacre.

1977

176.

180.

181.

182.

Fredrich **Cantor**

178.

June 17
July 8
78

FOTO
492 Broome Street
New York, NY 10013

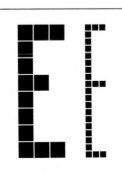

Emperor 8
Emperor 10
Emperor 15
Emperor 19

183.

184.
1990: David Carson, page from *Beach Culture.*

185.
1991: Ted Mader + Associates, book jacket.

Experimental digital typefaces:
186.
1990: Barry Deck, Template Gothic (Emigre).
187.
c. 1991: Jonathan Barnbrook, Exocet Heavy (Emigre).
188.
1993: Jonathan Hoefler, HTF Fetish No. 338.

1990: Reunification of Germany.

189.
1991: Erik Spiekermann, Meta (FontShop).

1991: Persian Gulf War.

1991: Fall of Communism in Russia; Apartheid ends in South Africa.

190.
1992: Robert Slimbach and Carol Twombley, Myriad, Adobe's first Multiple Master typeface.

191.
1992: Ron Kellum, Topix logo.
192.
1993: James Victore, Racism poster.
193.
1994: Netscape founded, early Web browser.

1990

184.

185.

186.

ABCDEFGHIJK

187.

ABCDEFGMOL

188.

EXCESSIVE?

189.

MetaMetaMeta**Meta**

M M M M M M M
M M M M M M M
M M M M M M M
M M M M M M M
M M M M M M M
M M M M M M M
M M M M M M M
M M M M M M M
M M M M M M M

190.

191.

193.

192.

194.
1994: Matthew Carter, Walker typeface with "snap-on" serifs.

195.
1995: Landor Associates, Xerox /The Document Company logo.

196.
1997: Frank Gehry, Guggenheim Museum, Bilbao, Spain.

1997: Dolly the sheep, first adult animal clone.

197.
1997: Paula Scher and Keith Daigle, book jacket.

Digital versions of classical typefaces:

198.
1989: Robert Slimback, Adobe Garamond.

199.
1994–95: Janice Fishman, Holly Goldsmith, Jim Parkinson, and Sumner Stone, ITC Bodoni.

200.
c. 1996: Zuzana Licko, Mrs. Eaves roman.

201.
1998: Neville Brody, conference poster.

A new century and millennium begin: 2000

202.
2001: Jennifer Sterling, calendar page (detail).

2001: Terrorists attack the World Trade Center towers and Pentagon.

1994

194.

196.

197.

201.

195.

198.

Adobe Garamond

199.

ITC Bodoni Roman

200.

Mrs. Eaves Roman

202.

Typographic design is a complex area of human activity, requiring a broad background for informed practice. This chapter explores the basic language of typography. Letterforms, the fundamental components of all typographic communications, are carefully examined. Nomenclature, measurement, and the nature of typographic font and family are presented.

The alphabet is a series of elemental visual signs in a fixed sequence, representing spoken sounds. Each letter signifies only one thing: its elementary sound or name. The twenty-six characters of our alphabet can be combined into thousands of words, creating a visual record of the spoken language. This is the magic of writing and typography, which have been called "thoughts-made-visible" and "frozen sounds."

1.
Strokes written with the reed
pen (top), and brush (middle),
and carved with a chisel
(bottom).

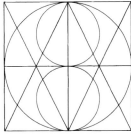

2.

3.
Capital and lowercase
letterform construction.

The four timelines in chapter one graphically present the evolution of letterforms and typographic design from the beginning of writing to the present. Our contemporary typographic forms have been forged by this historical evolution. Typography evolved from handwriting, which is created by making a series of marks by hand; therefore, the fundamental element constructing a letterform is the linear stroke. Each letter of our alphabet developed as a simple mark whose visual characteristics clearly separated it from all the others.

The marking properties of brush, reed pen, and stone engraver's chisel influenced the early form of the alphabet (Fig. **1**). The reed pen, used in ancient Rome and the medieval monastery, was held at an angle, called a cant, to the page. This produced a pattern of thick and thin strokes. Since the time of the ancient Greeks, capital letterforms have consisted of simple geometric forms based on the square, circle, and triangle. The basic shape of each capital letter can be extracted from the structure in Figure **2**, which is composed of a bisected square, a circle, a triangle, an inverted triangle, and two smaller circles.

The resulting vocabulary of forms, however, lacks several important attributes: optically adjusted proportions, expressive design properties, and maximum legibility and readability. The transition from rudimentary mark to letterforms with graphic clarity and precision is a matter of design.

Because early capital letters were cut into stone, these letters developed with a minimum number of curved lines, for curved strokes were difficult to cut (Fig. **3**). Lowercase letters evolved as reed-pen writing. Curved strokes could be written quickly and were used to reduce the number of strokes needed to write many characters.

The parts of letterforms
Over the centuries, a nomenclature has evolved that identifies the various components of individual letterforms. By learning this vocabulary, designers and typographers can develop a greater understanding and sensitivity to the visual harmony and complexity of the alphabet. The following list (Fig. **4**) identifies the major components of letterform construction. In medieval times, horizontal guidelines were drawn to contain and align each line of lettering. Today, letterforms and their parts are drawn on imaginary guidelines to bring uniformity to typography.

Baseline: An imaginary line upon which the base of each capital rests.

Capline: An imaginary line that runs along the tops of the capital letters.

Meanline: An imaginary line that establishes the height of the body of lowercase letters.

x-height: The distance from the baseline to the meanline. Typically, this is the height of lowercase letters and is most easily measured on the lowercase *x.*

All characters align *optically* on the baseline. The body height of lowercase characters align optically at the x-height, and the tops of capitals align optically along the capline. To achieve precise alignments, the typeface designer makes optical adjustments.

Apex: The peak of the triangle of an uppercase *A.*

Arm: A projecting horizontal stroke that is unattached on one or both ends, as in the letters *T* and *E.*

Ascender: A stroke on a lowercase letter that rises above the meanline.

Bowl: A curved stroke enclosing the counterform of a letter. An exception is the bottom form of the lowercase roman *g,* which is called a loop.

Counter: The negative space that is fully or partially enclosed by a letterform.

Crossbar: The horizontal stroke connecting two sides of the letterform (as in *e, A,* and *H*) or bisecting the main stroke (as in *f* and *t*).

Capline
Meanline
x-height
Baseline

Descender: A stroke on a lowercase letterform that falls below the baseline.

Ear: A small stroke that projects from the upper right side of the bowl of the lowercase roman *g.*

Eye: The enclosed part of the lowercase *e.*

Fillet: The contoured edge that connects the serif and stem in bracketed serifs. (Bracketed serifs are connected to the main stroke by this curved edge; unbracketed serifs connect to the main stroke with an abrupt angle without this contoured transition.)

Hairline: The thinnest stroke within a typeface that has strokes of varying weights.

Leg: The lower diagonal stroke on the letter *k.*

Link: The stroke that connects the bowl and the loop of a lowercase roman *g.*

Loop: See *Bowl.*

Serifs: Short strokes that extend from and at an angle to the upper and lower ends of the major strokes of a letterform.

Shoulder: A curved stroke projecting from a stem.

Spine: The central curved stroke of the letter *S.*

Spur: A projection – smaller than a serif – that reinforces the point at the end of a curved stroke, as in the letter *G.*

Stem: A major vertical or diagonal stroke in the letterform.

Stroke: Any of the linear elements within a letterform; originally, any mark or dash made by the movement of a pen or brush in writing.

Tail: A diagonal stroke or loop at the end of a letter, as in *R* or *j.*

Terminal: The end of any stroke that does not terminate with a serif.

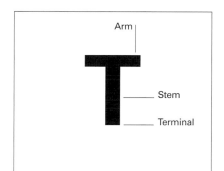

Arm
Stem
Terminal

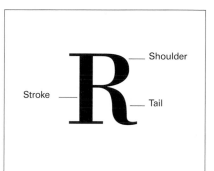

Shoulder
Stroke
Tail

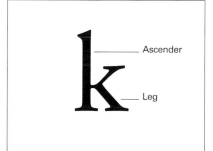

Ascender
Leg

Eye

Spine

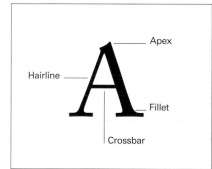

Apex
Hairline
Fillet
Crossbar

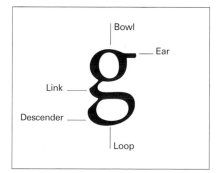

Bowl
Ear
Link
Descender
Loop

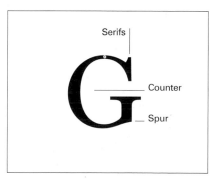

Serifs
Counter
Spur

4.

29

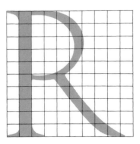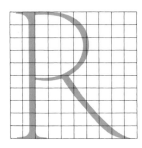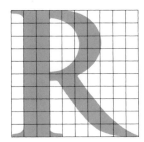

5.

1499 Old Style

1757 Baskerville

1793 Bodoni

1816 First sans serif

c. 1928 Ultra Bodoni

O

1957 Univers 55

6.

Proportions of the letterform

The proportions of the individual letterform are an important consideration in typography. Four major variables control letterform proportion and have considerable impact upon the visual appearance of a typeface: the ratio of letterform height to stroke width; the variation between the thickest and thinnest strokes of the letterform; the width of the letters; and the relationship of the x-height to the height of capitals, ascenders, and descenders.

The stroke-to-height ratio. The roman letterform, left, has the stroke-width-to-capital-height proportion found on Roman inscriptions (Fig. **5**). Superimposition on a grid demonstrates that the height of the letter is ten times the stroke width. In the adjacent rectangles, the center letter is reduced to one-half the normal stroke width, and the letter on the right has its stroke width expanded to twice the normal width. In both cases, pronounced change in the weight and appearance of the letterform occurs.

Contrast in stroke weight. A change in the contrast between thick and thin strokes can alter the optical qualities of letterforms. The series of *O*s in Figure **6,** shown with the date of each specimen, demonstrates how the development of technology and printing has enabled typeface designers to make thinner strokes.

In the Old Style typography of the Renaissance, designers attempted to capture some of the visual properties of pen writing. Since the writing pens of the period had a flat edge, they created thick and thin strokes. *Stress* is the term to define this

thickening of the strokes, which is particularly pronounced on curves. Note how the placement of weight within the Old Style *O* creates a diagonal axis. As time has passed, type designers have been less influenced by writing.

By the late 1700s, the impact of writing declined, and this axis became completely vertical in many typefaces of that period. In many of the earliest sans-serif typefaces, stress disappeared completely. Some of these typefaces have a monoline stroke that is completely even in weight.

Expanded and condensed styles. The design qualities of the typographic font change dramatically when the widths of the letterforms are expanded or condensed. The word *proportion,* set in two sans-serif typefaces, demonstrates extreme expansion and condensation (Fig. **7**). In the top example, set in Aurora Condensed, the stroke-to height ratio is one to nine. In the bottom example, set in Information, the stroke-to-height ratio is one to two. Although both words are exactly the same height, the condensed typeface takes up far less area on the page.

X-height and proportion. The proportional relationship between the x-height and capital, ascender, and descender heights influences the optical qualities of typography in a significant way. The same characters are set in seventy-two-point type using three typefaces with widely varying x-heights (Fig. **8**). This example demonstrates how these proportional relationships change the appearance of type. The impact of x-height upon legibility will be discussed in chapter four.

8.

On the same-size body (72 point), the x-height variation between three typefaces – Garamond 3, Bodoni, and Univers – is shown. The proportion of the x-height to the point size significantly affects the appearance of type.

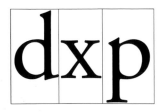

72 points

PROPORTION PROPORTION

A font is a set of characters of the same size and style containing all the letters, numbers, and marks needed for typesetting. A typographic font exhibits structural unity when all the characters relate to one another visually. The weights of thick and thin strokes must be consistent, and the optical alignment of letterforms must appear even. The distribution of lights and darks within each character and in the spaces between characters must be carefully controlled to achieve an evenness of tone within the font.

In some display faces, the font might include only the twenty-six capital letters. In a complete font for complex typesetting, such as for textbooks, it is possible to have nearly two hundred characters. The font for Adobe Garamond (Fig. **9**) includes the following types of characters.

Capitals: The set of large letters that is used in the initial position.

Lowercase: The smaller set of letters, so named because in metal typesetting these were stored in the lower part of a type case.

Small caps: A complete set of capital letters that are the same height as the x-height of the lowercase letters. These are often used for abbreviations, cross references, and emphasis.

Lining figures: Numbers that are the same height as the capital letters and sit on the baseline.

Old Style figures: A set of numbers that are compatible with lowercase letters; *1, 2,* and *O* align with the x-height; *6* and *8* have ascenders; and *3, 4, 5, 7,* and *9* have descenders.

Superior and inferior figures: Small numbers, usually slightly smaller than the x-height, used for footnotes and fractions. Superior figures hang from the capline, and inferior figures sit on the baseline.

Fractions: Common mathematical expressions made up of a superior figure, an inferior figure, and a slash mark. These are set as a single type character.

Ligatures: Two or more characters linked together as one unit, such as *ff.* The ampersand is a ligature originating as a letter combination for the French word *et* ("and") in medieval manuscripts.

Digraphs: A ligature composed of two vowels which are used to represent a dipthong (a mono-syllabic speech sound composed of two vowels).

Mathematical signs: Characters used to notate basic mathematical processes.

Punctuation: A system of standard signs used in written and printed matter to structure and separate units and to clarify meaning.

Accented characters: Characters with accents for foreign language typesetting or for indicating pronunciation.

Dingbats: Assorted signs, symbols, reference marks, and ornaments designed for use with a type font.

Monetary symbols: Logograms used to signify monetary systems (U.S. dollar and cent marks British pound mark, and so on).

7.

abcdefghijklmnopqrstuvwxyz
ABCDEFGHIJKLMNOPQRSTUVWXYZ
ABCDEFGHIJKLMNOPQRSTUVWXYZ
1234567890& 1234567890& 1234567890&
¼½¾ ⅛⅜⅝⅞ ⅓⅔‰ 1234567890/ 1234567890-

fffiflffiffl ÆŒßRpæœ√π=±+÷∞°-–—
ÂÅÁÇÍÎÏØÓÒÔÚ(.,;:'"!?^""''""¨·^˘˜‹›«»
áéíóú åäëïöüàèìòùâêîôûøÁÉÍÓÚÅÄËÏÖÜ
™©®@#$$$¢ᶜᴅ₡£¥%^*
{}[]¡¿¢§¶•†‡

15.

Optical relationships within a font

Mechanical and mathematical letterform construction can result in serious spatial problems, because diverse forms within an alphabet appear optically incorrect. These letterform combinations show the optical adjustment necessary to achieve visual harmony within a font.

AEVO

10.

Pointed and curved letters (Fig. **10**) have little weight at the top and/or bottom guidelines; this can make them appear too short. To make them appear the same height as letters that terminate squarely with the guidelines, the apexes of pointed letters extend beyond the baseline and capline. Curved letterforms are drawn slightly above and below these lines to prevent them from appearing too small.

HBESKX38

11.

In two-storied capitals and figures (Fig. **11**), the top half appears too large if the form is divided in the mathematical center. To balance these letters optically, the center is slightly above the mathematical center, and the top halves are drawn slightly narrower than the bottom half.

Horizontal strokes (Fig. **12**) are drawn slightly thinner than vertical strokes in both curved and straight letterforms. Otherwise, the horizontals would appear too thick.

Tight junctions where strokes meet (Fig. **13**) are often opened slightly to prevent the appearance of thickening at the joint.

Letters combining diagonal and vertical strokes (Fig. **14**) must be designed to achieve a balance between the top and bottom counterforms. Strokes can be tapered slightly to open up the

ETO

12.

M

13.

NK

14.

spaces, and adjustments in the amount of stroke overlap can achieve a harmony of parts. Letters whose vertical strokes determine their height (Fig. **15**) are drawn slightly taller than letters whose height is determined by a horizontal stroke. Optically, they will appear to be the same height.

MBNB

16.

The stroke weight of compact letterforms (Fig. **16**), such as those with closed counterforms, are drawn slightly smaller than the stroke weight of letterforms having open counterforms. This optically balances the weight.

17.

Curved strokes are usually thicker at their midsection than the vertical strokes, to achieve an even appearance (Fig. **17**).

These adjustments are very subtle and are often imperceptible to the reader. However, their overall effect is a more ordered and harmonious visual appearance.

Unity of design in the type font

Tremendous diversity of form exists in the typographic font. Twenty-six capitals, twenty-six lowercase letters, ten numerals, punctuation, and other graphic elements must be integrated into a system that can be successfully combined into innumerable words.

Letterform combinations from the Times Roman Bold font (Fig. **18**) demonstrate visual similarities that bring wholeness to typography. Letterforms share similar parts. A repetition of curves, verticals, horizontals, and serifs are combined to bring variety and unity to typographic designs using this typeface. All well-designed fonts of type display this principle of repetition with the variety that is found in Times Roman Bold.

DCGOQ

Curved capitals share a common round stroke.

The diagonal stokes of the *A* are repeated in *V W M*.

Lowercase letters have common serifs.

AVWM jiru

F E B demonstrates that the more similar letters are, the more common parts they share.

Repetition of the same stroke in *m n h u* creates unity.

FEB mnhut

Likewise, the letters *b d p q* share parts.

bdpq SCGH

Capital serifs recur in similar characters.

BRKPR atfr

ZLE MYX

Subtle optical adjustments can be seen. For example, the bottom strokes of the capital *Z* and *L* have longer serifs than the bottom stroke of the *E*. This change in detail compensates for the larger counterform on the right side of the first two letters.

bq bhlk ceo

18.

An infinite variety of type styles is available today. Digital typography, with its simple and economical introduction of new typefaces, has made the entire array of typefaces developed over the centuries available for contemporary use. Numerous efforts have been made to classify typefaces, with most falling into the following major categories. Some classification systems add a decorative, stylized, or novelty category for the wide range of fanciful type styles that defy categorization.

Old Style

Old Style type began with designs of the punchcutter Francesco Griffo, who worked for the famous Venetian scholar-printer Aldus Manutius during the 1490s. Griffo's designs evolved from earlier Italian type designs. His Old Style capitals were influenced by carved Roman capitals; lowercase letters were inspired by fifteenth-century humanistic writing styles, based on the earlier Carolingian minuscules. Old Style letterforms have the weight stress of rounded forms at an angle, as in handwriting. The serifs are bracketed (that is, unified with the stroke by a tapered, curved line). Also, the top serifs on the lowercase letters are at an angle.

Italic

Italic letterforms slant to the right. Today, we use them primarily for emphasis and differentiation. When the first italic appeared in the earliest "pocket book," printed by Aldus Manutius in 1501, it was used as an independent typestyle. The first italic characters were close-set and condensed; therefore, Manutius was able to get more words on each line. Some italic styles are based on handwriting with connected strokes and are called scripts.

Transitional

During the 1700s, typestyles gradually evolved from Old Style to Modern. Typefaces from the middle of the eighteenth century, including those by John Baskerville, are called Transitional. The contrast between thick and thin strokes is greater than in Old Style faces. Lowercase serifs are more horizontal, and the stress within the rounded forms shifts to a less diagonal axis. Transitional characters are usually wider than Old Style characters.

Modern

Late in the 1700s, typefaces termed Modern evolved from Transitional styles. These typefaces have extreme contrasts between thick and thin strokes. Thin strokes are reduced to hairlines. The weight stress of rounded characters is vertical. Serifs are horizontal hairlines that join the stems at a right angle without bracketing. The uppercase width is regularized; wide letters such as *M* and *W* are condensed and other letters, including *P* and *T*, are expanded. Modern-style typefaces have a strong geometric quality projected by rigorous horizontal, vertical, and circular forms.

Egyptian

In 1815, the English typefounder Vincent Figgins introduced slab-serif typestyles under the name Antique. At the time, there was a mania for ancient Egyptian artifacts, and other typefounders adopted the name Egyptian for their slab-serif designs. These typestyles have heavy square or rectangular serifs that are usually unbracketed. The stress of curved strokes is often minimal. In some slab-serif typefaces, all strokes are the same weight.

Sans Serif

The first sans serif typestyle appeared in an 1816 specimen book of the English typefounder William Caslon IV. The most obvious characteristic of these styles is, as the name implies, the absence of serifs. In many sans serif typefaces, strokes are uniform, with little or no contrast between thick and thin strokes. Stress is almost always vertical. Many sans serif typefaces are geometric in their construction; others combine both organic and geometric qualities.

The development of photo and digital technology has stimulated the design and production of countless new typefaces whose visual characteristics defy standard classification. The visual traits of these "hybrid" forms may fall into more than one of the historical classifications presented on the preceding two pages. The following is a classification system derived from the visual features common to letters throughout the typeface kingdom. It may be used for comparative purposes to pinpoint the most dominant traits of specific typefaces. Type designers use these variations to create a family of typefaces. The type family is discussed on pages 41–44.

Serifs:

Serifs provide some of the most identifiable features of typefaces, and in some cases they reveal clues about their historical evolution. The serifs shown are those that appear most frequently in typefaces.

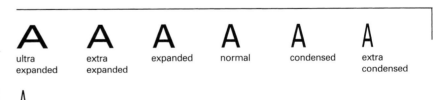

Weight:

This is a feature defined by the ratio between the relative width of the strokes of letterforms and their height. On the average, a letter of normal weight possesses a stroke width of approximately 15% of its height, whereas bold is 20% and light is 10%.

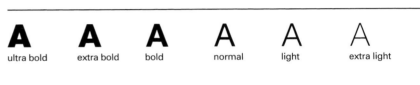

Width:

Width is an expression of the ratio between the black vertical strokes of the letterforms and the intervals of white between them. When white intervals appear larger, letters appear wider. A letter whose width is approximately 80% of its height is considered normal. A condensed letter is 60%, and an expanded letter is 100% of its height.

Posture:

Roman letters that slant to the right but are structurally the same as upright roman letters are referred to as oblique. Italic letters, which are based on handwriting, are structurally different from roman letters of the same type family. Italic letters with connecting strokes are called scripts. The angle of posture varies from typeface to typeface; however, a slant of approximately 12% is considered to be normal.

Thick/thin contrast:
This visual feature refers to the relationship between the thinnest parts of the strokes in letters and the thickest parts. The varying ratios between these parts produce a wide range of visual textures in text type.

A — high contrast A — medium contrast A — low contrast Ā — no contrast

x-height:
This proportional characteristic can vary immensly in different typefaces of the same size. Typically, x-heights are considered to be "tall" when they are at least two-thirds the height of capital letters. They are "short" when they measure one-half the height of capital letters.

d — extra tall d — tall d — rnedium d — short d — extra short

Ascenders/descenders:
Ascenders and descenders may appear longer in some typefaces and shorter in others, depending on the relative size of the x-height. Descenders are generally slightly longer than ascenders among letters of the same typeface.

dp — extra long dp — long dp — medium dp — short dp — extra short

Stress:
The stress of letters, which is a prominent visual axis resulting from the relationships between thick and thin strokes, may be left-angled, vertical, or right-angled in appearance.

O — left-angled O — vertical O — right-angled

Typographic measurement

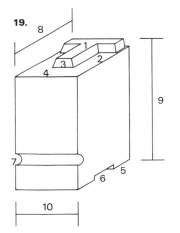

19.

1. Face (printing surface)
2. Counter
3. Beard
4. Shoulder
5. Feet
6. Groove
7. Nick

8. Point size (body size)
9. Type-high (.918″ height)
10. Set width

Our measurement system for typography was originally developed for the handset metal type invented by Johann Gutenberg around A.D. 1450. The rectangular metal block of type (Fig. **19**) has a raised letterform on top, which was inked to print the image.

Metal type measurement

The small sizes of text type necessitated the development of a measuring system with extremely fine increments. There were no standards for typographic measurements until the French type designer and founder Pierre Simon Fournier le Jeune introduced his point system of measurement in 1737. The contemporary American measurement system, which was adopted during the 1870s, has two basic units: the point and the pica (Fig. **20**). There are approximately 72 points in an inch (each point is 0.138 inches) and 12 points in a pica. There are about six picas in an inch.

Metal type exists in three dimensions, and an understanding of typographic measurement begins with this early technology. The depth of the type (Fig. **19,** caption 8) is measured in points and is called the point size or body size. All metal type must be the exact same height (Fig. **19,** caption 9), which is called type-high (.918 inch). This uniform height enabled all types to print a uniform impression upon the paper. The width of a piece of type is called the set width (Fig. **19,** caption 10) and varies with the design of each individual letter. The letters *M* and *W* have the widest set width; *i* and *I* have the narrowest. The length of a line of type is the sum of the set width of all the characters and spaces in the line. It is measured in picas.

Before the development of the point and pica system, various sizes of type were identified by names, such as *brevier, long primer,* and *pica;* these became 8-point, 10-point, and 12-point type. The chart in Figure **21,** reproduced from a nineteenth-century printers' magazine, shows the major point sizes of type with their old names.

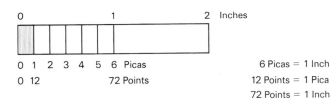

| 0 | | | | 1 | | | 2 | Inches |

0 1 2 3 4 5 6 Picas   6 Picas = 1 Inch
0 12   72 Points   12 Points = 1 Pica
                          72 Points = 1 Inch

20.

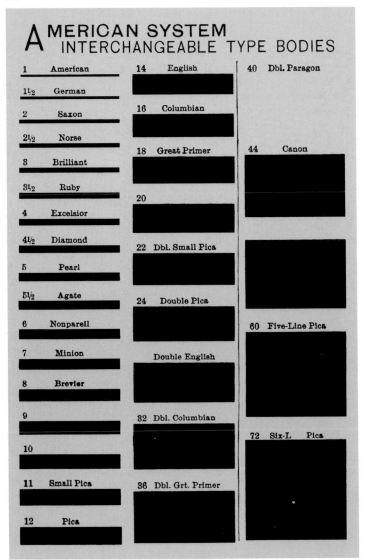

AMERICAN SYSTEM
INTERCHANGEABLE TYPE BODIES

1	American	14	English	40	Dbl. Paragon
1½	German	16	Columbian		
2	Saxon	18	Great Primer	44	Canon
2½	Norse	20			
3	Brilliant	22	Dbl. Small Pica		
3½	Ruby	24	Double Pica		
4	Excelsior			60	Five-Line Pica
4½	Diamond		Double English		
5	Pearl	32	Dbl. Columbian	72	Six-L Pica
5½	Agate	36	Dbl. Grt. Primer		
6	Nonpareil				
7	Minion				
8	Brevier				
9					
10					
11	Small Pica				
12	Pica				

21.

Reproduced actual size from
The Inland Printer, April 1885.

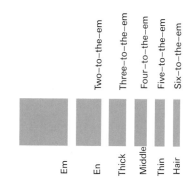

This line has word spacing with em quads.

This line has word spacing with en quads.

This line has word spacing with thick quads.

This line has word spacing with middle quads.

This line has word spacing with thin quads.

Thislinehaswordspacingwithhairquads.

Type that is 12 point and under is called text type and is primarily used for body copy. Sizes above 12 point are called display type, and they are used for titles, headlines, signage, and the like.

Traditional metal type had a range of text and display sizes in increments from 5 point to 72 point (Fig. **22**). The measurement of point size is a measurement of the metal block of type including space above and below the letters; therefore, one cannot measure the point size from printed letters themselves. This is sometimes confusing. Refer to the labels for x-height, cap height, and point size on Figure **22** and observe that the point size includes the cap height plus a spatial interval above and below the letters.

Spatial measurement
In addition to measuring type, the designer also measures and specifies the spatial intervals between typographic elements. These intervals are: interletter spacing (traditionally called letterspacing), which is the interval between letters; interword spacing, also called wordspacing, which is the interval between words; and interline spacing, which is the interval between two lines of type. Traditionally, interline space is called leading, because thin strips of lead are placed between lines of metal type to increase the spatial interval between them.

In traditional metal typography, interletter and interword spacing are achieved by inserting metal blocks called quads between the pieces of type. Because these are not as high as the type itself, they do not print. A quad that is a square of the point size is called an *em.* One that is one-half an em quad is called an *en.* In metal type, other smaller divisions of space are fractions of the em (Fig. **23**). These metal spacers are used for letter- and wordspacing, paragraph indentions, and centering or justifying lines of type.

5 Point
6 Point
7 Point
8 Point
9 Point
10 Point
11 Point
12 Point
14 Point
18 Point
24 Point
30 Point
36 Point
42 Point
48 Point
54 Point
60 Point
72 Point

Cap height | Body size

22.

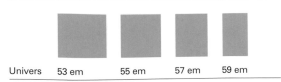

Univers   53 em   55 em   57 em   59 em

24.

This line is set with plus ten units of interletter spacing.
This line is set with normal, unaltered interletter spacing.
This line is set with minus five units of interletter spacing.
This line is set with minus ten units of interletter spacing.
This line is set with minus twenty units of interletter spacing.

26.

For design considerations, the em of a condensed type style can be narrower than a square, and the em of an expanded type size can be wider than a square. This is demonstrated by the em quads from four styles in the Univers family of typefaces (Fig. **24**).

While *em* and *en* are still used as typographic terms, spacing in digital typesetting and desktop publishing is controlled by a computer, using a unit system. The *unit* is a relative measurement determined by dividing the em (that is, the square of the type size) into equal vertical divisions. Different typesetting systems use different numbers of units; sixteen, thirty-two, and sixty-four are common. Some desktop publishing software even permits adjustments as small as twenty-thousandths of an em. The width of each character (Fig. **25**) is measured by its unit value. During typesetting, the character is generated, then the typesetting machine advances the number of units assigned to that character before generating the next character. The unit value includes space on each side of the letter for normal interletter spacing. Adding or subtracting units to expand or contract the space between letters is called *tracking.* Changing the tracking changes the tone of the typography (Fig. **26**). As will be discussed later, tracking influences the aesthetics and legibility of typesetting.

Some letter combinations, such as *TA,* have awkward spatial relationships. An adjustment in the interletter space to make the interval more consistent with other letter combinations is called *kerning.* In metal type, kerning was achieved by sawing notches in the types. Contemporary typesetting software can contain automatic kerning pairs, and the designer can manually change the kerning between characters when these awkward combinations appear.

| 13 Units | 10 Units | 9 Units | 5 Units | 10 Units | 11 Units |

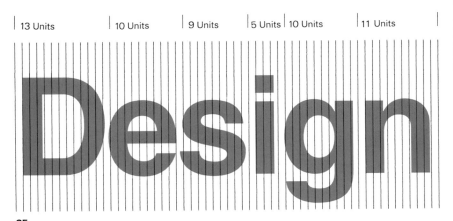

25.
The unit value of each letter in
the word *Design* is shown.

In this setting, minus one unit
is used for tighter interletter
spacing.

In this setting, minus two
units is used. The letters
almost touch.

A type family consists of a group of related type-faces, unified by a set of similar design character-istics. Each face in the family is an individual one that has been created by changing visual aspects of the parent font. Early type families consisted of three fonts: the regular roman face, a bolder version, and an italic. The roman, bold, and italic fonts of the Baskerville family (Fig. **27**) demon-strate that a change in stroke weight produces the bold version, and a change in stroke angle creates the italic. The bold font expands typographic possibilities by bringing impact to titles, headings, and display settings. Today, italics are primarily used for emphasis as a variation of roman. In addition to weight and angle changes, additional members of a type family are created by changing proportions or by design elaboration.

Weight changes. By simply changing the stroke width relative to the height of the letters, a whole series of alphabets, ranging from extremely light to very bold, can be produced. In England, a classifi-cation standard has been developed that contains eight weights: extralight, light, semilight, medium, semibold, bold, extrabold, and ultrabold. Most type families do not, however, consist of eight weights. Four weights – light, regular or book, medium, and bold – are often sufficient for most purposes. In the Avant Garde family (Fig. **28**), stroke weight is the only aspect that changes in these five fonts.

Proportion. Changing the proportions of a type style by making letterforms wider (expanded) or narrower (condensed), as discussed earlier, is another method for adding typefaces to a type family. Terms used to express changes in propor-tion include: ultraexpanded, extraexpanded, expanded, regular, condensed, extracondensed, and ultracondensed.

Sometimes confusion results because there is no standardized terminology for discussing the varia-tions in type families. For example, the regular face is sometimes called *normal, roman,* or *book.* Light weights are named *lightline, slim,* and *hairline. Black, elephant, massive, heavy,* and *thick* have been used to designate bold weights. Names given to condensed variations include *narrow, contract-ed, elongated,* and *compressed.* Expanded faces have been called *extended, wide,* and *stretched.*

27.

Baskerville

Baskerville

Baskerville

AVANT GARDE

AVANT GARDE

AVANT GARDE

AVANT GARDE

AVANT GARDE

28.

Futura Italic

Baskerville Italic

Bodoni Italic

29.

Angle. In our discussion about the basic classification of typefaces, italics were presented as a major independent category. They were first introduced four hundred years ago as a new style. Now italics serve as a member of type families, and they are used for contrast or emphasis. Italic fonts that retain curvilinear strokes inspired by handwriting are called cursives or scripts. In geometric typefaces constructed with drafting instruments, the italic fonts created by slanting the stroke angle are called obliques. Baskerville Italic (Fig. **29**) is a cursive, demonstrating a handwriting influence; Futura Italic is an oblique face; and Bodoni Italic has both cursive and oblique qualities. Although the Bodoni family was constructed with the aid of drafting instruments, details in the italic font (for example, some of the lower serifs) evidence a definite cursive quality.

Elaboration. In design an elaboration is an added complexity, fullness of detail, or ornamentation. Design elaboration can be used to add new typefaces to a type family. These might include outline fonts, three-dimensional effects, and the application of ornaments to letterforms. Some of the variations of Helvetica (Fig. **30**) that are available from the German firm of Dr. Boger Photosatz Gmbh include outlines, inlines, perspectives, rounded terminals, and even a chipped antique effect.

While many elaborations are gaudy and interfere with the integrity and legibility of the letterforms, others can be used successfully. Goudy

Handtooled (Fig. **31**) is based on Goudy Bold. A white linear element is placed on each major stroke. Dimensionality is suggested, and the face alludes to incised inscriptional lettering.

Decorative and novelty type styles should be used with great care by the graphic designer. At best, these can express a feeling appropriate to the content and can allow for unique design solutions. Unfortunately, the use of design elaboration is often a mere straining for effect.

The Cheltenham family
One of the most extensive type families is the Cheltenham series of typefaces (Fig. **32**). The first version, Cheltenham Old Style, was initially designed around the turn of the century by architect Bertram G. Goodhue in collaboration with Ingalls Kimball of the Cheltenham Press in New York City. When this typeface went into commercial production at the American Type Founders Company, designer Morris F. Benton supervised its development. Benton designed about eighteen additional typefaces for the Cheltenham family. Variations developed by other typefounders and manufacturers of typesetting equipment expanded this family to more than thirty styles. The design properties linking the Cheltenham family are short, stubby slab serifs with rounded brackets, tall ascenders and long descenders, and a moderate weight differential between thick and thin strokes.

Cheltenham
Cheltenham
Cheltenham
Cheltenham
Cheltenham
Cheltenham
Cheltenham
Cheltenham
Cheltenham
Cheltenham
Cheltenham
Cheltenham
Cheltenham
Cheltenham
Cheltenham
Cheltenham
Cheltenham
Cheltenham
Cheltenham
Cheltenham
Cheltenham

32.

Goudy Handtooled

31.

30.
Elaborations of
Helvetica Medium.

				39 Univers
45 Univers	46 *Univers*	47 Univers	48 *Univers*	49 Univers
53 Univers	55 Univers	56 *Univers*	57 Univers	58 *Univers*	59 Univers
63 Univers	65 Univers	66 *Univers*	67 Univers	68 *Univers*
73 Univers	75 Univers	76 *Univers*
83 Univers

33.

The Univers family

A full range of typographic expression and visual contrast becomes possible when all the major characteristics – weight, proportion, and angle – are orchestrated into a unified family. An exceptional example is the Univers family (Fig. **33**). This family of twenty-one type styles was designed by Adrian Frutiger. Instead of the usual terminology, Frutiger used numerals to designate the typefaces. Univers 55 is the "parent" face; its stroke weight and proportions are the norm from which all the other designs were developed. The black-and-white relationships and proportions of Univers 55 are ideal for text settings. Careful study of Figure **33** reveals that the first digit in each font's number indicates the stroke weight, three being the lightest and eight the heaviest. The second digit indicates expansion and contraction of the spaces within and between the letters,

which results in expanded and condensed styles. Roman fonts are designated with an odd number, and oblique fonts are designated with an even number.

In the design of Univers, Frutiger sparked a trend in type design toward a larger x-height. The lowercase letters are larger relative to ascenders, descenders, and capitals. The size and weight of capitals are closer to the size and weight of lowercase letters, creating increased harmony on the page of text. Because the twenty-one members of the Univers family share the same x-height, capital height, and ascender and descender length and are produced as a system, they can be intermixed and used together without limitation. This gives extraordinary design flexibility to the designer (Fig. **34**).

43

34.

Typographic interpretation of
The Bells by Edgar Allan Poe
using the Univers family.
(Designer: Philip Meggs)

Hear the

sledges with the **Bells**

SILVER Bells — —

What a world of **merriment** their *melody* foretells!

How they *tinkle,*

tinkle,

tinkle, in the icy air of night!

While the stars that

o v e r s p r i n k l e

All the heavens seem to t w i n k l e

With a *crystalline* delight:

Keeping *time, time,* **time,**

In a sort of **R**unic rhyme,

To the **tin**tin*nabu*la**t**ion that so *musically* wells

From the *bells,* bells,

Bells, Bells,

BELLS, Bells — —

From the *jingling* and the *tingling* of the bells.

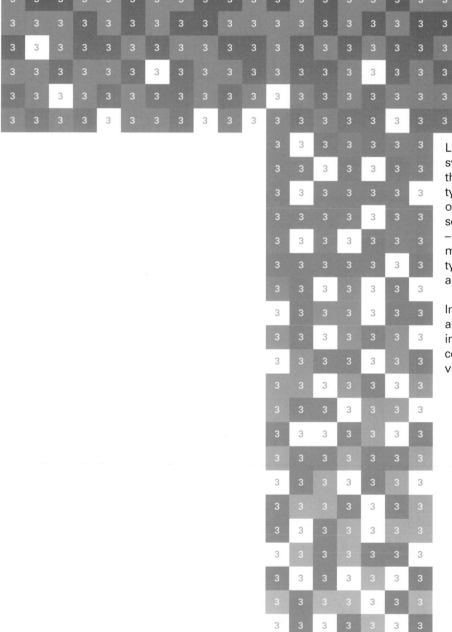

Like the anatomy of typography, typographic syntax and communication have a language that must be learned to understand typographic design. Syntax is the connecting of typographic signs to form words and sentences on the page. The elements of design – letter, word, line, column, and margin – are made into a cohesive whole through the use of typographic space, visual hierarchy, ABA form, and grid systems.

In this chapter, the relationship between form and meaning is also addressed. The imaginative designer can expand and clarify content through the communicative use of visual form.

Typographic syntax

In grammar, syntax is the manner in which words are combined to form phrases or sentences. We define typographic syntax as the process of arranging elements into a cohesive whole. The study of typographic syntax begins with its basic unit, the letter, and progresses to word, line, column, and margin.

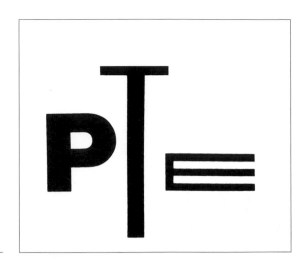

1.
This composition demonstrates contrasting visual characteristics of three letterforms. (Designer: Robert Boyle)

2.
Through precise letterform drawing and carefully considered form-to-counterform interaction, two dissimilar letters form a cohesive sign. (Designer: Gail Collins)

3.
Two letterforms are each broken into two geometric shapes of varying size and density, and the four resulting forms are combined into a delicate, asymmetrically balanced symbol (Designer: Frank Armstrong)

2.

The letter

Our initial discussion of typographic syntax addresses the intrinsic character of the individual letter. This well-drawn form, exhibiting subtlety and precision, is the unit that distinguishes one family of type from another. It exists in various weights, sizes, and shapes (Fig. **1**).

Although the letter typically functions as part of a word, individual letters are frequently combined into new configurations. As shown in Figures **2** and **3,** combinations of letters *A* and *g* and *P* and *Q* are unified to create a stable gestalt. In the illustrated examples, there is an expressiveness and boldness to the individual letters. The syntax displayed here is an example of letter combinations acting as signs, extracted from a larger system of signs.

A typographic sign is visually dynamic because of its interaction with the surrounding white space or void – the white of the paper. This form-to-void relationship is inherent in the totality of typographic expression. The repetition of the letter *T* in Figure **4** is balanced and complemented by its white space. In the title page for Hans Arp's book *On My Way,* the visual interplay between the three letterforms animates the page (Fig. **5**). This equilibrium and spatial interaction and the manner in which it is achieved will be discussed further in our study of typographic space.

Contemplating this ability of space to define form, Amos Chang observed, ". . . it is the existence of intangible elements, the negative, in architectonic forms which makes them come alive, become human, naturally harmonize with one another, and enable us to experience them with human sensibility."

4.
It is the figure/ground reversal in the repetition of the letter *T* that creates a balanced and expressive poster. (Designer: Willi Kunz)

5.
A dynamic composition is formed by the precise spatial location of the letterforms *a, r,* and *p,* which also spell the author's name. (Designer: Paul Rand)

4.

3.

5.

6.

6.

A star, a glass, and a word contribute to form a sign for *joy.* The word's meaning is expressed visually and poetically. (Designer: Frank Armstrong)

8.

This dissection of the word *Camerata* displays the letterform combinations and the relationships between consonants and their connecting vowels. Contrast and repetition create lateral movement within a word, and the overall arrangement relates to the word's meaning. (Designer: Sergio de Jesus)

8.

7.

Word-to-word interaction exhibits rhythmic recurrences of form and counterform. Individual letterforms are paired, and their corresponding interior counters are related here. (Designer: John Rodgers)

![olivetti olivetti]
9.

The word

By definition, a word has the potential to express an idea (Fig. **6**), object, or event. Word signs are independent of the things they represent, yet by design they can be made to signify and reveal their meaning.

Form and counterform relationships, found within individual letterforms, also exist within individual words. Speaking on the structural consideration of form and counterform and the designing of typefaces, Adrian Frutiger stated: "The material of typography is the black, and it is the designer's task with the help of this black to capture space, to create harmonious whites inside the letters as well as between them."

By observing this principle and by combining form and counterform into word units, the designer discovers subtle typographic connections and rhythms (Fig. **7**). The word unit is a constellation of individual letterforms, suggesting a union and forming a cohesive whole. Optically adjusted spaces and consistent counterform relationships assure the overall clarity of this union.

Discussing interletter spacing, the painter and graphic artist Ben Shahn tells about his training as an apprentice who lettered on lithographic stones in 1913. The shop foreman explained, "Imagine you have in your hand a glass that will hold only so much water. Now you must provide space between your letters – whatever their slants and curves may be – to hold just that much water, no more or less." The universal principle for spacing letters is this: the typographer, calligrapher, or designer attempts to make the interletter space

between each pair of letters appear equal to the space between every other pair of letters. Because these counterform spaces have such different configurations, this spacing must be achieved through optical balance rather than through measurement.

Figure **8** shows a dissection of the word *Camerata,* displaying various interletter relationships, including both geometric and organic features. In this example, the word's internal pattern is created by the visual properties of the individual letterforms and their various juxtapositions. This arrangement displays the nature of the internal pattern. *Camerata* is an Italian word meaning "a room full of people"; this meaning supplies yet another interpretation of the overall pattern. Such form-to-content relationships will be discussed later in this chapter.

A concern for form and counterform is evident in the equilibrium that is established among the letterforms comprising the word *Camerata*. It is extremely important to see the interior rhythms of a single word. In the example shown, the letters *C, m, r,* and *t* function as elements of contrast, while the three *a*s and the *e* act as the unifying elements. A similar use of contrast and repetition is demonstrated by the progression of letterforms within the corporate logotype for Olivetti (Fig. **9**).

Obviously, not all words offer the potential for such a rich typographic internal pattern. The complex and lively forms reproduced here clearly show the variety and fullness of form that exists in some deceptively simple word units.

9.
In the Olivetti logo, the x-height establishes continuity, and the five ascending vertical forms create a horizontal rhythm. The repetition of rounded forms (*o* and *e*) and the "echo effect" of a rounded form followed by vertical strokes create a lively unity; the angled strokes of the letter *v* introduce an element of contrast. (Designer: Walter Ballmer)

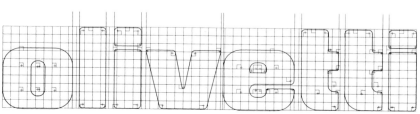
9.

*Of all the achievements
of the human mind, the birth of the alphabet
is the most momentous.*

13.

10.

Symmetrical placement
produces a quiet, balanced
configuration.

11.

Asymmetrical placement
achieves a dynamic division of
space on the page. (Designer:
Ivy Li)

The line

Words are joined to form verbal sentences and typographic lines. The configuration and placement of lines of type are significant structural concerns. In its most basic form, a line of type consists of a single point size and a single weight extended horizontally over a specific line width.

Lines of type can be arranged symmetrically (Fig. **10**), or asymmetrically (Fig. **11**). The viewer/reader must sense a clearly established relationship between individual lines of type and the surrounding space (Fig. **12**).

The smallest change in point size, weight, or line length controls the overall emphasis given to a line of type. The designer or typographer must determine when the overall effect is balanced and fully integrated. All design considerations – typeface selection, alignments, and spacing – should display connections that are apparent and distinct (Fig. **13**). Jan Tschichold states, "The relationship of the sizes must in any case be clearly visible, its effect must be lively, and it must always follow the sense of the text exactly."

The length of a group of lines of type can be equal justified) or unequal (flush left/ragged right, ragged left/flush right, or centered). The examples in this section illustrate various typographic alignments. Typographic form becomes lively and harmonious through these alignments, which enhance individual lines of type and activate the surrounding space (Figs. **14** and **15**).

The placement of punctuation marks is of special significance to these alignments. In Figure **16** punctuation marks extend into the margin. Slight adjustments and subtle refinements heighten the degree of unity.

Typographic rules are used in conjunction with type and separate one line of type from another or one group of typographic lines from another as in Figure **12**, or in footnotes. Rules are found in a variety of forms (Fig. **17**) and numerous sizes and weights. (The use of visual punctuation, including typographic rules, is detailed in *Visual Hierarchy*.)

Earlier, we discussed kerning and the optical spacing of letterforms. Control of these factors makes possible a judicious use of letterspacing in a line of type. The orientation of lines raises a multiplicity of other spacing concerns; for example, interword spacing, interline spacing, and line-to-page relationships, as well as the establishment of columns and margins.

12.

Type and rules combine to
bring a sense of unity to the
page. Note the recurrence of
similar space intervals and the
attention given to individual
line breaks (the rhythmic
pattern of line endings).
(Designer: Cheryl Van Arnam)

13.

This multiple-line composition
contains varying line weights,
yet expresses wholeness
through the careful placement
of all elements. It displays the
diversity possible in the
spacing of lines of type.
(Designer: Wolfgang
Weingart)

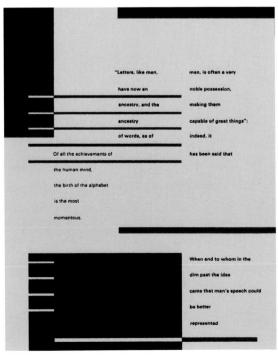

12.

"Bauhaus Masters"
Marcel Breuer
Paul Klee
Herbert Bayer

"Bauhaus Masters"
Marcel Breuer
Paul Klee
Herbert Bayer
16.

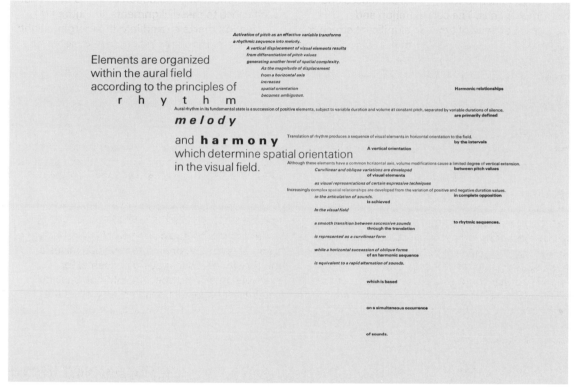

14.

14.
Complex and subtle relationships in interline spacing are achieved here by varying type size, weight, and spatial interval, which separate the statements for the reader. The overall effect is rhythmic and expressive. (Designer: Frank Armstrong)

15.
In this conversation, the placement of lines and intervals reflects the dialogue. (Designer: Warren Lehrer)

16.
In the top setting the lines are flush left, but the edge appears uneven because of the punctuation. In the bottom version, "hanging" the punctuation into the margin is an adjustment resulting in an optically aligned edge.

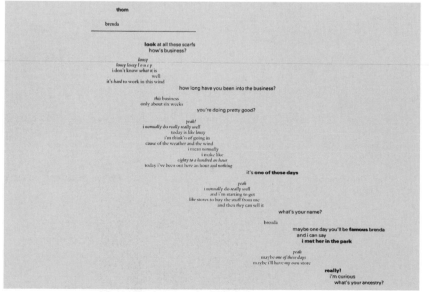

15.

	Straight-line rule
	Bar rule
	Bracket rule
	Swelled rule
	Oxford rule
	Leader

17.

18.

Six columns of type are arranged horizontally, allowing ample breathing space for the photographic image. Varying column depths make possible a clear integration of typographic and pictorial form. (Art Director: Bart Crosby; Designer: Carl Wohlt)

19.

Three columns of type create a vertical movement. Their uneven depths serve to balance other elements. The use of rules and bold headings breaks the overall grayness of the text. (Art Directors: Bart Crosby and Carl Wohlt)

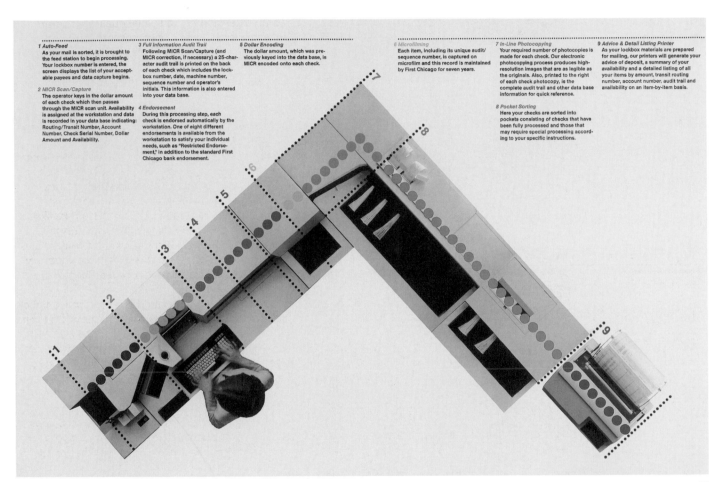

1 Auto-Feed
As your mail is sorted, it is brought to the feed station to begin processing. Your lockbox number is entered, the screen displays the list of your acceptable payees and data capture begins.

2 MICR Scan/Capture
The operator keys in the dollar amount of each check which then passes through the MICR scan unit. Availability is assigned at the workstation and data is recorded in your data base indicating: Routing/Transit Number, Account Number, Check Serial Number, Dollar Amount and Availability.

3 Full Information Audit Trail
Following MICR Scan/Capture (and MICR correction, if necessary) a 25-character audit trail is printed on the back of each check which includes the lockbox number, date, machine number, sequence number and operator's initials. This information is also entered into your data base.

4 Endorsement
During this processing step, each check is endorsed automatically by the workstation. One of eight different endorsements is available from the workstation to satisfy your individual needs, such as "Restricted Endorsement," in addition to the standard First Chicago bank endorsement.

5 Dollar Encoding
The dollar amount, which was previously keyed into the data base, is MICR encoded onto each check.

6 Microfilming
Each item, including its unique audit/ sequence number, is captured on microfilm and this record is maintained by First Chicago for seven years.

7 In-Line Photocopying
Your required number of photocopies is made for each check. Our electronic photocopying process produces high-resolution images that are as legible as the originals. Also, printed to the right of each check photocopy, is the complete audit trail and other data base information for quick reference.

8 Pocket Sorting
Here your checks are sorted into pockets consisting of checks that have been fully processed and those that may require special processing according to your specific instructions.

9 Advice & Detail Listing Printer
As your lockbox materials are prepared for mailing, our printers will generate your advice of deposit, a summary of your availability and a detailed listing of all your items by amount, transit routing number, account number, audit trail and availability on an item-by-item basis.

18.

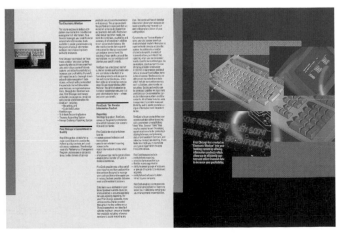

19.

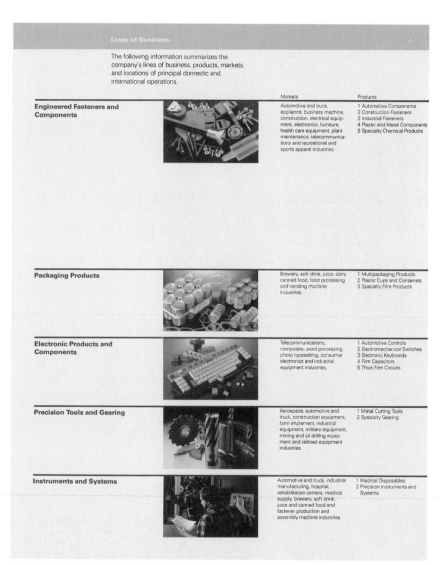

20.

Column and margin

As an extension of the spatial qualities inherent in single letters, pages also possess form and counterform relationships due to the interaction of columns and their surrounding spaces. Functional clarity and visual beauty are established in the harmonious relationships of these spaces.

Three specific variables related to columns govern these relationships: the proportion of column height to width, texture (the tactile appearance of the type), and tone (the lightness and darkness of type). It is through the manipulation of these contrasting variables that pages are spatially activated, optically balanced, and hierarchically ordered. Additionally, the height and width of columns (and their adjoining space intervals) should be carefully examined to ensure adequate legibility (for further discussion, see Chapter 4).

When organizing text columns, either horizontal or vertical movements may be emphasized. One will often dominate, as shown in Figures **18** and **19.** Eye movement across the page (side to side and top to bottom) is controlled by column rhythms, typographic weights, and rules functioning as visual punctuation. By the manipulation of these elements, the designer groups information according to its role in a given layout and guides the eye methodically through the space of the page. Each of the vertical columns in Figure **20,** for example, separates specific categories of information to make them easier to find. The first column, with bold-weight type, contains general information and is dominant; the two right-hand columns, with lightweight type, contain secondary information and are subordinate.

20.

Columns and margins are carefully balanced through the use of contrasting type sizes and weights and of two rule weights. (Art Director: Bart Crosby; Designer: Carl Wohlt)

2I.

In this annual report there are subtle spatial relationships. These include the form/counterform of the column to the margin; the placement of the heading and subheading, which extend into the margin for emphasis; and the column mass to rules, photograph, and caption. (Designer: Frank Armstrong)

22.

This magazine page exhibits the needed contrast between text and caption elements. The column width of the text is double the column width of the caption. (Art Director: Ben Day; Designer: Anne Stewart)

The one- and two-column arrangements shown in Figures **21** and **22** illustrate some of the possibilities for text-column placement. In the two-column arrangement, the column depths are equal. Vitality and contrast are achieved by the placement of the adjacent photograph, its caption, and the bar rule containing the title. In both examples, the caption-column width and the text column width are of different lengths, providing sufficient contrast to indicate to the reader that the caption is not part of the text. Such contrasts in column size, shape, texture, and tone are used to distinguish between different kinds of information and to provide visually luminescent pages.

Figure **23** is another example of how columns contrast with one another. Differences in the columns are produced by changing the interline spacing and the size and weight of the text type. Relative to one another, the columns can be seen as open or closed, light or dark.

The difference in tonality, which is an important design consideration, hierarchically leads the eye from one element to the next, and finally into the white of the page (for further discussion, see *Visual Hierarchy*). The critically determined spatial intervals create an engaging visual rhythm.

The size of type may vary from column to column (Fig. **24**) or within a column (Fig. **25**). As indicated in the latter diagram, type that is larger or heavier in weight appears more dense and is therefore emphasized on the page. Changes in density provide a kind of contrast that makes it possible to balance various typographic elements and add rhythmic qualities to the page.

The scale and proportion of columns, intervals between columns, and margins and their relationships to one another must be carefully adjusted as determined by the kinds of information they support. In Figure **21,** generous, unequal margins frame a single column of quiet text type for a hospital's annual report, while in Figure **19,** narrow margins surround quickly read narrow columns for an efficient-looking publication about computers. Margins not only

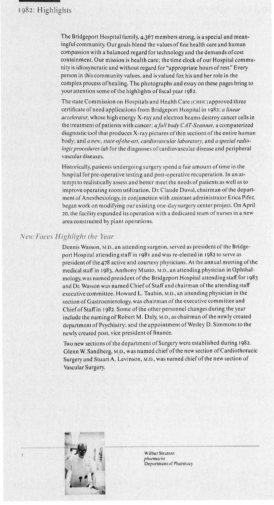

21.

23.

This experimental text composition reveals various combinations of typographic texture and tone.

24.

Variation in size, column to column.

25.

Variation in size within a column.

by Joseph Dyer

(Figure 22: text columns with article)

Haydn, Poulenc and the Princesses

22.

The whole duty of typography, as with calligraphy, is to communicate to the imagination, without loss by the way, the thought or image intended to be communicated by the author. And the whole duty of beautiful typography is not to substitute for the beauty or interest of the thing thought and intended to be conveyed by the symbol, a beauty or interest of its own, but,

The whole duty of typography, as with calligraphy, is to communicate to the imagination, without loss by the way, the thought or image intended to be communicated by the author. And the whole duty of beautiful typography is not to substitute for the beauty or interest of the thing thought and intended to be conveyed by the symbol, a beauty or interest of its own, but, on the one hand, to win access for that communication by the clearness and beauty of the

The whole duty of typography, as with calligraphy, is to communicate to the imagination, without loss by the way, the thought or image intended to be communicated by the author. And the

23.

frame parts within pages, they also contain supportive elements (marginalia) such as running heads, folios, and captions.

The elegant margins shown in Figure **26** have proportions identical to the page. The margin ratio is two margin units to three to four to six, as indicated. In other words, the bottom margin is twice as high as the top margin. Jan Tschichold has pointed out that this complex series of column-to-margin ratios, based on the golden section, is found in numerous medieval manuscripts. (For further discussion about margins, see *The Typographic grid,* page 70.)

Paragraph breaks within a column greatly influence the relationship between a column of text and its surrounding margins. A break may be introduced as an indention, as a space interval, or as a combination of both. Designers have also developed their own ways to indicate paragraphs (Fig. **27**). The overall page organization will determine the most suitable method.

When columns, margins, and their interrelationships are clear and appropriate to content, the result is a printed page of distinction. Every problem demands a fresh approach, yet an ordered unity that is responsive to the meaningful blend of form and counterform is always the goal.

independence in the student.

"Accordingly, handicraft in the workshops was right from the start, not an end it itself, but laboratory experiment preparatory to industrial production. If the initial products of the Bauhaus looked like individual craft products, this was a necessary detour for the groping student whom we avoided to prod with a foregone conclusion.

We salvaged the best of experimental education and added to it a carefully constructed program of information-based design that produced non-commercial products that worked. It was a different school with different people with different goals in a different time. Our aim was to produce designers who had the will, the ability, and the ethical base to change American production for the better.

I was somewhat concerned that this might be a middle of the road

27.

Placement of a bullet (a typographic dot used for emphasis) upon intercolumn rules designates new paragraphs in this booklet design. (Designer: Jeff Barnes)

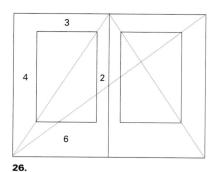

26.

Typographic space

28.

Spatial elements are balanced through the principle of visual compensation, achieving equilibrium and tension. Elements form relationships with other elements through carefully planned juxtapositions and alignments.

Tension exists between the edge of the composition and adjacent elements. These basic forces affect typographic organization and help achieve dynamic, asymmetrical composition. (Designer: Jean Brueggenjohn)

"Speech proceeds in time and writing proceeds in space." Applying Karl Gerstner's statement to typographic design, typographic space is the rhythmic and dimensional field in which typographic communication exists. This field consists of positive form (the typographic elements) and void (the spatial ground) upon which the elements are arranged. Unity within the space is achieved by visual compensation; that is, the spatial balance and arrangement of typographic elements. Amos Chang, discussing the relationship between compensation and visual dynamics, wrote, "This process of growth from deficiency to compensation brings inherent movement to physical form . . . we may borrow an important rule of balance from the anatomy of a zoological being, man in particular. . . man's body is in a state of balance when his arms and legs are in a position to be moved effectively to compensate for position changes of the body."

Visual compensation is achieved by balancing elements against each other, adjusting their sizes, weights, spatial intervals, and other visual properties until unity and equilibrium are achieved (Figs. **28–30**). In Figure **31**, two contrasting letterform pairs are balanced. The letterform pair *fj* suggests contraction and consonance, while *gv* expresses expansion and dissonance. Consonance is a harmonious relationship between similar or corresponding elements, while dissonance is a discordant relationship between dissimilar elements. In Figure **32**, dissonant elements are combined with consonant form-to-void relationships, resulting in a state of visual balance and unity.

29.

Pictorial and typographic elements are placed in asymmetrical balance. Two pointed arches balance three rounded arches, and the ruled line moving into the margin corresponds to the letterspaced word *Messiah*.

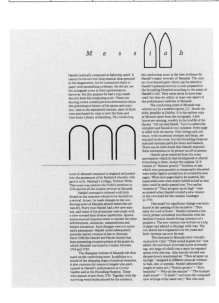

30.

This dynamic poster combines both large three-dimensional letterforms and a complex arrangement of two-dimensional elements. From the arrangement emerges a spatial wholeness: the over lapping of elements is precise and expressive. Compensation is achieved through careful placement, with attention given to the surrounding void. (Designer: Frank Armstrong)

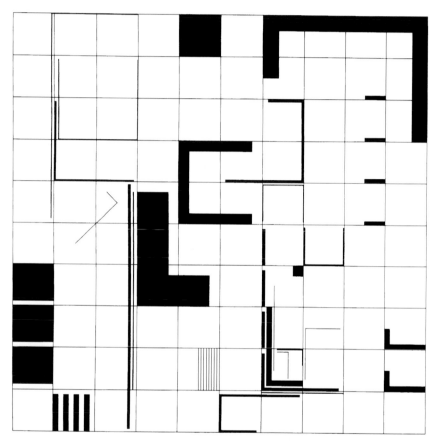

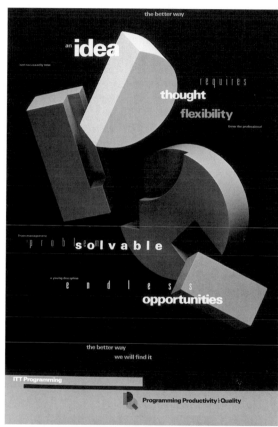

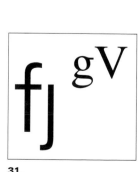

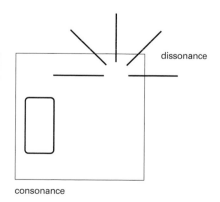

31.
(Designer: Lark Pfleegor)

consonance

32.

The contrast between geometric and gestural letterforms is dissonant. Unity is achieved by carefully planned shape correspondences and form-to-void relationships.

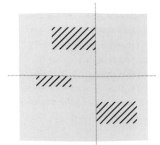

33.
Alignments create visual relationships between forms in space. (Designer: Jennifer Mugford Wieland)

34.
In this asymmetrically balanced composition, the edge of the type column aligns with the central axis of the circle. (Designer: Sergio de Jesus)

The structure of typographic space can be defined by alignments (Figs. **33–35**) and form-to-void relationships that establish a composition's underlying spatial order. This substructure is developed and enhanced through optical adjustment (Fig. **36**). Often inconspicuous, optical adjustment is the precise visual alignment of typographic elements in space based not on mathematical but perceptual alignment. The designer's understanding and use of optical adjustment is necessary for visual clarity.

Visual compensation and optical adjustment within the typographic space link printed elements and the spatial ground. This structural integration is not an end in itself; its order, simple or elaborate, acts as a stimulus, controlling the visual dynamics of the message transmission and response.

Nathan Knobler's observation in *The Visual Dialog* that "psychologists tell us that the need to understand, to find meaning in the world around us, is coupled with the need for stimulation and involvement" applies to design. To communicate with clarity and exactitude, the designer must be aware of the need to stimulate and involve the viewer. In typographic problem solving, the designer creates complex, highly interactive spatial environments (Fig. **37**) that establish coherence between the viewing experience and typographic form, between the verbal statement and written language.

35.
Typographic elements are aligned with the horizontal and vertical edges of the geometric configuration.

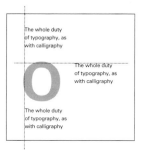

36.
Dotted lines indicate the use of alignments to relate forms to each other. Note the optical adjustment in relating the large *O* to the text type.

37.
In this exhibition catalog cover, horizontal and vertical alignment of elements bring order to a dynamic, asymmetrical design. Texture and tone create a vibrant luminosity. (Designer: Wolfgang Weingart)

Visual Hierarchy

A visual hierarchy is an arrangement of elements in a graduated series, from the most prominent to the least prominent, in an area of typographic space. When establishing a visual hierarchy, a designer carefully considers the relative importance of each element in the message, the nature of the reader, the environment where the communication will be read, and the need to create a cohesive arrangement of forms within the typographic space.

The study of visual hierarchy is the study of the relationships of each part to the other parts and the whole. When elements have similar characteristics, they have equality in the visual hierarchy, but when they have contrasting characteristics, their differences enable them to take dominant and subordinate positions in the composition.

Contrast between elements within the space is achieved by carefully considering their visual properties. Important contrasts used to create hierarchical arrangements include size, weight, color, and spatial interval. The location of an element within the space plays an important role in establishing a visual hierarchy. The spatial relationships with other elements can also influence an element's relative importance in the arrangement.

Principles used to achieve visual hierarchy through careful contrast between the elements are demonstrated by the nine small diagrams on this page (Figs. **38–46**). The nine typographic designs on the opposite page (Figs. **38a–46a**) correspond to these diagrams.

38.
Type style, size, color, weight, and spacing are consistent, resulting in an even texture and tone. Visual hierarchy is almost nonexistent in this arrangement.

39.
A spatial interval equal to one line space separates the title from the other information, giving it prominence in the composition.

40.
Setting the title in bolder type further separates it from the overall tone and texture, increasing the hierarchical contrast.

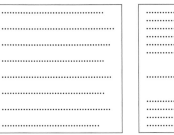

38.

39.

40.

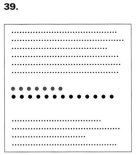

41.

42.

43.

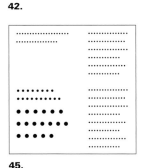

44.

45.

46.

41.
Changing the size and weight of the title makes it even more prominent in the visual hierarchy.

44.
The diagonal position of the title increases its prominence in the space. The smaller type elements align with the diagonals of the title's baseline and posture, unifying the composition.

42.
Color or value can create another level of contrast that can be controlled by the designer to create hierarchy.

45.
This composition demonstrates how extreme contrasts of type size and weight increase visual hierarchy and legibility from a distance.

43.
Two sizes and three weights of type are used to create subtlety and variety within the composition.

46.
Reversing the title from a black rectangle heightens contrast and increases the visual hierarchy. A ruled line separates the secondary type into two zones of information.

38a.

The Modern Literature

Society presents a lecture

by Raoul Ramirez,

Professor of Literature

Santaneo State University

Modern Hispanic Poetry

7:30 pm March 23

The Humanities Center Auditorium

Admission is free

39a.

The Modern Literature

Society presents a lecture

by Raoul Ramirez,

Professor of Literature

Santaneo State University

Modern Hispanic Poetry

7:30 pm March 23
The Humanities Center Auditorium
Admission is free

40a.

The Modern Literature

Society presents a lecture

by Raoul Ramirez,

Professor of Literature

Santaneo State University

Modern Hispanic Poetry

7:30 pm March 23

The Humanities Center Auditorium

Admission is free

41a.

The Modern Literature
Society presents a lecture
by Raoul Ramirez,
Professor of Literature
Santaneo State University

Modern
Hispanic Poetry

7:30 pm March 23
The Humanities Center Auditorium
Admission is free

42a.

The Modern Literature
Society presents a lecture
by Raoul Ramirez,
Professor of Literature
Santaneo State University

Modern
Hispanic Poetry

7:30 pm March 23
The Humanities Center Auditorium
Admission is free

43a.

The Modern Literature
Society presents a lecture

Santaneo State University
Professor of Literature

Raoul Ramirez
Modern Hispanic
Poetry

7:30 pm March 23
The Humanities Center Auditorium
Admission is free

44a.

The Modern Literature
Society presents
a lecture

Modern
Hispanic Poetry

by Raoul Ramirez,
Professor of Literature
Santaneo State University

7:30 pm March 23
The Humanities Center Auditorium
Admission is free

45a.

Santaneo State University
Professor of Literature

The Modern
Literature
Society
presents
a lecture

Raoul
Ramirez
Modern
Hispanic
Poetry

7:30 pm
March 23
The
Humanities
Center
Auditorium
Admission
is free

46a.

The Modern Literature
Society presents a lecture

by Raoul Ramirez,
Professor of Literature
Santaneo State University

Modern
Hispanic Poetry

7:30 pm March 23
The Humanities Center Auditorium
Admission is free

47.
The letters *f* and *j* are typographic counterparts because their forms correspond. Integration and equilibrium are achieved. (Designer: Lark Pfleegor)

When creating a visual hierarchy in typographic space, a designer balances the need for harmony, which unifies a design, with the need for contrast, which lends vitality and emphasis. As in music, elements can have a counterpart or a counterpoint relationship. Typographic counterparts are elements with similar qualities that bring harmony to their spatial relationship (Figs. **47** and **48**). Elements have a counterpoint relationship when they have contrasting characteristics, such as size, weight, color, tone, or texture. Counterpoint relationships bring opposition and dissonance to the design (Fig. **49**).

Typographic elements can have both counterpart and counterpoint relationships. In Figure **50,** extreme scale contrasts create a counterpoint relationship, while the modular letters, constructed from parallel horizontal and vertical elements, become typographic counterparts. Because the forms correspond, the *A*s (Fig. **51**) are counterparts, but their extreme scale contrast permits them to have a dissonant counterpoint relationship in the space. When organizing typographic elements into a visual hierarchy, it is useful to consider counterpart and counterpoint relationships.

48.
In this diagram, forms in the photograph and the letter *S* correspond. This counterpart relationship creates unity between these unlike elements. (Designer: Ivy Li)

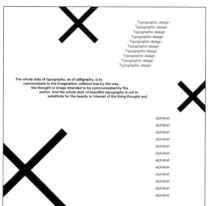

49.
In these arrangements, the dominant elements (addition and multiplication signs) have a counterpoint relationship to the text blocks due to contrasts of scale and weight. Because the text blocks echo the structure of the addition and multiplication signs, and the elements have a balanced arrangement in the space, unity is achieved. (Designer: Lark Pfleegor)

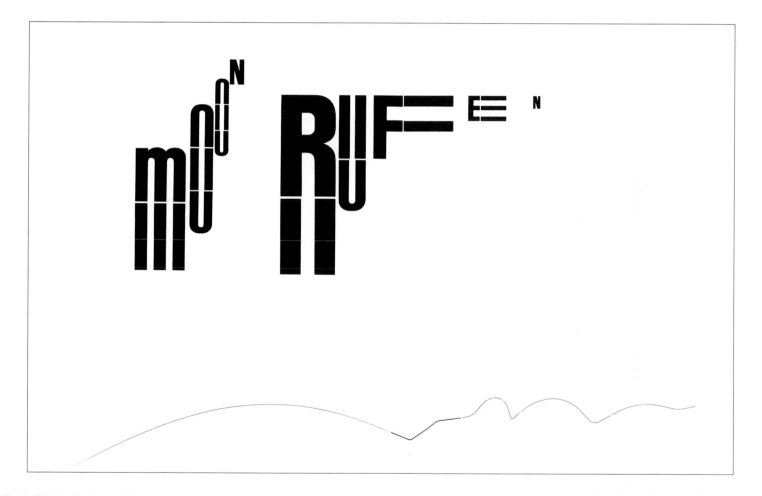

50.
A hierarchy of size gains unity and rhythm through the modular construction of letterforms. *"Moon rufen"* translates as "moon howling"; the type expresses the sound of a lone wolf howling at the moon. (Designer: Wolfgang Weingart)

51.
The repetition of the letter *A* in two different point sizes creates a dynamic hierarchical structure. (Designer: Paul Rand)

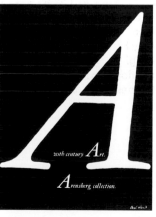

53.

In these typographic exercises, rules and space intervals are used as visual punctuation. (Designers: Bryan Leister and Rebecca Lantz)

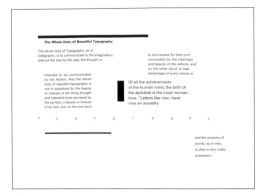 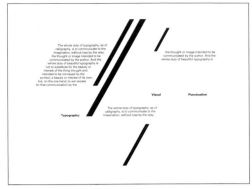

53.

52.

The word *sassafras* calls for a response, and the phrase *a flavoring agent* provides the reply. (Designer: Ivy Li)

Often, typographic elements in a visual hierarchy can be designated as questioning forms and answering forms (Fig. **52**). The typographic unit assigned the questioning role invites or calls for an answer. In a sense, the answering form has a counterpart relationship to the questioning form because it completes the communication. The most prominent visual element of a typographic hierarchy is frequently a questioning form. Consider the role of both typographic form and pictorial form: do individual components of a composition suggest a question or an answer? The questioning component expresses dissonance (unrelieved tension, while the answering component expresses consonance (relieved tension).

A typographic arrangement is partly governed by visual punctuation. As a writer uses standard punctuation marks to separate words and clarify meaning, a designer introduces visual punctuation (space intervals, rules, or pictorial elements) to separate, group, or emphasize words or lines. Visual punctuation (Figs. **53** and **54**) clarifies the reader/viewer's understanding of the content and structure of a typographic arrangement. Visual punctuation helps to clarify the meaning of the typographic message, while visual emphasis or accentuation is used to make one element more important. Emphasis is relative to the contrasting properties of elements; for example, in Figure **54** the word *collage* is dominant in the visual hierarchy due to its scale, weight, and position.

Visual accentuation is giving emphasis or stress to properties (round and straight, thick and thin, geometric and organic, etc.) of typographic and pictorial signs, usually through contrast with dissimilar elements. The bold and compelling mark combining the letter *A* and the scroll of a violin in Figure **55** is an example of visual accentuation through contrast. The geometric properties of the letter *A* are accentuated in opposition to the organic properties of the musical instrument. In this example, details in both the letter and pictorial form are accentuated or deleted, yet the legibility of the original letter and object has been retained. The letter *A* and the violin are incomplete, yet each retains its essence.

Typographic joinery is the visual linking and connecting of elements in a typographic composition through structural relationships and form repetition. The assembly of separate typographic elements to form a unified sign is seen in the logotype for the American Broadcasting Corporation (Fig. **56**). The pronounced geometry and emphasis given to the circular forms joins the forms through the use of the repetition. The shape of the circle is common to every part of this mark. The three letterforms and their circular container are blended to become one sign.

Some typographic designs are seen from different distances (far, middle, close). The viewer's perceptions are greatly influenced by shifts in the viewing experience. Attention to visual hierarchy and the perceptual environment is vital in graphic media (signage, posters, and exhibitions) where the viewing experience is in constant flux (Fig. **57**).

Typography's hierarchical order derives from the basic process of pattern-forming found in nature, in verbal and written language, the arts, and computer technology. This is aptly described by Gyorgy Doczi, speaking of his research on proportional harmonies in art and design, "The rhythms of writing are created by the same pattern-forming process of sharing that creates rhythms of dance, music, and speech. Movements shared make dance, patterns shared make music and speech."

The shared patterns of typography find expression through visual dynamics that enable it to function as both a message-carrier and a rhythmic, visual structure. The typographic message, with all its limitless thought and diversity of form, is shaped by this subtle and meaningful hierarchical language.

ABC abc abc abc

56.
As typographic joinery becomes more developed, the unity of a mark is enhanced dramatically. (ABC logo, Designer: Paul Rand)

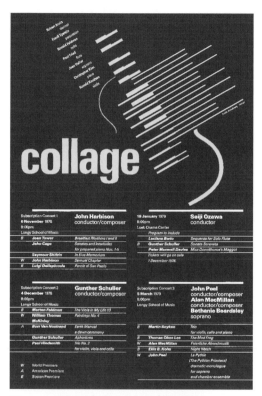

54.

55.

54.
In this poster, a complex system of rules separates, connects, and emphasizes the names of composers, conductors, and other information about numerous events. In the top area of the poster, ruled lines perform a different function: they combine to create a rhythmic visual sign for music. (Designer: Frank Armstrong)

55.
Visual accentuation is demonstrated by this symbol. Striking visual contrast is achieved through the opposition of straight and curved edges and shapes. (Designer: Nick Schrenk)

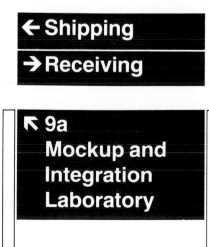

57.

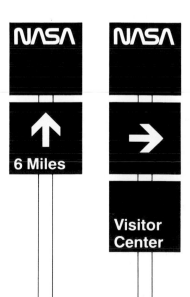

57.
In this signage for NASA, viewing context determines the visual hierarchy. For example, the size and position of the arrow in the interior directional signage are quite different from the size and position of the roadside signage. (Designer: Danne and Blackburn)

ABA form

In typographic communication, visual relationships are established through an active dialogue between two fundamental design principles: repetition and contrast. It is through these principles that the typographic designer imbues messages with visual order and rhythmic variety.

Music structure is also based upon repetition and contrast, and because it is linear in nature, a quality that is common also to typography, it provides an excellent model for understanding basic typographic structure. The primary structural pattern of music is the three-part form of statement-departure-return (ABA). The unifying components (the two *A*s) function as repetition, while the middle component (the *B*) functions as contrast. Arnold Schoenberg observed that "the principle function of form is to advance our understanding. It is the organization of a piece which helps the listener to keep the idea in mind, to follow its development, its growth, its elaboration, its fate." This quote also clarifies the mission of typographic form, where relationships between visible typographic elements are guided by the dynamics of ABA form.

The viewer of typographic communication perceives form relationships as being either in opposition or correspondence. This principle suggests that a fully integrated typographic composition depends upon the successful blending of elements of contrast and repetition. The viewer seeks a variety that stimulates both eye and mind, while structuring the communications experience. This is the dual basis of ABA form.

59.
Even though the functions of the small text block and the photograph are unrelated, these elements correspond to one another because of their similar sizes.

60.
Letters, when combined together as text, provide a treasury of textural contrasts. Corresponding textures reveal visual links between elements.

61.
When typographic elements possess contrasting tonal qualities, the eye perceives an implied three-dimensionality.

A   B   A   B

59.

A   B   A   B

60.

A   B   A   B

61.

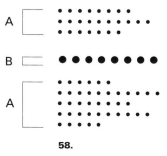

A

B

A

58.

ABA form in typography, as in music, is based upon a fundamental three-part structure where two *repeating* parts are in correspondence, and a third *contrasting* part stands in opposition (Fig. **58**). This fundamental structure, however, may be found in abundant variation. This is true because contrasting and repeating typographic elements within a composition are governed by the dynamic principles of proportion and rhythm. It is via these principles that ABA form grows in complexity and diversity. By definition, proportion in ABA form is the ratio determined by the quantity, size, weight, texture, tone, shape, color (or other syntactic quality) of similar and dissimilar typographic elements (A**A**BA**A**BA**A**). Rhythm is established in the intervals of space separating these elements (A**A** . B . A**A** . B . A**A**). The following examples illustrate this idea:

When typographic elements are similar in size to one another, an immediate correspondence between these elements is established (Fig. **59**). This correspondence is heightened because the tonality of the photograph and small text block is darker than the tone of the larger text block. In the middle diagram, the correspondence between the smaller text blocks is also magnified (Fig. **60**). A third variation is created by altering the tone of the elements: a bold typeface is introduced in the smaller text blocks, linking them together. Here, the factors of both scale and tone establish a distinct pattern of repetition and contrast (Fig. **61**). In an applied example – the design of a concert poster – the recurrence and contrast of typographic tone and texture are demonstrated (Fig. **62**).

Further variations in ABA form are discovered when elaborations (ABa, ABAb or AbAc) of corresponding elements occur to establish subtle contrasts (Fig. **63**), or when primary and

62.

This poster is zoned into three spatial corridors: two columns of text, finely textured and light in tonal value, flank a dynamic arrangement of music-related visual signs, coarser in texture and darker in tone.

Orchestra

Bass
Thomas Coleman
Anthony Beadle

Flute
Elinor Preble

Oboe
Peggy Pearson
Raymond Toubman

Clarinet
William Wrzesien
Andre Lizotte

Violin I
Carol Lieberman,
concertmaster
Victor Romanul
Joseph Conte
Karen Van Sant
Sharan Leventhal
Judith Eissenberg

M o z a r t

S Y M P H O N Y

H A L L

Violin II
Wilma Smith
Lynn Newdome
Martha Edwards
Elizabeth Field
Elsa Miller

Viola
Endel Kalam
Katherine Murdock
Mary Ruth Ray
Virginia Haines

Bassoon
Francis Nizzari
Ronald Haroutunian

French Horn
Pamela Paikin
Jean Rife

B O S T O N

Violoncello
Bruce Coppock
Joan Esch
Corinne Flavin
Olivia Toubman

a   b   a   b   a

A   B   A

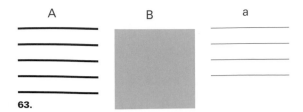

63.

secondary relationships occur in compositions simultaneously (Fig. **64**). The foregoing examples show the influence of proportion upon the relationships between typographic elements. The rhythmic patterns in each of these examples are identical, with equal or nearly equal intervals of space separating the elements. In a detail of the concert poster (Fig. **65**), a distinct rhythm composed of unequal spatial intervals between typographic elements can be observed. This rhythmic pattern may be viewed on two levels: the major group (A . BA), and the minor group (**a** . bb . . **a** . b . . **a** . bb . . **a,** etc.). The intervals between these elements facilitate the functional grouping of the parts of the message: the "instruments" are separated from the "performers" by a "1X" interval of space, and each of these groupings is separated one from another by a "2X" interval of space. Other syntactic traits bind and isolate the parts: the "instruments" are bold in typographic weight, linking them together, while the "performers" are light in weight. At the same time, all these typographic elements share the same type size to distinguish them from the location of the event, which is presented in a larger, italic, all-capitals typeface.

In this example, it is also possible to observe a phenomenon that appears at first as a contradiction in terms, but nonetheless is a condition in typographic design: perceiving typographic forms that are *simultaneously* in correspondence and opposition. This is a concept that is linked to a fundamental design notion: achieving unity within diversity (Fig. **66**). ABA form variations are capable of unifying diverse forms through visual correspondence, while at the same time bringing variety to similar forms through opposition. The skilled designer manipulates typographic elements to achieve this essential balance.

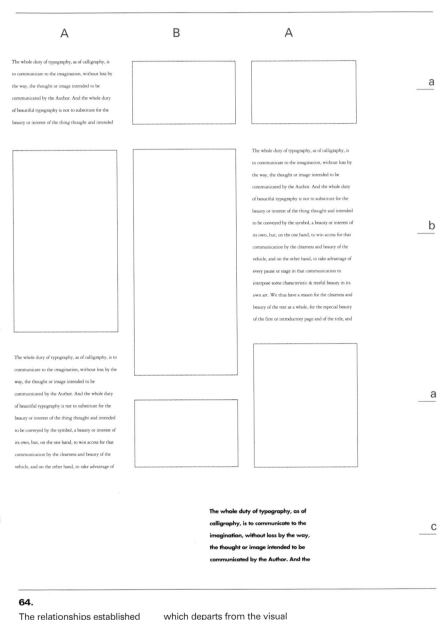

64.
The relationships established by the three vertical columns of equal width (ABA) achieve visual dominance over the three horizontal bands (aba). The small column of text (c), which departs from the visual pattern of the main unit in position and type weight, provides an additional variation.

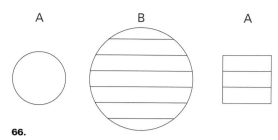

A   B   A

66.
Shape relates the first and
middle forms; texture relates
the middle and right forms;
and size relates the left and
right forms.

ABA form is comprised of both simple and complex patterns that give order and emphasis to the visual linking of typographic elements. These are not fixed systems but are a way of understanding the interrelationships of typographic form. About music Joseph Machlis stated, "The forms . . . are not fixed molds into which the composer pours his material. What gives a piece of music its aliveness is the fact that it adapts a general plan to its own requirements."

a   **Bass**

b   Thomas Coleman
b   Anthony Beadle

a   **Flute**

b   Elinor Preble   a

a   **Oboe**

b   Peggy Pearson
b   Raymond Toubman

a   **Clarinet**

S Y M P H O N Y

H A L L   b

a   **Bassoon**

b   Francis Nizzari
b   Ronald Haroutunian   a

a   **French Horn**

b   Oaneka Oaujub

65.

The typographic grid

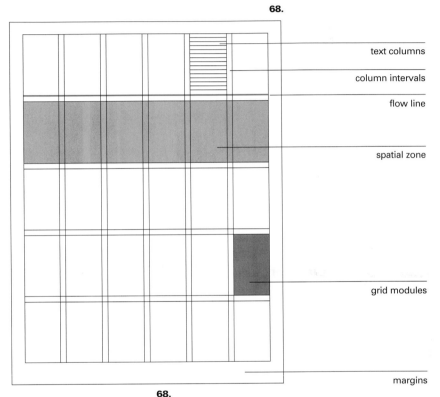

An elemental grid is based upon a "Cartesian" co-ordinate system of intersecting, perpendicular axes. It consists of rectangular modules defined by a network of horizontal and vertical lines (Fig. **67**). The typographic grid, which is an adaptation of this basic structure, possesses unique anatomical characteristics. These include margins that provide boundaries for typographic elements and define the "active" space of the page; grid modules that provide a framework for the designer in placing type and image; columns and the intervals of space between them that accommodate text settings; spatial zones that provide a means of organizing the various parts of information; and flow lines that establish a dominant flow of elements through alignment (Fig. **68**). The proportional relationships of these features, as well as the number of modules incorporated in a grid are influenced by the specific nature of the content, legibility considerations (see Chapter 4), and desired visual effect. Each of these considerations should be given the utmost attention by the designer.

An important consideration in determining an appropriate grid is that of margins. Regardless of the typographic application, these spatial zones, which surround the type area, can provide a sense of spatial stability if sensitively proportioned. For proportional harmony, margins should be at least as wide as the i intervals of space between columns. Narrow margins create compositional tension as typographic elements interact dynamically with the edges of the page, whereas wide margins provide a sense of calm (Fig. **69**). No rules govern the use of margins; however, when margin intervals are unequal, the resulting visual tension can provide a pleasing asymmetrical appearance. In publications involving spreads, the gutter margins should take into account the amount of space needed for binding. Text columns should not appear as though they are being swallowed by the gutter. Also, margins should be generous enough to prevent printed elements from being improperly trimmed during the printing process. (For further discussion, see *"Column and margin,"* pp. 53–55.)

Typographic grids exist in a nearly infinite number of configurations, accommodating a wide range of design needs. Figure **70** presents a small sampling of grids that range from one to sixteen modules.

68.

text columns

column intervals

flow line

spatial zone

grid modules

margins

68.
The typographic grid is a structure with features specifically suited to the physical properties of typographic elements.

69.
Margins function within grids to set the typographic stage; they may be dynamically asymmetrical or quietly symmetrical.

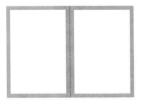

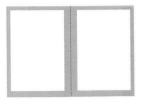

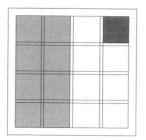
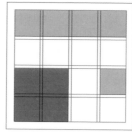
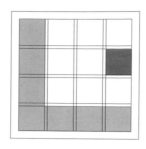

71.
Spatial interaction and compositional balance are achieved when modules define void spaces that are integral to the geometry of the page.

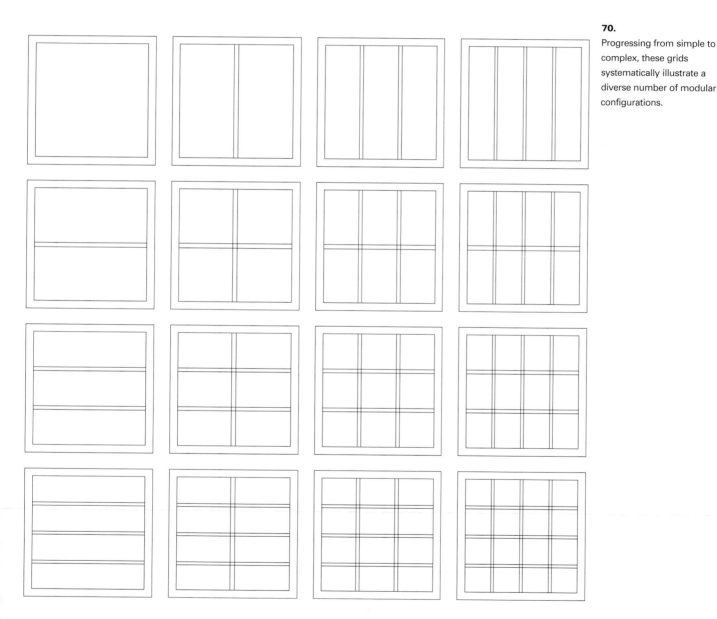

70.
Progressing from simple to complex, these grids systematically illustrate a diverse number of modular configurations.

These modules, which are constructed with horizontal and vertical lines, represent the type and image areas of the grid. Variations in both the size and shape of modules and the intervals of space separating them are shown. Modules may be combined into a variety of sizes and configurations. It is the designer's task to transform the rigid structure of the grid into a lively pattern of positive and negative modular combinations (Fig. **71**). Generally, as the number of modules within a grid increases, so too does the designer's flexibility in organizing the elements and achieving dynamic scale contrasts. However, a point of diminishing returns is reached when a grid is inappropriately complex for the content. Careful study of the content will reveal the most appropriate grid for the occasion.

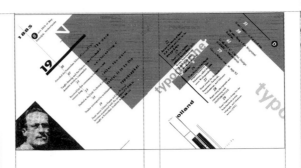

Modular relationships can be established without the use of the traditional typographic grid. A grid ratio, which is a mathematical relationship between two or more grid measurements, governs the size and placement of typographic elements. The ratio X:2X (one unit to two units) indicates the relative size of grid dimensions (Fig. **72**). This stepped progression of X:2X establishes an underlying modular system among the parts.

The type area within a grid is comprised of vertical columns. The width of text columns and the intervals between them should promote optimum legibility when required. The size of type should be measured on the column width to achieve the ideal number of characters per line. Once these factors are considered, column widths may comprise any number of modules within the grid (Fig. **73**).

Grids may consist of primary and secondary divisions of space. For example, the grid used in this book consists of two columns as the dominant structure, with an optional structure of five columns (note the visible grid lines on this page). Concurrent grids not only provide added flexibility, they also enable the designer to layer typographic elements, achieving an illusion of three-dimensionality.

Departing from the conventions of the traditional grid, which is characterized by horizontal and vertical relationships, it may be desirable to employ dynamic structural divisions based upon the diagonal and the circle, or hybrid combinations of spatial divisions (Fig. **74**). Again, the designer should be aware of the appropriateness of such approaches in light of the context of the problem.

Grids allow for the distribution of typographic elements into a clearly intelligible order. Within the internal structure created, headlines, text, captions, images, and other parts of the message are integrated. The areas occupied, which correspond to specific modules or groups of modules, are referred to as spatial zones. After identifying all the parts of a message, the designer assigns them to specific zones. The result is a logical hierarchy of parts and information that is more accessible to the reader.

The book *American Graphic Design Timelines* features a highly flexible grid that makes it possible for readers to compare and contrast timelines of several design and related themes, including major events in world and U.S. history, cultural events, American graphic designers, companies, organizations, and publications (Figs. **75–77**). In addition to the timelines, each section contains a number of other informational components that are accommodated by the grid. The American graphic designers section, for example, includes a headline (the designer's name), quotation, reproductions of characteristic work, captions describing the work, a narrative reviewing significant contributions to the field,

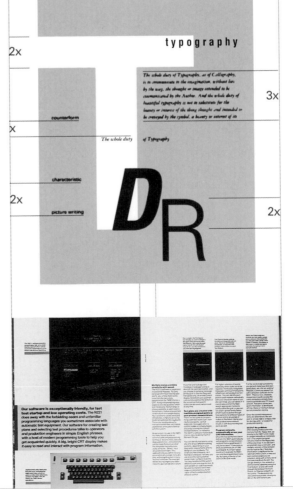

72.

This exploratory composition exhibits modular relationships among elements. (Designer: Debra Thompson)

73.

This layout, characterized by a rhythmic tension of typographic and photographic elements, demonstrates legible text settings on columns of single and triple module width. (Designer: John Kane)

As the pages of the book turn, timelines can be compared one with another due to the interactive grid system

and a biographical timeline. Timelines in all sections are organized in a nine-column grid, with each column corresponding to a decade in the twentieth century. As readers turn the pages, this time-oriented structure remains constant from section to section, making it possible for information to be studied in context. Events on the timeline related to topics elsewhere in the book are keyed by a page number printed on a color-coded square. Depending upon need, several pathways through the book may be taken by readers. It may be read traditionally as a linear narrative from section to section, or it may be used as a reference book where readers make specific connections by comparing the information found on the timelines.

Flow lines are boundaries that divide pages or spreads into major zones. When applied consistently throughout a publication, these boundaries unify pages and promote visual flow. In *American Graphic Design Timelines,* flow lines establish essential boundaries for the major zones of the book. As a result, the information flows naturally through the publication, and readers confidently move from one section to another without getting lost.

In the tradition of modern design, the spatial zones within a typographic grid are not violated. The designer works within the grid framework to objectively present information, while utilizing the principles of ABA form to establish relationships between the parts and to embue the composition with rhythmic and textural variety. But rules can be broken and risks are possible; skilled designers are capable of violating the grid to optimize clarity and maximize visual effect.

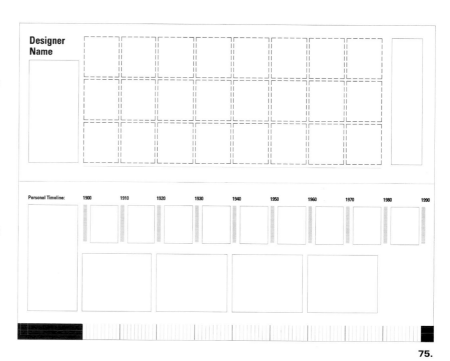

75.

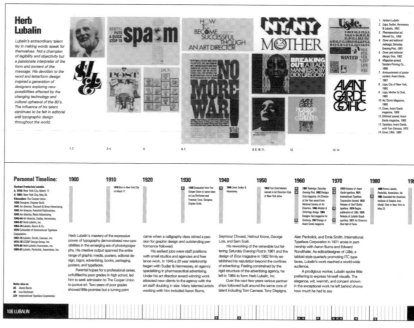

76.

75.

All parts of the information are assigned a "home" in the publication. While these zones are separated from one another spatially, the grid unifies them through visual alignments. (Designer: Keith Jones)

76.

This spread demonstrates how the typographic and photographic information is applied to the grid. Events in the timeline related to subjects elsewhere in the book are keyed by page numbers located in an index at the bottom of the page.

DE STIJL

ping pong
ping pong ping
pong ping pong
ping pong

78.

The typographic message is verbal, visual, and vocal. While typography is read and interpreted verbally, it may also be viewed and interpreted visually, heard and interpreted audibly. It is a dynamic communication medium. In this sense, early twentieth-century typography became a revolutionary form of communication, bringing new expressive power to the written word. Consider the concrete poem "ping pong" (Fig. **78**). The geometric structure of this poem is composed of a repetition of the words *ping* and *pong*. As these words are repeated, they signify the sound of a bouncing ping-pong ball, and the circular letters *p, o,* and *g* reflect the shape of the ball. The full impact of this poem is achieved when it is read aloud. By hearing the sounds and viewing the typographic forms, the typographic message is strengthened.

Significant departures from the use of conventional typographic forms occurred in Europe at the beginning of the twentieth century. During this activist period, experimentation in all the visual and performing arts was affected by potent social and philosophical changes, industrial and technological developments, and new attitudes about aesthetics and modern civilization. Typographic design was pulled into this artistic revolution as poets and visual artists realized that both meaning and form could be intensified in typographic communications.

The Futurist manifesto, written by the Italian poet Filippo Marinetti in 1909, profoundly influenced thinking in Europe and Russia. Futurism praised technology, violence, danger, movement, and speed. Futurist typography, known as "free typography," demonstrated these ideas in a highly expressive manner (Fig. **79**; and see Chapter 1, Fig. **125**). The chill of a scream was expressed in bold type, and quick impressions were intensified through italics. Letters and words raced across the page in dynamic motion.

Among the movements affected by Futurism were Dadaism in France, Switzerland, and Germany; de Stijl in Holland; and Constructivism in Russia. Each of these historical movements has had a penetrating effect upon typography. Artists and

designers associated with these movements saw typography as a powerful means of conveying information relating to the realities of industrialized society (Figs. **80–82;** also see Chapter 1, Figs. **129–35**). They disdained what typography had become: a decorative art form far removed from the realities of the time. The architect Otto Wagner further emphasized that "all modern forms must be in harmony with the new requirements of our time. Nothing that is not practical can be beautiful." Written in 1920, the second de Stijl manifesto clearly demonstrated the concern for a new, expressive typography (Fig. **83**). With dramatic changes taking place in the form and content of typography, the typographic message became a multifaceted and expressive form of communication. Typography needs to be read, seen, heard, felt, and experienced.

78.
"ping pong" (Poet: Eugen Gomringer)

81.
Title lettering for *De Stijl.* (Designer: Theo van Doesburg)

79.
Les mots en liberte futuristes. (Designer: Filippo Marinetti)

80.
Cover of the first issue of *Der Dada.* (Editor: Raoul Hausmann)

82.
Constructivist cover design for *Veshch, Gegenstand, Objet.* (Designer: El Lissitzky)

BERLIN 1922

OBJET

ВЕЩЬ

GEGENSTAND

1-2

REVUE • INTERNATIONALE • DE L'ART • MODERNE
МЕЖДУНАРОДНОЕ • ОБОЗРЕНИЕ • СОВРЕМЕННОГО • ИСКУССТВА
INTERNATIONALE • RUNDSCHAU • DER GEGENWART

84.
Solidarity logotype. (Designer:
Jerzy Janiszewski)

THE WORD IS DEAD…
THE WORD IS IMPOTENT
asthmatic and sentimental poetry
the "me" and "it"
   which is still in common use
    everywhere…
is influenced by an individualism fearful of space
    the dregs of an exhausted era…

psychological analysis
and clumsy rhetoric
have KILLED THE MEANING OF THE WORD…

the word must be reconstructed
    to follow the SOUND as well as
    the IDEA
if in the old poetry
    by the dominance of relative and
    subjective feelings
the intrinsic meaning of the word is destroyed
we want by all possible means
    syntax
    prosody
    typography
    arithmetic
    orthography
to give new meaning to the word and new force
to expression

the duality between prose and poetry can no longer
be maintained
the duality between form and content can no longer
be maintained
Thus for the modern writer form will have a directly
spiritual meaning
it will not describe events
it will not *describe* at all
but ENSCRIBE
it will recreate in the word the common meaning of
events
a constructive unity of form and content…

Leiden, Holland, April 1920.

  Theo van Doesburg
  Piet Mondrian
  Anthony Kok

As a dynamic representation of verbal language, typography must communicate. This functional role is fulfilled when the receiver of a typographic message clearly and accurately understands what is in the mind of the transmitter. This objective, however, is not always accomplished. With a proliferation of typographic messages littering the environment, most are missed or ignored. The messages that are noted, possessing effective qualities relating to form and content, are appropriate to the needs of both message transmitter and message receiver.

The impact of an effective typographic message cannot be easily measured. Some may assume that since printed and broadcast messages are ephemeral, they have little impact upon their audience. This assumption is false. Because typographic ephemera are rhetorical, they often have a long-range effect upon a message receiver, influencing change within the context of social, political, and economic events. The symbol of solidarity expressed by Polish workers (Fig. **84**), the social statements made with graffiti in urban environments, and the typography on billboards aimed at passing motorists all operate as purposeful messages directed toward a predetermined audience within a specific context.

Effective typographic messages result from the combination of logic and intuitive judgment. Only the neophyte approaches this process in a strictly intuitive manner; a purely logical or mechanical procedure undermines human expression. Keeping these two extremes in balance requires the use of a functional verbal/visual vocabulary capable of addressing a broad spectrum of typographic communication.

83.
De Stijl manifesto of 1917.

87.

to scrape   to crease   to peel   to melt   to splinter

Verbal/visual equations

Language, in any of its many forms, is a self-contained system of interactive signs that communicate ideas. Just as elocution and diction enhance and clarify the meaning of our spoken words, typographic signs can be manipulated by a designer to achieve more lucid and expressive typographic communication.

Signs operate in two dimensions: syntactic and semantic. When the mind is concerned with the form of a sign, it is involved with typographic syntax. When it associates a particular meaning with a sign, it is operating in the semantic dimension.

All objects in the environment can potentially function as signs, representing any number of concepts: a smog-filled city signifying pollution, a beached whale representing extinction, and confetti implying celebration – each functions as a sign relating a specific concept.

Signs may exist at various levels of abstraction. A simple example will illustrate this point. Let us consider something as elemental as a red dot. It is a sign only if it carries a particular meaning. It can represent any number of things: balloon, ball, or Japanese flag. The red dot becomes a cherry, for example, as the mind is cued by forms more familiar to its experience (Fig. **85**).

The particular syntactic qualities associated with typographic signs determine a specific meaning. A series of repeated letters, for example, may signify motion or speed, while a small letter in a large void may signify isolation. These qualities, derived from the operating principles of visual hierarchy and ABA form, function as cues, permitting the mind to form concepts. Simple syntactic manipulations, such as the repetition of letters, or the weight change of certain letters, enable words visually to mimic verbal meaning (Fig. **86**). In another example, the letter *E* has been visually altered, relating it to the meaning of specific descriptive words (Fig. **87**).

85.
Signs exist at various levels of abstraction. A form is a sign, however, only when it carries a message. As the mind is cued by forms familiar to experience, information is conveyed.

86.
Simple syntactic manipulations are controlled by such factors as repetition, size change, position change, or weight change. These enable words to mimic verbal meaning visually.

87.
These elaborations of the letter *E* express a variety of concepts. (Designers: Carol Anthony, Linda Dronenburg, and Rebecca Sponga)

leav e

in ter val

di e t

ststutter

dro p

86.

85.

88.
Typographic signs combine to
form a more complex sign,
suggesting a decorated
Christmas tree. (Designer:
Donna Funk)

In language, signs are joined together to create messages. Words as verbal signs, grouped together in a linear fashion, attain their value vis-á-vis other words through opposition and contrast. Words can also evoke meaning through mental association. These associative relations are semantically derived. Since typography is both visual and verbal, it operates in a linear fashion, with words following each other in a specific sequence, or in a nonlinear manner, with elements existing in many syntactic combinations. For example, in the visual poem "O Christmas Tree," the choice of the typeface, Futura Light, is very important. The capital letter *O* is a perfect circle, signifying ornaments; the linear strokes of other letterforms suggest the texture of evergreen needles (Fig. **88**). This typographic message is derived from the mental associations formed by contrasting typographic signs.

Two terms important to the understanding of signs are denotation and connotation. When considering the meaning of typographic signs, denotation refers to objective meaning, the factual world of collective awareness and experience. For example, a denotative interpretation of a yellow *O* would be: "This is a yellow letter *O*" or "This is a yellow circle." Connotative interpretations of the yellow *O* might be: "This is the sun, a slice of lemon, or a golden ring." Connotative observations are often conditioned, for they relate to overtones and are drawn from prior personal experience.

Typographic signs are both verbal and visual. The associations formed between the verbal and visual attributes are verbal/visual equivalencies, which are found in a variety of configurations. These reveal the associative nature of signs composing the typographic message and help us further understand its multifaceted attributes. Figures **89–101** illustrate the nature of some of these verbal/visual equations.

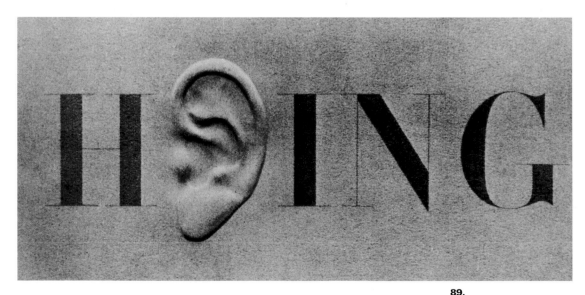

89.
Visual substitution: The visual
sign of an ear is substituted
for the letters *E, A,* and *R.*
(Designer: Lou Dorfsman)

91.

Simultaneity: The numeral *8* functions as the letter *g* in this logotype used for a group exhibition of paintings by the early-twentieth-century American art group The Eight.

92.

Visual transformation: A mother, father, and child are suggested through the visual transformation of the letters *I* and *i*. (Designer: Herb Lubalin)

Families

Taking Things Apart and Putting Things Together

what chemistry is what chemists do and what the results have been

sponsored by the American Chemical Society on the occasion of its 100th anniversary

Union Carbide 270 Park Ave. New York, N.Y. 10017

April 5-May 28, 1976 9:30-4:30 weekdays Closed April 16,17 and Sundays Admission: free

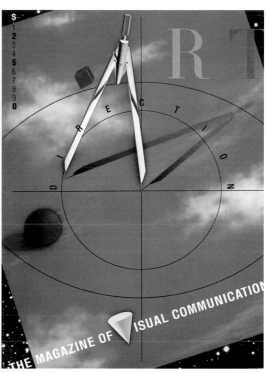

90.

Visual substitution: The visual sign of a compass is substituted for the letter *A* and an inverted cone is substituted for the letter *V*. (Designer: Harold Burch)

93.

Visual exaggeration: The irregular syntactic treatment of typographic signs exaggerates the process of taking things apart and putting things together. (Designer: Steff Geissbuhler)

the American premiere at the Depot in Urbana
of the play by Marcel Achard

translated by Sue Huseman Moretto
directed by Jose Moretto

October 31, November 1, 2, 3 1974
November 7, 8, 9, 10
at 8:00 pm, Friday and Saturday also at 10:30 pm

tickets at Record Service
704 South Sixth Champaign
and at the Depot 223 North Broadway
on nights of performance

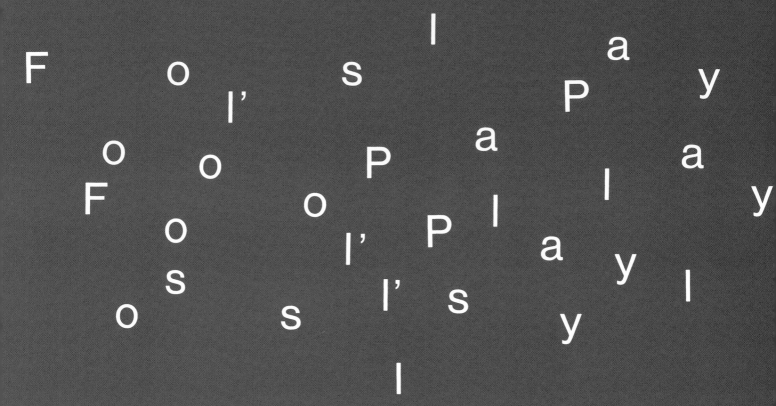

95.

Form combination: Visual and verbal signs are combined into a single typographic statement, creating trademarks that suggest the nature of various industries: an electrical contractor, a maker of plastic fibers for carpets and draperies, and a lithographic printer. (Designer: Don Weller)

95.

96.

Form combination: Verbal signs are combined with visual signs (cables). The resulting forms suggest the qualities of cable transmission. (Designers: Jerry L. Kuyper and Sheila de Bretteville)

97.

Parallel form: The Olivetti logotype and electronic calculator have similar visual characteristics that parallel each other. (Logotype design: Walter Ballmer)

98.

Verbal/visual correspondence: The syntactic qualities of this typographic sign correspond to the graffiti found in an urban environment. (Designer: Jeff Barnes)

99.

Verbal/visual correspondence: The visual characteristics of this typographic sign correspond to the form of a zipper. This is achieved by a repetition of letters and a horizontal shift within the word. (Designer: Richard Rumble)

96.

CABLE

97.

94.

Visual exaggeration: The repetition and playful treatment of typographic forms effectively reinforces the content of the drama *Fool's Play,* for which this poster was designed. (Designer: David Colley)

ZIIIIIIIIIIIIPPPER

99.

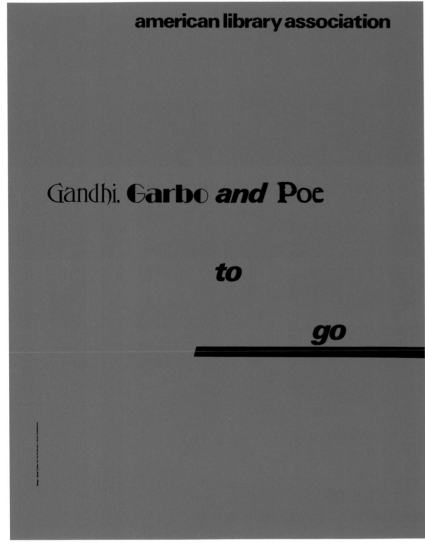

101.

100.

100.
Verbal/visual correspondence:
The visual qualities of the
typefaces chosen for the signs
Gandhi, Garbo, and *Poe* make
direct reference to time and
culture. The message is
further strengthened by the
sounds associated with the
words. (Designer: David
Colley)

101.
Verbal/visual correspondence:
The visual repetition of this
word – unified by the shared
letters *u* and *n* – express the
concept of unity. (Designer:
Steff Geissbuhler)

Function and expression

Functionalism is a term used to describe the utilitarian and pragmatic qualities of designed objects. During the early twentieth century, functionalism was generally equated with designed objects of clarity, purpose, and unornamented simplicity. However, it has since evolved as a subjective notion that varies widely according to the needs of the audience and the objectives of the designer.

For example, if comfort in the design of a chair is defined as plushness and cushiness, an upholstered automatic recliner complete with footrest and vibrator might satisfy the criteria of a functional chair.

In contrast to the automatic recliner is the red/blue chair, a central artifact of the de Stijl movement, designed in 1918 by Gerrit Rietveld (Fig. **102**). Members of de Stijl sought a restrained expression and a new philosophy for living. With its hard, flat surfaces, the red/blue chair appears very uncomfortable; however, Rietveld's desire was for the chair to promote alert mental activity through rigid support. The seat and backrest planes are attached at only one edge, enabling the pliable wood to adjust to the user's weight. In this regard, the chair functions according to Rietveld's intentions. In an interior environment, Rietveld's red/blue chair has the presence and visual harmony of a piece of sculpture. The needs for a functional object (seating) and for aesthetic experience are fulfilled in this one object.

In typography, function is the purposeful communication of information to a specific audience. Although the range of possible typographic design solutions is infinite, the appropriateness of a solution always depends upon the purpose for which it was intended. Varying degrees of formal reduction or elaboration can be effective when solving specific typographic problems.

102.
Red/blue chair, 1918.
(Designer: Gerrit Rietveld)

103.

The elemental shape and sequence of letters in the word *eye* visually suggest two eyes and a nose. Set in News Gothic, this typographic configuration serves as the masthead for *eye, The International Review of Graphic Design.* (Designer: Stephen Coates)

104.

Required to appear on all food packaging in the United States, the standardized *Nutrition Facts* label clearly provides consumers with important information about the nutritional value of foods. Typography responsibly assumes an objective, informational role. (Designer: Berkey Belser)

105.

The "A" stamp is the official priority stamp of the Swiss Post Office. A simple configuration of three interlocking shapes suggests an uppercase *A.* The trilogy of shapes represents the co-dependent parts of the mailing process: message, sender, and receiver. (Designer: Jean-Benoît Lévy)

106.

The vitality of *Rolling Stone* magazine is revealed in this monumental, three-dimensional letterform, a deconstructed element used in the traveling exhibition *The 30th Anniversary Covers Tour.* (Designer: J. Abbott Miller)

107.

This sequence of frames represents the animated "splash page" of a Web site designed to teach children how to read. The letter *O,* containing the remaining vowels, rolls onto the screen. As the letterforms transform in color, they roll off of the screen and disintegrate. (Designer: John Stratiou)

Formal reduction can be used to create optimum clarity and legibility, presenting complex information, such as news or scientific data, in a clear and straightforward manner. Orderly presentation guides the eye from one element to another, preserving reader interest and attention (Figs. **103** and **104**).

Another approach, expressionism, accomplishes its purpose through formal elaboration and ornamentation, creating visual impact. When appropriate, attention can be given to experimental, expressive, and ornamental possibilities. Ornament serves a variety of practical needs. Because it is semiotic, iconographic, and historical, it identifies the object with which it is associated. Expressive and ornamental typographic forms place objects in time, reveal their purpose, and clarify their structures (Figs. **105–107**). The formal elaboration of objects in architecture, industrial design, and the fine arts can significantly influence typographic possibilities. Figures **71** and **119** (Chapter 1) and **108–110** possess strong ornamental qualities. Innovative typography can emerge when a designer fully understands communication needs and is able to assimilate a diversity of visual ideas.

On this subject, Ladislav Sutnar commented that "an eccentric visual scandal or visual shock of the outrageous and of the unexpected can catch the attention of the astonished eye . . . it may also delight the eye to see a fresh design concept or a message so orderly presented as to make comprehension fast and easy." A designer can avoid conventional solutions to typographic problems when innovation is appropriate. A single approach to typographical design, induced by stylistic convention and predetermined formulas, is a routine activity lacking the vitality of meaningful typographic invention. Sound principles and a trained vision should supersede dependency upon preconceived formulas. For typography to be truly functional, satisfying the needs of an audience, a designer must understand both the verbal and visual attributes of a typographic message.

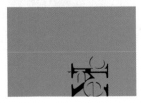

103.

104.

107.

105.

108.

The wheel of a farm tractor provides a substitute for the letter *o* in the word *tomato*. The large scale and oblique angle of the type, and the hot color set the stage for a summer event at a farmer's market. (Designer: John Malinoski)

109.

This view book acquires its robust and expressive quality through vivid color, varying typographic textures, and structural complexity.

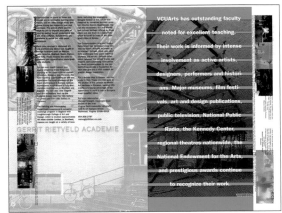

110.

Expressive text type is achieved on a spread of the book *Elvis+Marilyn* by its configuration into the letter *A*. (Designer: Mirko Ilić)

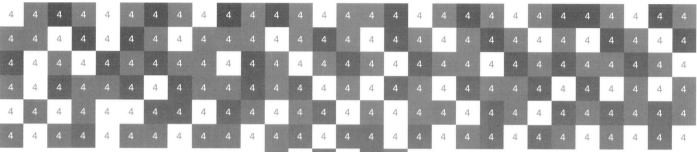

Typographic legibility is widely misunderstood and often neglected by designers. Yet it is a subject that requires careful study and constant evaluation. Legibility is achieved by controlling the qualities and attributes inherent in typography that make type readable. These attributes make it possible for a reader to comprehend typographic forms with the least amount of difficulty.

Typographers and designers have a definite responsibility to their readers to communicate as clearly and appropriately as possible. This responsibility is suggested by Henry David Thoreau in *Walden:* "A written word is the choicest of relics. It is something at once more intimate with us and more universal than any other work of art."

a a a d d d

1.
As the top stroke of the letter *a* rises to become the ascender of the *d*, the intermediate forms are not easily deciphered by the reader.

As signs representing sounds in spoken language, letters are basic to legible typography. The primary purpose of a letterform is to convey a recognizable meaning to the mind. Therefore, letterforms must be designed with clarity, each being distinct within the alphabet. The contrast among individual characters makes it possible for the reader to decipher written information without confusion.

The most legible typefaces are those timeless examples characterized by three qualities upon which legibility is dependent: contrast, simplicity, and proportion. These typefaces exemplify beautiful and functional letterforms. A close look at typefaces such as Garamond, Baskerville, and Bodoni will reveal why their forms are as vital now as when they were first designed. (See the type specimens in Chapter Eight.) The use of well-designed typefaces, however, is no guarantee that typography will be legible. Effective typography depends upon such factors as the communications context and the subtle adjustment of letterforms and their spatial relationships, each of which may have an effect upon how easily typography is read. Making type legible is a masterful achievement, requiring a process of intelligent decision making.

In the strictest sense, legible typography is a means of communicating information objectively. However, typographic designers sometimes bend the traditional criterion of legibility for expressive purposes. Designers, with their instinctive curiosity, have experimented with typography, playing with forms, imposing new meaning, and changing the standards of typographic communication. Innovative typography always poses fresh questions, challenges edicts of the past, and redefines the concepts of legibility and functionality.

This chapter approaches legibility as an art of spatial synthesis. As an art, it is not absolute. Therefore, information derived from legibility research should be considered only a guideline. The knowledge designers have of legibility is based upon a legacy of typographic history and a keen awareness of the visible world. This knowledge will continually evolve, creating new standards for readability and functional typography.

Distinguishing characteristics of letters

The alphabet consists of twenty-six letters, each of which has evolved over the centuries to a unique place within this system of signs. This evolution has occurred gradually. It is no accident that the individual shapes of letterforms have developed out of a need to improve the communication process. As the alphabet has evolved, it has become a flexible system of signs in which all letters are distinct, yet all work together harmoniously as visible language.

In spite of the innumerable variations of size, proportion, weight, and elaboration in letterform design, the basic structure of each letterform must remain the same. For example, the capital *A* always consists of two oblique strokes joined at the top and connected by a horizontal stroke at their midsection. Sufficient contrast must exist between the letters in a font so that they can be easily distinguished (Fig. **1**).

2.
Four groupings show the structural relationships of all letters in the alphabet. The divisions are based upon the dominant strokes of each letter.

il

acegos

bdfhjmnpqrtu

kvwxyz

EFHILT

COQS

BDGJPRU

AKMNVWXYZ

Letters can be clustered into four groups, according to their contrasting properties. These are letterforms with strokes that are vertical, curved, a combination of vertical and curved, or oblique (Fig. **2**). From these groupings, one notices that letters are not only similar in many ways but that there are also some important differences. Obviously, letters with similar characteristics are more likely to be confused, while letters with distinct qualities provide contrast within a word. Letters within a word are most legible when they are taken, in equal number, from each group.

A closer look at the alphabet reveals additional characteristics distinguishing letters. The upper halves of letters provide more visual cues for letter recognition than the lower halves (Fig. **3**). Likewise, the right halves of letters are more recognizable than the left halves (Fig. **4**). Dominant letters within the alphabet that aid in word recognition are those that have either ascenders or descenders. Through tests, researchers have contributed valuable information about the comparative legibility of each letter in the alphabet. Findings vary only slightly. Lowercase letters can be rank ordered according to their distinctiveness as follows: *d k m g h b p w u l j t v z r o f n a x y e i q c s.* This varies, however, with different typefaces.

The most frequently used letters, such as the vowels *a e i o u,* are among the most illegible, and *c g s x* are easily missed in reading. Other letters that often cause confusion and are mistaken for one another are *f i j l t.* For example, the words *fail, tail,* and *jail* each begin with letters of similar shape and could easily be misread. The eye could possibly perceive *f* as *t,* or *t* as *j* (Fig. **5**). The designer should carefully study the words in display typography to identify such potential problems in legibility.

fail
tail
jail

5.
Words have a tendency to be misread and confused with each other when composed of letters of similar shape.

As with the changing position
of the dancer, subtle changes
in the drawing of the forms
and counterforms significantly
affect perception.

6.

7.

DANCER
DANCER
DANCER

G
DANCER
DANCER
G

shape

SHAPE

8.
Word recognition is based on
word structure, a combination
of word shape (defined by the
contours of the letters) and
internal word pattern. The
word set in lowercase letters is
more distinct than the word
set in all capitals, because its
irregular word shape makes it
more recognizable.

The perception of a letter is based upon the
form/counterform relationship. Counterforms are
as significant to legibility as the shapes of the
letters themselves. This principle relates to all
aspects of visual phenomena. A dancer
manipulates space with the body, "making
shape," defining, and redefining space (Fig. **6**).
If the shape of a letter is changed, so is the way
in which that letter is perceived. Letter shapes are
cues that distinguish one letter in the alphabet
from another (Fig. **7**).

Much controversy has surrounded the issue of
the comparative legibility of serif and sans-serif
typefaces. One argument claims that serif text type
is more readable because the serifs reinforce the
horizontal flow of each line. Serif typefaces also
offer more character definition: for example, the
serif on the bottom horizontal stroke of a capital *E*
accentuates the difference between it and a capital
F. However, the relative legibility between serif and
sans-serif typefaces is negligible. Reader familiarity
and the control of other legibility factors (to be
discussed later) are far more significant than the
selection of a serif or sans-serif typeface. (See the
text-type specimens in Chapter Eight to compare
the legibility of serif and sans-serif type.)

The nature of words
While individual letters as discrete units, affecting
all other spatial and aesthetic considerations, are
the basis for a discussion of legibility, one reads
and perceives words and groups of words and not
just letters. In discussing typographic legibility,
Frederic Goudy observed that "a letter may not be
considered apart from its kinsmen; it is a mere
abstract and arbitrary form far remote from the
original picture or symbol out of which it grew,
and has no particular significance until it is
employed to form part of a word."

There are two important factors involved in the
reading process: word shape and internal pattern.
Words are identified by their distinctive word
shapes, strings of letters that are instantaneously
perceived, permitting the reader to grasp content
easily (Fig. **8**). Counterforms create internal word
patterns that provide cues for word recognition.

```
O R D W
R D W O
D W O R
R O W D
W O R D
O W R D
```
9.

When these internal spaces are altered sufficiently, the perceptual clarity of a word may also be altered. The weight of letters is vital to word recognition and influences an adequate internal pattern. The combination of word shape and internal pattern creates a word structure, an all-inclusive term describing the unique composition of each word (Fig. **9**).

Capital and lowercase letters
If a text is set entirely in capital letters, it suffers a loss of legibility and the reader is placed at a significant disadvantage. Type set in this manner severely retards reading – more so than any other legibility factor. Figure **8** demonstrates that a word set in all capital letters is characterized by a straight horizontal alignment, creating an even word outline with letters of similar shape and size. A reader is not provided with the necessary visual cues that make words recognizable.

TEXT SET IN ALL CAPITAL LETTERS ALSO USES A SIGNIFICANTLY GREATER AMOUNT OF SPACE THAN TEXT SET IN LOWERCASE LETTERS OF THE SAME SIZE. AS MUCH AS 35 PERCENT MORE SPACE CAN BE CONSUMED WHEN USING ALL CAPITAL LETTERS.

On the other hand, text set in lowercase letters forms words that are distinct, based upon their irregular word shape and internal pattern. A variety of letter shapes, ascenders, and descenders provides rich contrasts that assure satisfactory perception. Once a specific word shape is perceived, it is stored in the reader's memory until the eye confronts it again while reading. A reader can become confused if a word takes on an appearance that differs from the originally learned word shape.

Interletter and interword spacing
The spacing of letterforms has a significant impact on legibility. Most readers are unaware of the typographic designer's attention to this detail. Minute spatial relationships are controlled to create not only readable but beautiful and harmonious typographic communication. It takes great skill to specify spaces between letters and

words, determining proper spatial relationships. Letters must flow rhythmically and gracefully into words, and words into lines.

Typographic texture and tone are affected by the spacing of letters, words, and lines. When the texture and the spatial intervals between typographic elements are consistent, the result is an easily readable text. Texture is also affected by qualities unique to the design of specific typefaces. Sometimes designers arrange type for specific spatial effects, sensitively balancing norms of legibility with graphic impact. (See the text-type specimens in Chapter Eight.)

Too much or too little space between letters and words destroys the normal texture intended by the typeface designer. As you read this sentence, notice that the narrow letter and word spacing causes words to merge together visually. L i k e w i s e, t h e e x t r e m e l y w i d e l e t t e r s p a c i n g o f t h i s s e n t e n c e i s a l s o d i s r u p t i v e f o r t h e r e a d e r.

There is often a danger of misfit letter combinations, which, in earlier typesetting systems such as Linotype, could not be easily corrected. (If the type size is small and evenly textured, this is a minor problem.) With phototypesetting and digital typesetting, these details can be corrected easily. The kerning of specific letter combinations can be programmed into the typesetting system. As type is set, appropriate letterspacing appears automatically (Fig. **10**).

SPACING
SPACING

9.
Letters can be grouped in myriad combinations. Words that are perceived as having meaning are those with which we have become familiar over time. They form a distinct and familiar shape.

Reading is disrupted by inappropriate wordspacing.

10.
Misfit letter combinations and irregular spacing can be a problem, particularly for display type. Optical adjustments should be made to achieve spatial consistency between elements.

EdwardoJohnston,oaocalligrapher, advocatedoaowordospaceoequaloto aolowercaseoo.
11.

AaronrBurns,ranrinfluential typographer,rsuggestedrwordrspacing equalrtorarlowercaserr.

Space between letters and words should be proportional to the width of letters. This proportion is often open to personal judgment (Fig. **11**). With experience and practice comes an understanding of the spacing that is suitable to a particular design project.

Type size, line length, and interline spacing
Critical to spatial harmony and legibility is an understanding of the triadic relationship of type size, line length, and interline spacing. When properly employed, these variables can improve the legibility of even poorly designed letterforms or enhance the legibility of those forms considered highly legible.

It is difficult to generalize about which sizes of type should be used, how long lines should be, or how much space should be inserted between lines. These decisions are based upon comparative judgments. The guidelines discussed in this section can never replace the type designer's sensitively trained eye for typographic detail. The normal reading distance for most printed matter is from twelve to fourteen inches, a fact to be kept in mind when making decisions about type size, since it affects the way in which a specific type size is perceived.

Text type that is too small or too large makes reading difficult. Small type reduces visibility by destroying counterforms, which affect word recognition, while large type can force a reader to perceive type in sections rather than as a whole. According to legibility research, the most legible sizes of text type at normal reading distances range from 9 to 12 point. This range results from the wide variation of x-height in different typefaces. That is, when typefaces of the same

point size are placed side by side, they may appear to be different sizes, because their x-heights vary radically. This is important to keep in mind when selecting typefaces and sizes.

An interesting comparison is the relationship between Univers 55 and Baskerville. Univers 55 has a very large x-height, with short ascenders and descenders. It appears much larger than Baskerville set in the same size, which has a smaller x-height and large ascenders and descenders. (See text column specimens in Chapter Eight.)

Type sizes larger than 12 point may require more fixation pauses, making reading uncomfortable and inefficient. A fixation pause occurs when the eye stops on a line of type during reading, actually perceiving the meaning of groups of words. When there are fewer fixation pauses, there is greater reading efficiency and comprehension. When text type is smaller than 9 point, internal patterns can break down, destroying legibility. The reading audience is also a major consideration. For example, children learning to read need large type sizes in simple formats, as do adults with poor eyesight.

An appropriate line length is essential for achieving a pleasant reading rhythm, allowing a reader to relax and concentrate on the content of the words. Overly short or long lines will tire a reader. Excess energy is expended when reading long lines, and it is difficult to find the next line. A short column measure requires the eye to change lines too often, and there is an inadequate supply of horizontal perceptual cues. Compare the legibility of this paragraph with the legibility of Figures **12** and **13**.

An appropriate line length is essential for achieving a pleasant reading rhythm, allowing a reader to relax and concentrate on the content of the words. Overly short or long lines will tire a reader. Excess energy is expended when reading long lines, and it is difficult to find the next line. A short column measure requires the eye to change lines too often, and there is an inadequate supply of horizontal perceptual cues.
13.

An appropriate line length is essential for achieving a pleasant reading rhythm, allowing a reader to relax and concentrate on the content of the words. Overly short or long lines will tire a reader. Excess energy is expended when reading long lines, and it is difficult to find the next line. A short column measure requires the eye to change lines too often, and there is an inadequate supply of horizontal perceptual cues.
12.

Interline spacing intervals

Interline spacing intervals

14.

Certainly, every typographic problem has its own legibility requirements. The following data can serve as a point of departure in determining how to create legible typography. Line length is dependent upon both the size of type and the amount of space between lines. When working with the optimum sizes of 9-, 10-, 11-, and 12-point text type, a maximum of ten to twelve words (or sixty to seventy characters) per line would be acceptable. This would equal a line length of approximately 18 to 24 picas. An optimum line length for the average 10-point type is 19 picas.

The amount of interline spacing is dependent upon several factors. Generally, lines with no added space between them are read more slowly than lines with added space. Proper interline spacing carries the eye naturally from one line to the next. When there is inadequate space between lines, the eye takes in other lines as well. If lines are too widely spaced, a reader may have trouble locating the next line. As column measure increases, the interline spacing should also increase to maintain a proper ratio of column length to interline spacing.

Typefaces with larger x-heights need more interline spacing than those with smaller x-heights. Also, when working with display types, the frequency with which ascenders and descenders occur makes a difference. They can optically lessen the amount of white space between lines. Optical adjustments in display types should be made when spaces between lines appear inconsistent because of ascenders and descenders (Fig. **14**). Generally, the maximum line length for text type with a small x-height – used without interline spacing – is about sixty-five characters. When text type with a large x-height is used without interline spacing, legibility is diminished when line length exceeds about fifty-two characters.

Research has shown that for the optimum sizes of text type (9, 10, 11, and 12 point), one to four points of interline spacing can be effectively added between lines to increase legibility. Remember, this is not to say that type set outside these optimum specifications will be illegible, for critical judgment can ensure legible typography without inhibiting fresh approaches.

Weight
When considering the legibility of a typeface, the thickness (weight) of the strokes should be examined. A typeface that is too light or too heavy has diminished legibility. Light typefaces cannot be easily distinguished from their background, while a typeface that is too heavy has a tendency to lose its internal pattern of counterforms.

Weight can be used advantageously to provide contrast and clarity between typographic page elements such as titles, headlines, and subheads. A heavier or lighter weight can emphasize one piece of information over another, thereby making information more comprehensible.

Extreme thick and thin strokes within letters of a particular typeface make reading more difficult, preventing smooth transitions from one word or group of words to the next. Thin strokes are less visible, creating confusion with letters of similar shape. When a typeface with extreme contrasts between thick and thin strokes is used in a text setting, a dazzle or sparkle effect is created. The reader begins to have difficulty distinguishing the words, and legibility decreases significantly.

Character Width
The shape and size of the page or column can influence the selection of character width. For example, a condensed typeface might be selected for a narrow page or column, achieving proportional harmony and an adequate number of characters and words to the line.

The width of letters is also an important legibility factor. Generally, condensed type is more difficult to read. A narrower letter changes the form/counterform relationship, causing letters to have an extreme vertical posture that can alter eye movement and reading patterns, diminishing legibility.

Italics
Similar to other situations where typeforms deviate from a reader's expectations, italics impede reading. An extreme italic slant can slow the reading process and is disliked by many readers. However, italic type can be very effective when used as a means of providing emphasis.

Typefaces of median weight are most legible.

In text type, weight change significantly affects legibility.

In text type, legibility is affected when condensed or expanded typefaces are used.

93

15.
Black type on a white
background and on a light
gray background prove highly
legible. Legibility suffers as the
contrast between type and its
background diminishes. The
color temperature of the paper
upon which type is printed
and the choice of typeface
also have a relative affect
upon legibility.

16.
Legibility is greatly
compromised when type and
background are assigned
complementary colors.
Adjusting the value of either
color improves contrast and
thus legibility. In this example,
the backgrounds of the
complementary colors blue
and orange are lightened,
for improved legibility.

Black type on
a white background

Black type on
a light gray background

White type on
a light gray background

White type on
a dark gray background

White type on
a black background

15.

Blue type on
an orange background

Orange type on
a blue background

Blue type on
a light orange background

Orange type on
a dark blue background

16.

Legibility and color

Incorporating color into type significantly affects legibility, and the most important consideration when working with type and color is to achieve an appropriate contrast between type and its background. The degree of legibility sought depends entirely upon the intent of the designer and the nature of the content.

It has long been considered that black type on a white background is most legible. While this combination remains an excellent choice, other alternatives may offer equal if not improved legibility due to improved digital and printing technologies, and the fact that color is a relative phenomenon (Fig. **15**). When applied to type, color should be evaluated in relationship to the conditions in which it is read. In print, for example, one should consider the specific nature of the paper. If the paper is white, is it a warm or cool white? Is the surface of the paper rough or smooth? Is it coated or uncoated? What typeface is being considered, and in what size will it appear?

Generally, all legibility guidelines related to working with color and type in print apply also to type appearing on a computer screen. However, the use of color and type on a screen should also take into consideration the conditions of screen resolution and luminescence, as well as whether the type is static or in motion. Digital technologies have vastly changed the way in which designers use color and type, making it possible to easily assign color from palettes containing millions of colors. Also, the range of typographic applications continues to expand, with type asserting a role not only in printed and environmental communications, but also in on-screen media such as the Internet.

Appropriate contrast between type and its background requires that designers carefully weigh the three basic color properties of hue, value, and saturation. By definition, *hue* and *tone* are simply more specific names for color. *Value* refers to the lightness or darkness of a color, and *saturation* – also called *chroma* or *intensity* – is the relative brightness of a color.

17.
The analogous hues yellow-green and blue are sufficiently different in value, resulting in an acceptable combination. A moderate adjustment of the yellow-green to a lighter value further improves legibility.

18.
Red and orange hues exist very close to each other on the color wheel, and when used for type and background do not offer sufficient contrast. A tint or shade of one of the colors, however, improves legibility.

19.
By scrutinizing the roles of value and hue contrast, the legibility of most typefaces can be improved. Typefaces that are visually challenging due to extreme proportions (heavy, light, wide, or thin) can be made more legible by assigning appropriate color combinations.

All colors possess characteristics of hue, value, and saturation, and when combining color and type, balancing these properties is a critical legibility concern. For example, the highly saturated, complementary colors blue and orange offer maximum hue contrast, but when applied to type and background the effect is one of vibration that quickly tires the eye. These colors compete in brightness and vie for attention. If the type or background is lightened or darkened by selecting a tint or shade of the hue, legibility is improved (Fig. **16**).

But not all fully saturated hues are of the same value. Two highly saturated, analogous colors, for example, such as blue and green, provide sufficient contrast without a dizzying effect. (Analogous colors are those that appear in close proximity on a color wheel.) Because the green is actually lighter in value and brighter in saturation than the blue, there may be no need for further adjustment (Fig. **17**). However, if analogous colors are too close to each other on the color wheel, adjustments in contrast will be necessary (Fig. **18**).

Of all the contrasts of color, value affects legibility most significantly. Value contrasts effectively preserve the shapes and formal details of letters, thus making them more easily recognizable.

Typefaces possess unique shapes, proportions, and individual characteristics that should be taken into consideration when selecting color. A typeface with fine serifs, ultrathin strokes, small counters, or any number of other visual eccentricities may appear illegible if color is not carefully articulated. By turning value or intensity up or down in these situations, legibility can improve greatly (Fig. **19**).

Blue type on
a green background

Blue type on
a light green background

17.

Violet type on
a blue background

Light violet type on
a blue background

18.

Univers 49, an ultracondensed typeface

Univers 49, an ultracondensed typeface

**Bauer Bodoni Black, a typeface
with extreme thick and thin strokes**

**Bauer Bodoni Black, a typeface
with extreme thick and thin strokes**

19.

7-point Minion Regular

10-point Minion Regular

20.

The smaller and more delicate the type, the more contrast is needed to ensure adequate legibility.

color color

color color

color color

21.

If you find it necessary to present large amounts of text type in color, try increasing slightly the amount of space between lines. Even an additional point of space can make a significant difference, and a reader might be encouraged to continue rather than stop.

22.

If you find it necessary to present large amounts of text type in color, try increasing slightly the amount of space between lines. Even an additional point of space can make a significant difference, and a reader might be encouraged to continue rather than stop.

The type size is also an important consideration in the planning of color. At smaller sizes, type requires backgrounds that are significantly different in hue and/or value (Fig. **20**).

Whether type is printed on paper or appears on-screen, an optical effect referred to as "typographic color" occurs. Not to be confused with the particular hue of a typographic element, this effect is the result of the visual qualities inherent in individual typefaces and the spacing of letters, words, and lines of type (Fig. **21**). Typographic color is an important tool, for it is an effective means by which hierarchical order and emphasis are achieved between different typographic elements. Also, if a large amount of text is set in an elaborate or unusual color setting, an increase in the space between lines can significantly improve legibility (Fig. **22**).

The reading process can be severely retarded when reading type on textured or photographic backgrounds, for they potentially interfere with the internal patterns of words and their distinctive word shapes. This problem is further exacerbated when such backgrounds and the type appearing on them are incompatible in color for reasons stated earlier in this discussion.

21.

Words set in various typefaces appear different in "color." As interletter spacing increases, the words also appear lighter in tone.

22.

The illusion of "lighter" or "darker" text is achieved with the introduction of additional interline spacing, and in some situations, legibility is improved.

Compare the legibility of
the justified and unjustified
columns.

justified

unjustified
(flush-left, ragged right)

Justified and unjustified typography

Traditionally, it was common practice to set type in a justified alignment. This was done for reasons of efficiency; in addition, it was more familiar and was considered to be more refined. In the 1920s, designers began to question this typographic convention and experiment with alternative text-setting styles. Unjustified and asymmetrical typography began to find widespread acceptance. Among experimental typographic designers was Herbert Bayer, who said, "I have long believed that our conventional way of writing and setting type could be improved for easier reading. In my first typographic works in the early twenties, I started to abandon the flush-left-and-right system for short lines of text and have introduced the flush-left system, leaving a ragged-right outline."

There are appropriate reasons for setting either justified or unjustified typography, but type set flush left and ragged right promotes greater legibility. If properly used, flush-left, ragged-right typography provides visual points of reference that guide the eye smoothly down the page from line to line. Because each line is either shorter or longer than the next, the eye is cued from one to another. In a justified setting, all lines are of equal length. Lacking are visual cues that promote easy reading.

With the use of unjustified typography, wordspacing is even, creating a smooth rhythm and a consistent texture. The indiscriminate placement of additional space between words in order to justify lines causes awkward gaps or "rivers" in paragraphs, which are disruptive to reading. Hyphenations at the end of lines should be used whenever possible to keep wordspacing consistent.

When setting ragged-right text, care should be taken not to rag the type too much. Uncontrolled line breaks of erratic rhythm can create awkward spaces that inhibit reading. In ragged-right type, care should be given to the selection of interline spacing, for it influences legibility and appearance. Spatial consistency and rhythmic line breaks result from careful typographical decisions.

The breaking of lines can be determined by the author's meaning rather than by appearance. This method, sometimes referred to as "thought-unit" typography, arranges lines into discrete parts related to the meaning of the text. Ragged-right lines may be of any length, with line breaks that are logical and focus on the intended message of the writer (Fig. **23**).

Paragraphs and indentions

An important goal for a designer is to distinguish typographically one thought from another, clarify content, and increase reader comprehension. Clear separation of paragraphs in a body of text is one way to accomplish this goal.

It is common practice in the design of books, magazines, and newspapers to indent each paragraph, usually with moderate indention of one to three ems. It is also typographic practice not to indent the first paragraph in an article, chapter, or advertisement so that the square corner of the first column can be maintained.

Paragraphs can also be separated by inserting additional space between them. This space should be proportional to the amount of interline spacing, which corresponds to the vertical measurement of the typographic grid. Paragraphs are often separated by one line space. This method should be avoided if the original copy is full of short, choppy paragraphs. Spaces between such paragraphs could be very disturbing, consuming too much space. Indentions and additional linespace are also used to establish order within complex tabular matter, such as financial charts and scientific data.

1:1 In the beginning
God created the heaven and the earth.
2 And the earth was without form, and void;
and darkness was upon the face of the deep.
And the Spirit of God
moved upon the face of the waters.

3 And God said,
Let there be light:
and there was light.
4 And God saw the light, that it was good:
and God divided the light from the darkness.
5 And God called the light Day,
and the darkness he called Night.
And the evening and the morning
were the first day.

6 And God said,
Let there be a firmament
in the midst of the waters,
and let it divide the waters from the waters.
7 And God made the firmament,
and divided the waters
which were under the firmament
from the waters
which were above the firmament:
and it was so.

8 And God called the firmament Heaven.
And the evening and the morning
were the second day.

9 And God said,
Let the waters under the heaven
be gathered together unto one place,
and let the dry land appear:
and it was so.
10 And God called the dry land Earth;
and the gathering together of the waters
called he Seas:
and God saw that it was good.
11 And God said,
Let the earth bring forth grass,
the herb yielding seed,
and the fruit tree yielding fruit after his kind,
whose seed is in itself, upon the earth:
and it was so.
12 And the earth brought forth grass,
and herb yielding seed after his kind,
and the tree yielding fruit,
whose seed was in itself, after his kind:
and God saw that it was good.

This is Garamond
This is Garamond
This is Garamond

24.

a b c d e f g
h i j k l m n
o p q r s t u
v w x y z

25.

Legibility and electronic page design

New legibility issues emerged when the digital revolution occurred in typography and design. This includes concerns relating to software, discussed in this section, and problems related to on-screen display, covered in the following section. Electronic page design offers designers more possibilities for type manipulation than ever before, resulting in an obligation to know more about the cultural and formal evolution of typography than in times past. Without adequate knowledge of typographic legibility, it is easy for designers to blindly follow fads, succumb to common visual clichés provided by software, or thoughtlessly yield to the built-in defaults of a computer application. Legibility is a concern that should be continually addressed as technology changes. Because designers now work at a keyboard, they are directly responsible for composing legible type – a task once accomplished by sending specifications to a compositor at a typesetting firm.

As a result of desktop technology and type-design software, new typefaces and revivals of old typefaces are being released at an unprecedented rate. Some of these are well designed, but others are not. Many different typefaces from various digital foundries have the same name, yet the design of some of these faces is far removed from the original (Fig. **24**). It is not enough to make typeface selections on the basis of a name; designers should make visual comparisons before deciding which typefaces are most suitable.

Well-drawn typefaces possess the following optical characteristics: crisp edges without stair-stepping, no out-of-control pixels, curves with smooth and flowing thick-to-thin transitions, bowls of curved characters that slightly extend beyond the baseline and meanline, form and counterform relationships that provide consistent texture and color, characters that do not "dance" up and down on the baseline, optically equal spacing, and the absence of "black sheep" characters that visually stray from the rest of the letters due to an anomalous shape (Fig. **25**).

Tools available in desktop software enable type to be outlined, stretched, rotated, skewed, mirrored,

placed on a curved baseline, and manipulated in innumerable other ways. Upon determining the objectives, requirements, and limitations of the typographic problem at hand, designers can creatively employ these tools while also addressing legibility needs. These tools are best used to express ideas visually, rather than to merely embellish type. When using such tools, it is desirable to make typography as legible as possible by adhering to the legibility factors discussed earlier in this chapter, and to maintain the proportional integrity of letterforms. Even though type set on a curved baseline, for example, is not as legible as type set on a horizontal baseline, it can be made more legible by carefully spacing the letters and choosing a well-designed typeface. Figures **26–28** present a variety of electronic type manipulations with accompanying alterations for improved legibility.

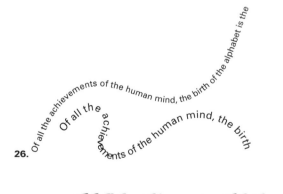

26.

27.

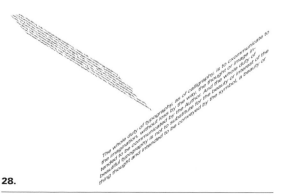

28.

24.

Three typefaces have the same name, but significantly different properties. The size, weight width, and shape of characters differ from one to the other.

25.

The lowercase i, j, and l appear out of place due to the presence of serifs in an otherwise sans-serif typeface. Also, the m and w appear darker in tone than their neighbors.

26.

Type improperly scaled on a tightly curved baseline causes characters to awkwardly bump into each other (bottom). Smaller type on a similar curve flows smoothly and consistently (top).

27.

Type skewed to the degree that it is no longer readable (top). Type similarly skewed, but word pictures are preserved enough to ensure legibility (bottom).

28.

Several skewed lines of type suggest a textural plane floating in space. Due to the degree of skew and the proximity of the lines one to another, the type is totally unreadable (left). By increasing interline spacing, changing the type weight, and reducing the degree of skew, lines can still be read (right).

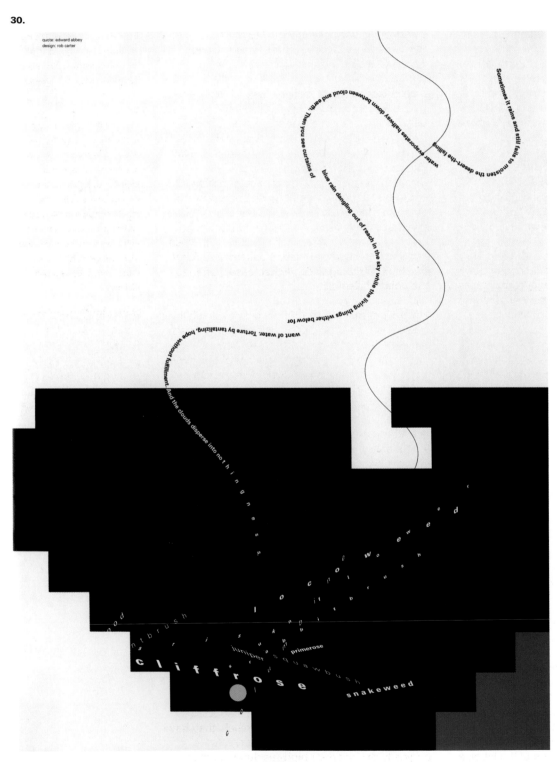

EOA EOA a a a a

EOA
EOA a a a

29.

31.

32.

33.

34.

30.

quote: edward abbey
design: rob carter

Sometimes it rains and still fails to moisten the desert–the falling
water evaporates halfway down between cloud and earth. Then you see curtains of
blue rain dangling out of reach in the sky while the living things wither below for
want of water. Torture by tantalizing, hope without fulfillment. And the clouds disperse into no t h i n g n e s s

snakeweed
cliffrose
juniper squawbush
primerose

29.
When letters are stretched horizontally or vertically on a computer to create condensed and expanded letterforms, their proportions change. The optical relationships of the original typeface design are destroyed.

30.
Experimental typography exploring computer manipulation of type. (Text: Ann Zwinger; Design: Rob Carter)

31.
Digital letterforms have decreasing resolution as the number of pixels is reduced.

32.
This enlargement of an *a*, displayed on a computer screen at a five-pixel height, shows the distortion that resulted. (Designer: Matt Woolman)

33.
Enlargement of a screen display of an *a* shows "the jaggies" caused by pixels. (Designer: Matt Woolman)

34.
Anti-aliasing smooths out the hard, stair-stepped diagonal and curved edges. (Designer: Matt Woolman)

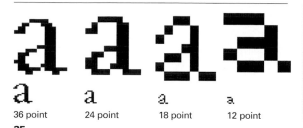

a a a a

36 point   24 point   18 point   12 point

35.

36.

Gross distortion of the optical relationships within a font occurs when only one axis, such as its width or height, is changed as shown in Figure **29**. Adobe introduced its multiple-master font technology around 1992 to address the need to alter letterforms by changing more than one axis while maintaining their design integrity. Multiple-master type is discussed in Chapter Five.

Typographic experimentation on the computer allows designers to probe the relationship between type, space, and expression. Syntactic exploration reveals boundless potential to inform, amuse, and astonish. In recent years designers have extended their range of possibilities by approaching work as play and tools as toys. One example of the expressive potential of computer-manipulated type is seen in a page from a series of experiments created to document wanderings in canyons of the Utah desert (Fig. **30**).

Legibility and the Internet

The Internet is a challenging environment for good typography, especially at text sizes. Its problems are inherent in all on-screen font displays, whether designing typography for a CD-ROM, cell-phone display, interactive kiosk, or Web site. When designing on a computer screen – even when the final production will take another form, such as offset printing – the same legibility issues apply to the on-screen type. Screen fonts are bitmaps, which are digitized images made up of tiny dots. To render a letterform on a computer screen, it must be rasterized, or converted into tiny dots called pixels, which is short for picture elements. The relatively low resolution of many contemporary computer screens, which typically have a bitmap matrix of 72 or 96 pixels per inch, cannot display the subtle nuances of a beautifully designed font. When type is rendered on a screen, details such as stroke weight, subtle curves, and serif detail are reduced to a coarse approximation of the refined forms found in the original design. This occurs because curved and diagonal edges rendered as pixels on a raster-scan display have a jagged stair-step quality, called "the jaggies." The more pixels used to generate the letterform, the higher the resolution (Fig. **31**). When small type appears on-screen with too few pixels to accurately display the subtle forms of the letter, a

catastrophic decrease in legibility can occur (Fig. **32**). Several methods are used to improve on-screen font display.

Anti-aliasing is a technique used to replace the jagged stair-step edges (Fig. **33**) created by pixels with an illusion of the smooth curves found in a well-designed typeface. Pixels around the edges of curved or angled letterforms are rendered in an intermediate tone or color. These pixels are displayed in a blend of the type color and the background color, resulting in an appearance of smoother, more refined letterforms (Fig. **34**). The drawbacks of anti-aliased type are that it looks fuzzy and it is only effective in larger sizes. When text-size type is anti-aliased, it becomes so fuzzy that legibility is significantly decreased, often to the point of illegibility.

Hinting. A major factor influencing the legibility of on-screen type is resolution. Where fewer pixels are available to describe letters, resolution decreases. To compensate for this problem, type designers reshape the outlines of characters – a process called "hinting"– to create the best possible image at various point sizes. Hints alter the actual outlines of letters by selectively activating pixels, thus improving the legibility of letters on the screen and from low-resolution output devices. An *unhinted* typeface will typically instruct the computer to turn on a pixel if more than half of its area is covered by the letterform. A *hinted* typeface has the pixels activated to display each letter adjusted to more accurately display it at various sizes (Fig. **35**). Hinting information is built into the software that generates the typeface on the screen and automatically occurs when the type is displayed on the screen.

Two widely used on-screen typefaces were specifically created for use as Web-page text. These are Verdana and Georgia (Fig. **36**), designed by Matthew Carter and hinted by Thomas Rickner. Most digital typefaces are designed as outline fonts that are used to generate bitmapped screen fonts. Verdana and Georgia were first designed as bitmaps of pixels (Fig. **37**), *then* they were translated into outline fonts. As a result, they have better on-screen fidelity than most typefaces originally designed for high-resolution output.

35.
Four sizes of a hinted letter *a* are shown enlarged and at on-screen reproduction sizes. (Designer: Matt Woolman)

36.
Verdana (left) and Georgia (right) are shown at 9-, 14-, 24-, and 36-point on-screen sizes. Hinting improves legibility by adjusting the design for each size. Note that the 9-point type is bitmapped, while the computer applied anti-aliasing to the larger sizes. (Font designer: Matthew Carter, hinted by Thomas Rickner)

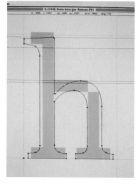

37.
This screen photograph shows a text-size Georgia *h* as a bitmapped letterform and as an outline letterform. (Photographer: Matthew Carter)

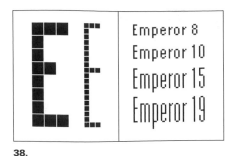

38.

39.

Pixel fonts are typefaces specifically designed as bitmapped type. These are designed to the pixel; for example, the characters in Emperor 15 (Fig. **38**) are exactly 15 pixels high. On a 72-dpi screen, these will be the same height as a 15-point typeface, since there are also 72 points in an inch. On a 96-dpi screen, however, a 15-pixel tall bitmap font will appear smaller, about the size of 11-point type. Pixel fonts can degrade when used at larger or smaller sizes than the size for which they have been designed. Pixel fonts are especially useful for very small on-screen text, as they can be designed to maximize legibility when pixellated. The distinctive appearance of these fonts has led to their occasional use as display fonts because their character is expressive of computer technology.

On-screen typefaces often face the problem of platform inconsistency. People will often view Web pages set in typefaces that are not installed on their computer. This results in a carefully designed Web page being rendered on many viewers' screens in a different font than the one used in the original design. The different set width and letterform designs can totally change the appearance of the page layout and type. Fonts can be imbedded into Web pages, but often these are not downloaded and displayed. Some Web-design software permits a designer to list a string of commonly available fonts (for example, Georgia, Times New Roman, Times) that are frequently installed on computers. The computer will set the text in the first available font from the list.

HTML and CSS are two programming possibilities for generating font and size selection on the Web. HTML (Hyper Text Markup Language) is the primary programming language used to produce Web pages. An HTML designer can only specify general type category and an approximate size measure. Tracking, linespacing (sometimes called line height by Web designers), and wordspacing are usually arbitrary. CSS (Cascading Style Sheets) allow designers to specify exact type

size, letter-, line-, and word-spacing. As discussed earlier in this chapter, these characteristics are major determinates of text type legibility. CCS also have the capability to specify different style sheets for different output devices. For example, one type style can be specified in pixel size for on-screen viewing, while another can be specified in points for printing on a laser printer. When developing a Web site in HTML and CSS, designers do not yet have control over anti-aliasing.

Type as image. Type, especially display type, is often converted to a picture file (for example, a GIF), and downloaded as an image on a Web site (Fig. **39**). The benefits are fidelity to the designer's intent and compatibility with almost all Web-browser software. Since images require more file size than plain text, this slows the downloading of the Web page. If a large number of typographic elements are downloaded as images, this further increases the time required for a browser to display the Web page. Type downloaded as an image is fixed in size and cannot be selected or copied as text. It cannot be scaled or changed in size. Revisions are difficult, because an image, rather than the words in running text, must be revised. When the design of a Web site is changed or updated, each text treated as an image has to be revised individually.

The rapid pace of computer technology holds promise for greater on-screen type resolution, faster download speeds on the Internet, and more sophisticated software. Newer vector-based software (for example, the FLASH plug-in) permits the downloading of a font's outline data, not just the pixels. More accurate letterforms can be downloaded and rendered on-screen.

The legibility problems and design difficulties facing designers creating on-screen graphics are gradually diminishing. The resolution of computer screens and output devices such as printers will continue to improve, and the gap between printed and on-screen type legibility will lessen over time.

38.

Emperor is a pixel font with a different design for display at different point sizes, with each pixel equaling one point. Emperor 19, for example, is nineteen pixels tall. (Designer: Zuzana Licko)

39.

This element from a Web site timeline demonstrates that typography downloaded as an image – rather than as a text file – maintains its fidelity to the original fonts. A detail of the element is reproduced at screen size (above), with the complete element shown below. (Designer: Lois Kim)

The invention of typography has been called the beginning of the Industrial Revolution. It is the earliest mechanization of a handicraft: the handlettering of books. Typographic design has been closely bound to the evolution of technology, for the capabilities and limitations of typesetting systems have posed constraints upon the design process. At the same time, typesetting has offered creative challenges as designers have sought to explore the limitations of the available systems and to define their aesthetic and communicative potential.

From hand composition to today's electronically generated typography, it is important for designers to comprehend the nature and capabilities of typographic technologies, for this understanding provides a basis for a thoughtful blending of design and production.

1.
Composing stick.

Hand composition

The traditional method of setting foundry type by hand is similar to the method used by Gutenberg when he invented movable type in 1450. For centuries, hand composition was accomplished by assembling individual pieces of type into lines. A typographer would hold a composing stick (Fig. **1**) in one hand while the other hand placed type selected from a type case (Fig. **2**) into the stick. Type was set letter by letter, line by line, until the desired setting was achieved. When it was necessary to justify a line, additional spaces were created in the line by inserting metal spacing material between words. Letterspacing was achieved by inserting very thin pieces of copper or brass between letters until words appeared to be evenly spaced. When additional space between

lines was desired, strips of lead were inserted between the lines until the type column was the proper depth. By adding lead, the exact proportion and size of the column could be formed, assuring readability through consistent spacing.

Once type was set, it was "locked up" in a heavy rectangular steel frame called a *chase* (Fig. **3**). This was done on a table called a *stone.* The type was surrounded by wood or metal spacing material, called *furniture,* and the contents of the chase were made secure by tightening steel, wedgelike devices called *quoins.* After the type was secured in the chase, it was ready to be transferred to a

2.
Type case.

Chase

Wood furniture

Type

Quoins

3.
A chase containing type "locked up" and ready for printing.

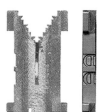

4.
Linotype machine.

press for printing, and after printing, the individual pieces of type were distributed back into the type case by hand.

Hand composition was tedious and time consuming. When typesetting became automated as a result of the invention of Linotype and Monotype machines, hand composition was used only for setting small amounts of type or for display type. Currently, hand composition is obsolete as a practical means of setting type, but as an art form there has been a revival. Private presses produce limited-edition books and a variety of experimental materials by hand. Many of our typographic conventions and traditions have their origins in the rich heritage of handset metal type.

Linotype

One of the most profound developments in typesetting technology was the invention of the Linotype machine (Fig. **4**) by Ottmar Mergenthaler in 1886. This machine represented the first great step toward typographic automation. Its name was coined because it produced a single line of type to a predetermined length specified by the keyboard operator.

The operation of the Linotype was based on the principle of a circulating matrix. Each time a key was pressed, a single brass matrix (Fig. **5**) was released from an overhead magazine, divided into ninety vertical channels, each containing matrices for one character. The magazine was the character storage case for the machine. Once an entire line had been typed, the matrices moved into an automatic casting mechanism where the line of type was cast from molten lead. As each line was being cast, the operator typed the next line. After the casting process was complete, cast lines of type called slugs (Fig. **6**) were ejected from the mold, and the matrices were automatically returned to their appropriate slot in the magazine for reuse.

The advantages of machine composition as compared to hand composition were obvious. It was faster and more accurate; the problem of type distribution (returning characters to the type case) was eliminated, for the cast lines of type were

6.
A Linotype slug.

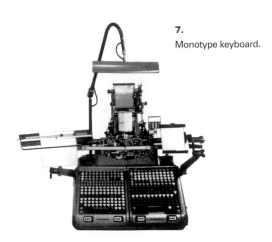

7.
Monotype keyboard.

simply melted, and the lead was reused. Justification of type was automatic, eliminating the tedious process of inserting spaces between letters and words. A standard Linotype could cast lines up to thirty picas in length.

An important development for linecasting type was the Teletypesetter. This perforated tape-driven machine – an attachment to Linotype and Intertype – was introduced in 1928. Tape, which was punched by a machine similar to a standard typewriter, could be generated from a distant office and transmitted to the linecaster by wire, which made the machine invaluable to news services.

Monotype

Another significant achievement leading to fully automated typesetting was the Monotype machine, invented by Tolbert Lanston in 1887. This machine cast one character at a time rather than an entire line. it was composed of two parts: a keyboard and a typecaster (Figs. **7**). When an operator typed at a keyboard, a perforated paper tape was generated. This coded tape was used to drive the second part of the system – the typecaster. Compressed air, blown through the punched holes of this revolving spool of coded paper, determined which characters would be cast by the typecaster. Actual casting of type occurred when hot metal was forced into matrices from the matrix case (Fig. **8**). Once the cast characters had cooled, they were placed into a metal tray called a galley, where the lines were assembled. Monotype lines could reach a maximum length of about sixty picas.

Monotype became an efficient way to set type for several reasons. Corrections could be made by changing individual letters instead of complete lines. Therefore, complex typesetting, such as scientific data and tabular information, was easier. The Monotype matrix case held many more characters than a Linotype magazine, and the casting machine was relatively fast, casting one hundred fifty characters per minute. Since the system consisted of two separate machines, an operator could generate type away from the clatter of the casting machine. In fact, several operators could keyboard information for later setting.

8.
Monotype matrix case.

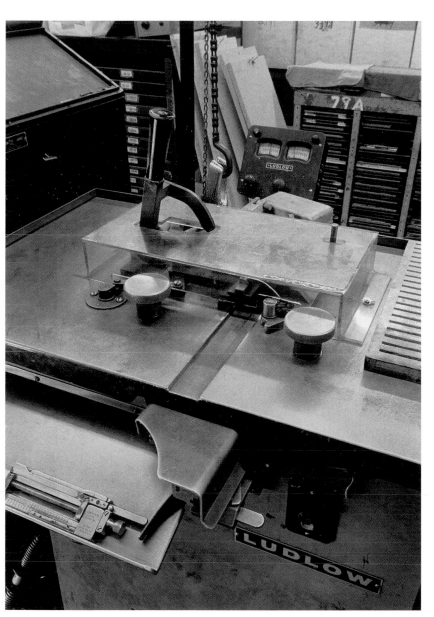

Ludlow

Ludlow, a semiautomatic linecaster, is another machine that found a place in the development of automated typesetting (Fig. **9**). Unlike the Linotype and Monotype, the Ludlow did not have a keyboard but combined both hand and machine production. An operator took matrices from a matrix case similar to a handset type case and placed them into a special composing stick, one by one. The stick would automatically justify or center lines by inserting blank matrices where necessary. Once a line of matrices was assembled, it was placed into a casting device where it was automatically cast into slugs. If a correction was necessary, matrices were inserted into the stick, cast, locked up, and printed. Although partially automated, this process was time consuming. Distributing the matrices back into the type case by hand added to the production time.

Type produced by the Ludlow machine ranged from 6 to 144 points. Its major use was to produce display type for headlines and other purposes requiring larger typefaces. As was true in the case of handset composition, the Ludlow was neither practical nor efficient for setting large volumes of type.

9.
Ludlow linecaster.

Phototypesetting

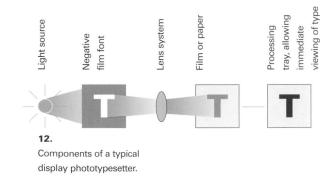

12.
Components of a typical display phototypesetter.

Phototypesetting is a cold-type process, for type is set not from molten cast metal, but by exposing film negatives of characters onto photographic paper. Although photographic typesetting was explored as early as the 1880s, its potential was not fully recognized until after World War II. As printing advanced from letterpress to offset lithography, typography underwent a similar evolution. Hand composition of metal display type, and cast metal machine-set text type, yielded to photographic typesetting. Two kinds of phototypesetting systems were developed: display phototypesetters, for larger headlines and titles; and keyboard phototypesetters, used to set text type through keyboard input. Phototypesetting gradually replaced metal type during the 1960s, as the technology improved rapidly.

Display phototypesetting

In display phototypesetting machines (Fig. **10**), light is projected through film negatives and a lens to expose letters, numbers, and other symbols onto a strip of photographic paper. While a font of type in hand composition consisted of a drawer full of raised metal letters, a font for display photo composition consists of clear images on a long strip of film (Fig. **11**) wound on two reels. This film font slides between an amber safe light and a lens. Characters are projected onto a strip of photo paper resting in a shallow tray of developer. An operator uses hand cranks to roll the strip from one drum to another, putting the next letter in position to be exposed. By pressing a button, the operator causes a bright white light to flash thorough the lens, exposing the character to the photo paper (Fig. **12**). The character immediately begins to develop, so the operator sees it while using a lever to advance the photo paper. The projected image for the next character is positioned by winding the film strip on the reels with hand cranks. Character by character, a line of display type is exposed on the photo paper, then developed and fixed. Because the operator can view recently set characters as they develop, letterspacing is precisely controlled (Fig. **13**). This spacing flexibility was a major innovation. Many design advantages of display phototypesetting made it the dominant method for setting headlines by the late 1960s. No longer constrained by the

fixed sizes of metal type, the designer could now specify display type set from the film font (whose capitals were about an inch tall) in a wide range of sizes. Type could be enlarged up to two times the master font size, for two-inch capitals, or reduced to a one-fourth size, with capitals as small as a quarter inch high. Enlarged and reduced type retained perfect sharpness, unlike metal type, which became very ragged when enlarged. Metal fonts had a limited number of characters, while photo type had an unlimited number of characters, because the same negative could be exposed over and over again.

The constraints of metal blocks yielded to the elasticity of photographic processes, and innovative designers rapidly explored new possibilities. The lens system permitted photographic distortion. Characters could be expanded, condensed, italicized, and even backslanted (Fig. **14**). The tremendous expense of introducing new metal typefaces, requiring punches, cast letters, and matrices, was replaced by the cost of one economical film font. As a result, many new display typefaces – as well as revivals of earlier styles that were no longer available – were introduced at a rapid pace.

11.
Film font for a display phototypesetter.

10.
A display phototypesetter.

Typography
Typography
Typography
Typography

13.
Unlike hand composition, where every letter is cast on a block of metal and can not be easily kerned, display phototype interletter spacing is visually controlled by the operator and can be set wide, normal, tight, or even touching.

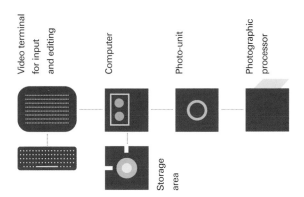

Video terminal for input and editing

Computer

Photo-unit

Photographic processor

Storage area

16.
Components of a typical
keyboard phototypesetter.

14.
Normal, expanded,
condensed, backslant, and
italic (top to bottom).

aaaaaaaa

aaaaaaa
aaaaaaa
aaaaaa

aaaaaaaaa
aaaaaaaaaa
aaaaaaaaaa

aaaaaaaa
aaaaaaaa
aaaaaaaa

aaaaaaaa
aaaaaaaa
aaaaaaaa

Keyboard phototypesetters

Keyboard phototypesetters were introduced in 1950. Two major types of phototypesetting systems (Fig. **15**) were developed: photo-optical and photo-scanning systems. They have the same basic components (Fig. **16**); the primary difference is how the photo paper or film is exposed.

Photo-optical systems store characters as a master font on film discs, drums, grids, or strips. The letters, numbers, and other symbols in the text are input on a keyboard. A typical film disc or drum spins at several thousand revolutions a minute, and a computer controls the exposure of light through the negative characters and a lens, onto light-sensitive paper or film. At the same time, the computer advances the paper or film in a transport device, moving it forward by the set width of the previously exposed character and into position for the next character to be exposed. Different lenses are used for different magnifications, so the typesetter can set different sizes of type. The computer makes very precise adjustments in spacing for the specific type size, and increases interletter and interword spacing when setting justified text columns. These systems are capable of setting hundreds of characters per minute. Early phototypesetting systems used a special keyboard to code punched paper tape that was fed into the phototypesetter to control the typesetting process. Paper-tape systems were replaced by magnetic tape systems, then by magnetic disks and diskettes.

A newer generation of photo-scanning typesetters replaced the photo-optical systems with an electronic system. Fonts are stored as electronic data. These digitized characters are projected as typeset text on a cathode ray tube (CRT) screen. A lens focuses the type on the CRT screen onto light-sensitive film or paper. A full page of type including many different sizes and typefaces can be divided into a grid of several blocks, each the size of the CRT screen, and stored in the computer's memory. Photo-scanning typesetters are much faster than photo-optical systems. They reproduce sections of the page rapidly, one block at a time, setting up to ten thousand characters per second.

Phototypesetters are flexible and fast, compared to hot-metal typesetting machines, which could set only about five characters per second. Hot-metal machines had many mechanical parts, while phototypesetters were operated electronically. Photo type needs little storage space because it is stored on flat photographic paper or film, while metal slugs are very heavy and require enormous amounts of storage space. Phototypesetting permits electronic editing, with corrections and changes made at the keyboard.

Phototypesetting freed designers from the physical restrictions of metal type. Increased flexibility in spacing typographic elements included greater control over kerning, interletter and interline spacing, overlapping, and special effects such as runarounds (type running around elements such as images). Designers who understood the potential of this technology used it to great advantage.

15.
A keyboard phototypesetter.

Digital typesetting

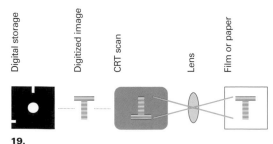

19.

Digital-scanning typesetter.

The digital computer in combination with the high-resolution cathode ray tube (CRT) and laser revolutionized the communications industry. Because digital computers have no mechanical parts and are entirely composed of electronic components, they set and process type at speeds never thought possible. In addition, the text type from digital typesetters has now been developed to rival the quality of phototype.

Knowledge of digital-computer functions is critical to an understanding of digital typesetting. A digital computer is an electronic device that uses electricity to process information. It can perform repetitive logical and arithmetic operations and store the results in memory. A computer system is composed of hardware and software. Hardware consists of the physical components of a computer; software is the program data that controls the operation of the hardware.

The computer component that controls all other parts, performs logical operations, and stores information is the central processing unit (CPU). All components that do not belong to the CPU are called peripherals. A typical digital-typesetting system is composed of a CPU and various peripherals that perform the functions necessary to the setting of type – for example, editing and storing text, displaying text on a screen, and printing typeset copy. In the main memory of a computer, called random access memory (RAM), data is stored and retrieved.

In digital typesetting, when an operator punches a key to enter a letter or issue a command (such as line length or paragraph indent), the computer receives it as binary code. Once information has been entered, it can be stored, edited, and sent to a peripheral device for typesetting.

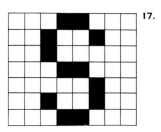

17.

Digital typesetting systems encode typographic characters digitally on a grid, defining the shape of each letter as a certain number of distinct points. Every detail of a letter is defined, including horizontal strokes, vertical strokes, and curves. The coded characters are stored electronically as digital instructions designating the x and y coordinates of the character on the grid. In the earliest digital typesetters, these instructions were sent to a CRT, where the character is generated onto the computer screen.

A CRT has a vacuum tube with a cathode at one end and a plate of phosphorous and aluminum at the other. When the CRT receives the digital instructions from the computer, defining the shape of the characters, the cathode emits a beam, which scans the tube in a series of parallel back-and-forth sweeps. The light emitted by the plate defines each character being typeset. The type is then digitally exposed to photographic paper.

The degree of resolution in digital letterforms is an important consideration. Basically, the more dots or lines used to describe a letterform, the higher the resolution. Because letters are constructed on a grid, the curved lines consist of a series of stair-stepped contours (Fig. **17**). When more dots are used to represent a curve, the curve appears smoother to the eye. The quality of letterforms is determined not only by their design but also by their digital resolution (Fig. **18**).

Resolution is improved through a process called *hinting* (see Chapter Five), which mathematically encodes letterforms in a manner true to their original design. Each size of a well-designed typeface possesses characters with unique proportional characteristics, and hinting preserves these characteristics, a concern particularly relevant for typefaces of smaller size. Details of curves, strokes, and serifs maintain optical integrity.

Scanning and laser systems
There are two classes of digital typesetters: digital-scanning systems, first introduced in 1972, and digital-laser systems. In digital-scanning systems (Fig. **19**), photographic characters were digitally

18.

Examples of digital letterforms, demonstrating decreasing resolution, from top to bottom, as the number of elements is reduced.

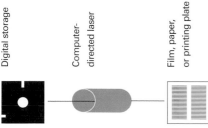

Digital storage

Computer-directed laser

Film, paper, or printing plate

20.
Digital-laser typesetter.

21.
A morphology of multiple-master fonts, originating with four master fonts interpolated along the axes of weight, width, and optical size. Weight and optical size occur along the vertical axis; width occurs along the horizontal axis. Though the variations seem very subtle, each represents an individual font.

22.
Walker, a typeface designed by Matthew Carter, enables designers to "snap-on" five variations of serifs at will.

scanned and recorded electronically on a magnetic disk or tape. The characters were translated into a grid of extremely high resolution and then transmitted as a set of instructions to a CRT. Next, the characters were generated onto the CRT by a series of scan lines. The letterform images were then projected from the CRT onto paper, film, or an electrostatic drum. Because the output type is digital, it could be modified automatically to reflect a number of typographic variations. For example, it could be made heavier, lighter, slanted, condensed, or expanded at the command of the operator.

Rather than employing a CRT to generate characters, digital-laser systems (Fig. **20**) used a laser beam that scanned photographic paper as it read digital information stored in the typesetter. As the paper was scanned, a series of dots forming the characters were exposed to the paper. The information controlling the laser included the font, as well as spacing, paragraph configuration, hyphenation, and kerning.

Digital typesetting technology continues to improve and evolve, and with the introduction of electronic page design, and the responsibility for typesetting having shifted from a compositor to the designer, the nature of typographic communication has changed drastically. The ability of a designer to dynamically edit and alter individual letterforms and entire fonts with the aid of new software has in many ways redefined the way type is used. For example, multiple-master typefaces, developed by the Adobe Corporation in 1991, readily enable designers to interpolate and therefore change fonts along several design axes (Fig. **21**). These axes include weight, width, optical size, stroke shape, and serif configuration.

Other developments depart entirely from traditional typesetting methods. The typeface Walker, for example, designed in 1995 by Matthew Carter for the Walker Art Center provides "snap-ons," that is, variant serifs treated as separate characters that can be added to or removed from letters as desired (Fig. **22**). Future innovations in digital typesetting will continue to shape and define typographic culture.

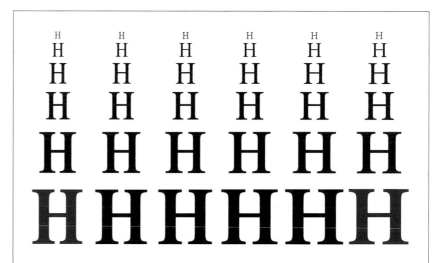

21.

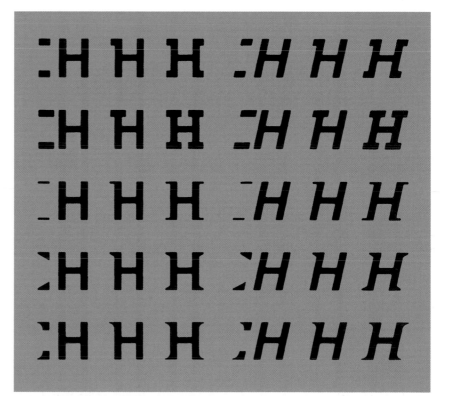

22.

Electronic page design

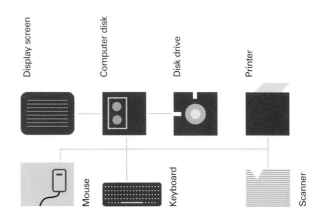

Display screen
Computer disk
Disk drive
Printer
Mouse
Keyboard
Scanner

24.
Electronic page design workstation.

23.
This laptop computer screen displays type in true WYSIWYG, for it accurately shows the image as it will print.

Digital typesetting moved onto the designer's desktop with the development of more powerful personal computers and software applications during the last decade. This major leap forward in typographic technology makes it possible to design entire pages on a computer screen, then electronically output them onto paper, film, or even printing plates. Electronic page design, also called desktop publishing, eliminates the need for pasteup, which is the hand-assembly of elements in position for reproduction as a page. Type size, style, spacing, and position can be changed, then viewed on the screen immediately, bringing unprecedented control and freedom to typographic design. Advances in technology are bringing typography closer to WYSIWYG, an expression meaning "what you see is what you get;" that is, the image on the computer monitor (Fig. **23**) is identical to the image that will be printed as final output.

Hardware components

Hardware, the physical components of the system, consists of the computer and the peripheral devices (Figs. **24** and **25**) that connect to it. Available peripherals include input devices, which are used to feed information into the computer, and output devices, which produce the final product.

Central processing unit. This electronic microprocessor chip does the actual work of the computer by receiving, processing, and storing information. It functions in a manner similar to the CPU of a digital typesetter, discussed earlier.

Input devices. These generate information for processing by the CPU and display on a screen, which uses a cathode-ray tube to produce a visual display of data. The keyboard contains alphabetical and numeric keys to input data. In addition, it contains special keys to perform specified functions, such as arrow keys to direct a pointer around the screen, and a command key that is held down while other keys are pressed, enabling them to send commands to the computer. The mouse is a handheld device that is moved about the desktop; it controls the movement of a pointer on the screen. A button on

the mouse is clicked on elements to select them. When the mouse button is held down, elements on the screen can be moved by moving the mouse. Graphics tablets operate in a manner similar to a mouse, but use a stylus or pointer touched to a flat surface to input information. Scanners are devices that convert images or text into digital form so that they can be stored and manipulated by the computer.

Information storage devices. A disk is a round platter with a magnetic coating similar to recording tape, on which information from the computer is stored in the form of magnetic impulses. A disk drive reads information from and writes information onto disks. Floppy disks are portable and housed in a 3.5-inch hard plastic case; they are inserted into a disk drive, which reads the information on the disk. Hard-disk drives have large rigid disks permanently mounted within the computer or in a separate case. Hard disks have large storage capacity and fast operating speed. Removable hard-disk cartridges combine the portability of floppy disks with the large storage capacity of hard-disk drives. The development of new information storage devices using compact disks and optical, rather than magnetic, systems promises even greater speed and the storage of massive amounts of data.

Output devices. After a design is completed, output devices are used to convert the screen image to printed output. A dot-matrix printer composes characters and image into a pattern of dots. The measure of quality for typographic output is the number of dots per inch (dpi); this determines the resolution of the image. A pin-strike printer uses a series of small pins that strike against an inked ribbon, transferring dots of ink onto paper to form the image. Many pin-strike printers have 72 dpi resolution, identical to the dpi of low-resolution screens.

A laser printer creates images by drawing them on a metal drum with a laser. Dry ink particles are attracted to this image, which is then transferred to paper in a process similar to a photocopying machine. The first-generation laser printers' 300 dpi resolution was called "near typeset quality." The ability of laser printers to output pages combining text and images was made possible by the development of interpretive programming languages that provide a software interface between page-design programs, discussed below, and output devices. The first page-description programming language, PostScript™ by Adobe Systems, Inc., was specifically designed to handle text and graphics and their position on the page; QuickDraw™ by Apple Computer is another programming language that enables the rapid display of typographic elements on a screen.

Imagesetters are high-resolution output devices (Fig. 26) that consist of two components, a raster image processor (RIP) and a recorder or exposure unit. The RIP is a computer that uses a page-description language (see below) to convert the data files from the designer's workstation into an electronic pixel pattern of the page. Every single

point on the page, whether part of a letterform or a pictorial image, is positioned in this pattern, which is sent to the exposure unit as a bitmap of raster lines. A bitmap is a computerized image "made up of dots." Exposure units from various manufacturers use different technologies – such as cathode-ray tube (CRT), gas laser, laser diode, or light-emitting diode (LED) – to record the RIP-composed page on photographic paper or film, plain paper, or even a printing plate.

Imagesetters produce very high resolution 1270 or 2540 dpi output. Imagesetters output type and halftone images in their final reproduction position, and some can output color separation negatives as well. The speed of digital typesetters is rated in characters per second, but imagesetters are rated in inches per minute since they output an entire bitmapped page. Early imagesetters were not capable of the typographic refinement of digital typesetters; however, steady improvement in hardware and software has closed the gap in quality. Imagesetter output of electronically designed pages has rapidly replaced traditional composition and pasteup.

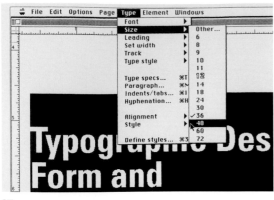

27.

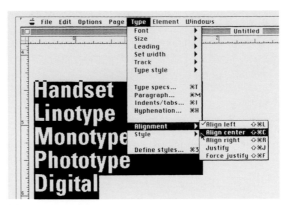

28.

Many typesetting firms have service bureaus to offer imagesetter output for their clients, and large advertising agencies and graphic-design offices have installed imagesetters within their firms. Typefaces are stored electronically in either bitmapped or outline data form. Bitmapped fonts are made up of dots and usually require a separate data set for each size of the typeface. Outline fonts are stored as instructions for drawing the outline of each character, using bezier curves to drawn nonuniform curves (as opposed to uniform curves, which are called arcs). Bezier curves are defined by four points, and their use enables computers to generate smooth images of complex letterforms.

Software
The instructions that tell the computer what to do are called software. An application program is software used to create and modify documents. The principle types of applications used in typographic design are word processors, drawing and painting programs, and page-layout software.

Word-processing programs are used to type in text, then edit, change, move, or remove it. Word-processing software can check grammar and spelling and suggest synonyms. Most text is written with a word-processing program, then transferred to a page-layout program for design.

Drawing and painting programs are used to create images. Early paint programs created images as a series of bitmapped dots, while drawing programs generated objects that are treated as mathematically defined line and arc segments rather than a series of dots. A rectangle created in a paint program can have its corner erased, but in order to move it, all the dots composing it must be selected; by contrast, an object-oriented rectangle can be selected by clicking anywhere on it, then moving it about the space. However, you cannot erase or change details. Most drawing and painting programs can generate and manipulate

type, and advanced versions often combine the features of object-oriented draw programs along with bitmapped paint programs.

Page-design programs are used to design pages of typography and combine images with them. The type font, size, and leading can be selected, and text type can be flowed into columns running from page to page. Elements can be moved about the page, and templates of grid lines and standard repeating elements such as page numbers can be established. The screen image provides immediate feedback about the page design because all the elements are visible in their final sizes and spatial positions, and their attributes are capable of infinite change. The paper or film output is in final form, ready for reproduction.

The differences between word-processing programs and page-design programs are decreasing as each incorporates features from the other in updated versions. In general, word-processing programs have greater control over the editing process, whereas page-design programs have greater control over page composition. For example, in page-design programs an element can be selected with the mouse and moved anywhere on the page, but word-processing programs do not have this capability.

Page-design programs were made possible by the development of interpretive programming languages that provide a software interface between page-design programs and output devices.

The new computer-graphics technology has rapidly expanded the range of typeface design as well, for typeface design programs permit more rapid development of a new font than was possible with earlier technologies, while font editors allow the customization of individual letters or entire fonts to meet the needs of a user.

27.
The type menu lists parameters that can be changed on type that has been selected. Here the user has chosen *Size* and clicked the mouse button on *48* to change the selected type from *36-* to *43-*point.

28.
The type menu is being used to change the alignment of the selected type from *Align left* to *Align center.*

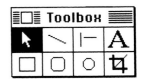

29.
When toolbox icons are selected, the mouse-controlled pointer becomes the selected tool. Top row: pointer tool, diagonal line drawing tool, perpendicular line drawing tool, and text tool. Bottom row: Rectangle drawing tool, round-cornered rectangle drawing tool, oval drawing tool, and cropping tool.

The history of writing is, in a way, the history of the human race, since in it are bound up, severally and together, the development of thought, of expression, of art, of intercommunication, and of mechanical invention.

The history of writing is, in a way, the history of the human race, since in it are bound up, severally and together, the development of thought, of expression, of art, of intercommunication, and of mechanical invention.

30.

The top specimen has an undesirable widow. By changing the tracking of the second line in the bottom example by -1.5 (-1.5/200 em), the spatial interval between characters is deleted slightly, setting the type tighter and pulling the widow up to the last full line.

31.

Using a drawing program, the designer has joined the baseline of the type with an oval and a curved line.

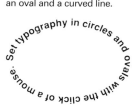

The user interface

A typographic designer's computer workstation has an intuitive user interface; this means the tools are easy to use, permitting the user to focus upon the task at hand. A desktop pasteup metaphor is employed. The user sees the page surrounded by a desktop where elements can be created, held to one side, and then placed into position on the page. This metaphor to traditional pasteup has made it easier for the designers accustomed to traditional methods to design and assemble pages.

In page-design programs, a menu bar across the top of the screen lists major titles. The user moves the mouse to place the pointer on an item on the screen to be changed, then selects it by clicking the mouse button. Then, the pointer is placed on a menu title, and the mouse button is clicked, causing a list of commands to pop down. Under the type menu in one page-design program, for example, a list of commands for making changes to type that has been selected pops down. The user can change the type style, size (Fig. **27**), color, or alignment (Fig. **28**). Page-layout programs also have a palette of tools that are represented by icons (Fig. **29**). After a tool icon is selected, the mouse is used to perform that operation.

Advanced page-design programs permit unprecedented flexibility in typographic design. Minute adjustments of typographic spacing are possible.

Type can be set in sizes from 2 points to 720 points and leaded from -1080 to +1080 points. Letterspacing can be controlled by manually kerning in increments of 1120 or 1/200 em. The user can create kerning tables that automatically kern letter pairs. Tracking can be edited by selecting a range of characters (Fig. **30**), then changing the tracking in increments of 1120 or 1/200 em as well.

Many programs provide the designer with unique capabilities for the manipulation and distortion of typographic forms. Lines of type can be joined to circular, oval, or irregular baselines (Fig. **31**); letterforms can be stretched and distorted in numerous ways (Fig. **32**). Page-design programs compose elements on a page in layers, so elements can be overlapped and layered in space (Fig. **33**). These electronic page-design capabilities are a mixed blessing, for though they can expand the creative range of typography, they can also produce awkward spatial arrangements and typographic forms that are hard to read.

DISTORT TYPE
DISTORT TYPE
DISTORT TYPE
DISTORT TYPE

32.

The bottom letterforms have been stretched excessively, causing the optical relationships to become distorted. The crossbar of the *T* has become too thick; the *S* and *O* extend too far above and below the baseline.

33.

In contrast to the two-dimensional plane of traditional typographic technology, computer software permits the layering of information in space. (Designer: Erika Maxwell)

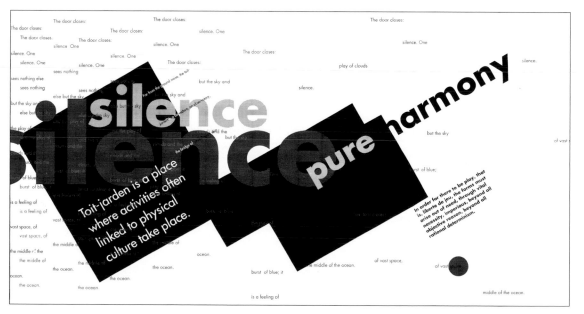

Each major typographic process has its own place in the evolution of technology. Increased efficiency, control, flexibility, and the design of letterforms have been affected by continuous research and innovation. The nature of the typographic image has been changed as well (Fig. **34**). The microphotographs by Mike Cody demonstrate the differences. Letterpress printing of metal type impressed the letterform into the fibers of the paper. Phototype, usually printed by offset lithography, provides a precise image with a comparatively smooth contour. As the microphotographic enlargement shows, digital type evidences the stepped contour caused by the digitization of the image into discrete elements.

In the most advanced digital-typesetting systems, the discrete elements are so small that they become indiscernible to the naked eye.

Technology develops rapidly, and designers must work to keep abreast of innovations that influence the design process and the typographic image. Designers should view typographers as partners in the design process, for their specialized knowledge of the typesetting system and its capabilities, along with an understanding of typographic refinements, can help the designer achieve the desired quality of typographic communication.

34.
Microphotographic enlargement of letterforms.

Metal type on newsprint

Metal type on coated paper

Phototype

Digital-photo type

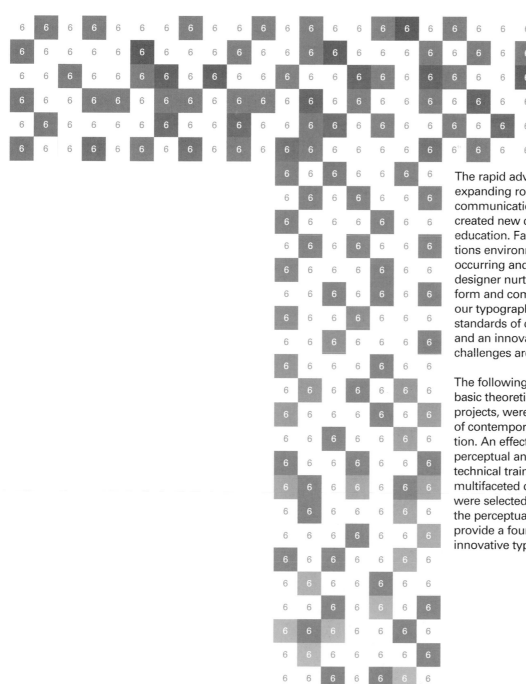

6   Typographic Design Education

The rapid advance of technology and the expanding role of visual and audio-visual communication in contemporary society have created new challenges for typographic education. Faced with a complex communications environment, and the changes that are occurring and are anticipated, how can a designer nurture sensitivity to typographic form and communication? An appreciation of our typographic heritage, an ability to meet the standards of contemporary design practice, and an innovative spirit in facing tomorrow's challenges are required.

The following assignments, ranging from basic theoretical exercises to complex applied projects, were selected to provide an overview of contemporary typographic design education. An effective curriculum is composed of perceptual and conceptual development, technical training, and processes for solving multifaceted design problems. These projects were selected with emphasis upon building the perceptual and conceptual abilities that provide a foundation for effective and innovative typographic design practice.

Generation of a typographic sign from a gestural mark

P. Lyn Middleton

North Carolina
State University

Students were asked to make gestural question marks (Figs. **1–3**), giving consideration to the visual-design qualities of their sketches. Proportion, stroke weight, negative space, and details such as the relationship of the dot to the curved gesture were evaluated. One of the student's question marks was selected and became the basis for designing a freehand typographic sign.

Students generated a variety of graphic signs, exploring a range of forms that can function as a question mark. Executing the typographic version develops visual and manual acuity, and an understanding of the differences between written and typographic signs.

1.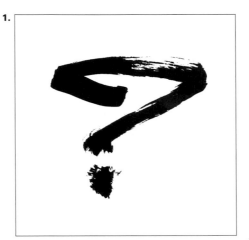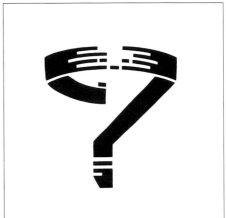

2.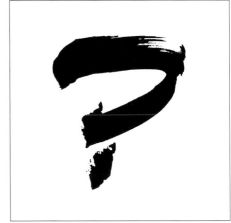

3.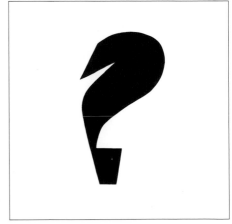

1.
Designer: Alexandre Lock
2.
Designer: Maxine Mills
3.
Designer: Angela Stewart

Letter/digit configurations

Urban letterform studies

Rob Carter

Virginia Commonwealth University

Thomas Detrie

Guest Lecturer
Winter Session in Basel
Rhode Island
School of Design

Visual configurations were invented by combining a letter from the English alphabet with a single-digit number (Figs. 4–7). Scale, proportion, weight, and shape relationships between two different signs were explored.

Objectives of this exercise include introducing letterform drawing and drafting skills, using typographic joinery to unify the two distinct forms into a visual gestalt, and understanding the variety of spatial relationships that can exist among characters.

4.
Designer: Penny Knudsen
5.
Designer: Penny Knudsen
6.
Designer: Colene Kirwin
7.
Designer: Linda Evans

8.

Letterforms in an old section of a European town were studied and documented through drawing, rubbings, and found material. A black-and-white letter composition was developed, depicting graphic qualities found in the assigned area.

On a formal level, compositional issues such as dynamic asymmetrical composition and form-counterform relations are explored. On an interpretive level, the ambience of a historical area is translated into a typographic configuration.

4.

8.
Designer: J. P. Williams

5.

6.

7.

Inventing sign systems

Greg Prygrocki

North Carolina
State University

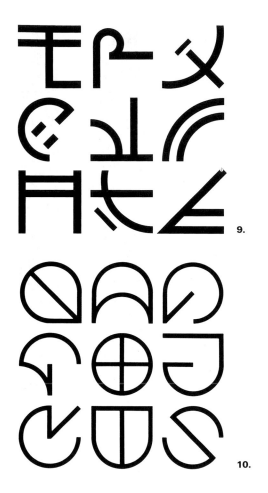

9.

10.

A set of nine signs were invented (Figs. **9–10**). Each was required to be a distinctive mark, with unique optical characteristics, yet harmonious with all the other signs and clearly recognizable as part of the set.

The focus of this project is to make students aware of the properties that bring unity to any typographic system. These include stroke weight and direction, stress, form repetition, and intersection.

9.
Designer: Joe Easter
10.
Designer: Paul Dean

Letterform analysis

Ben Day

Boston University

A modular grid of horizontal, vertical, and diagonal units was established and used to draw variations of a letterform (Fig. **11**). The sans serif *E* has been transformed into expanded and condensed variations. A grid sequence from four to twelve vertical units and from five to ten horizontal units was used. In Figure **12,** the form has been elaborated upon by opening the space between the vertical stroke and the three horizontal strokes.

The purpose of this project is to understand the allowable tolerance for the alteration of letterform proportions without losing sign legibility. In addition, the internal structure of a letter is analyzed and manipulated. This project introduces students to the formal variety that is possible and to the process of logo design.

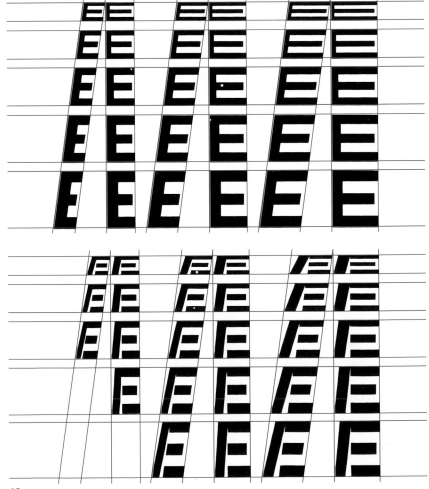

12.
Designer: Tim Barker

Flowering typography

13.

Dennis Y. Ichiyama

Purdue University

Selected letters of the alphabet were combined with images of flowers that have been reduced into visually simplified forms. Each letter is coupled with a flower whose generic name begins with the chosen letter. In the examples shown, *A* is for Alyssum (Fig. **13**), *K* is for Kirengeshoma (Fig. **14**), *J* is for Jalap Root (Fig. **15**), and *H* is for Hollyhock (Fig. **16**).

A primary objective of this project is to achieve a harmonious synthesis between type and image, and in the process create a new visual configuration. It is essential in the process of creating this hybrid form that the recognizability of both the letterform and flower be preserved. Another fundamental concern is to explore the dynamic relationship between positive and negative space.

13–17.
Designer: Li Zhang

14.

15.

16.

Sequential typographic forms in space

Akira Ouchi

Virginia Commonwealth University

By cropping, shifting, rotating, and scaling a large sampling of single letterforms within square modules, students discover the dynamic relationships between form and counterform and the resulting effect upon visual space. Students then proceed with a study of typographic kinetics by organizing selected modules into a linear sequence of ten modules (Figs. **18–21**). Similar to musical scores, diagram sketches enable students to articulate and test sequences with respect to rhythmic patterns, shape and value transitions, and the flow of typographic elements (Fig. **22**).

18–22.
Designers: Virginia Commonwealth University sophomores

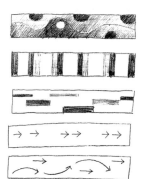

22.

18–21.

17.

Visual organization and grid structures

Greg Prygrocki

North Carolina State University

Students developed linear grid structures, then created a series of plates, organizing found typographic materials into spatial compositions based upon this underlying structure (Figs. **23** and **24**).

This project introduces the grid structure as a formal design element. The grid module is the basic compositional unit, bringing order to the arrangement. Students consider contrast, structure, positive and negative space, balance, texture and tone, and rhythm as design properties.

23.
Designer: Craig McLawhorn
24.
Designer: Matt Monk

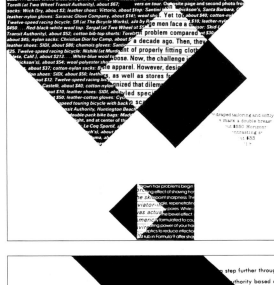

23.

24.

Introduction
to systems design

Lisa Fontaine

Iowa State University

Using letterforms as the primary visual elements, students learned how individual designs can function as a cohesive system. Six square compositions were designed (Figs. **25–30**) using a limited range of colors and letterforms. The success of each individual design relied not only on its composition but also on its systematic potential: each square had to bring both unity and variety to the series to result in a cohesive visual system.

To prove the systematic integrity of their six designs, students create a series of nine-unit grid patterns (Figs. **31** and **32**), where any combination of the smaller designs are placed in the larger grid. If the system is successful, a wide range of patterns is possible through repetition and rotation of the six designs. If the patterns generated are too similar, the system needs more variation of font, color, size, or placement. When the patterns lack continuity, the student needs to more clearly define or limit the visual elements of their system.

25–32.
Designer: Jasmine Friedl

25–30.

31–32.

Designing with a single letter

Typography and image transformations

Cece Cutsforth

Portland Community College

Gordon Salchow

University of Cincinnati

A series of designs each used one or more copies of a single letter to demonstrate a series of design concepts: *scale,* communicating large and small by comparison; *positive and negative space,* with the spaces surrounding the letter becoming equal to the letter itself; *pattern,* using repetition to create a distinctly articulated pattern; *congestion,* where letters encroach upon one another's space; *tension,* with placement and angle conveying instability; and *playfulness,* with letters conveying a carefree sensation.

The examples shown here are from the pattern segment of the project. The choice of letterform, size, angle, and figure/ground relationships determine the tonal density and degree of consonance or dissonance.

33–35
Designers: Portland
Community College students

33.

34.

35.

36.

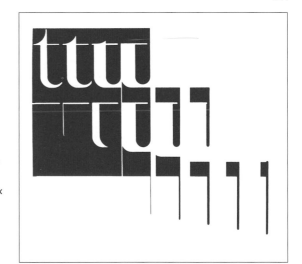

37.

A letter has been altered in a series of steps until it is transformed into a simple object, an abstract shape, or another letterform (Figs. **36–38**). An understanding of typographic sequencing, permutation, and kinetic properties is developed. Students can gain an awareness of form and counterform relationships, and the unity that can be created in complex configurations.

38.

36–38
Designers: University of
Cincinnati sophomores

Experimental compositions
with found typography

Katherine McCoy

Cranbrook Academy of Art

Using all of the typography found on a product label, a grid-based composition was produced exploring size relationships, spatial interval, and weight (Fig. **39**). A second composition was generated with more dynamic movement and scale change (Fig. **40**). Visual notations were made of each, analyzing eye movement, massing, and structure (Figs. **41** and **42**). Tone, texture, and shape are substituted for the typographic elements.

This project is designed to encourage an understanding of the abstract properties inherent in existing typographic forms. An exploratory attitude toward space and visual organization is developed.

39.

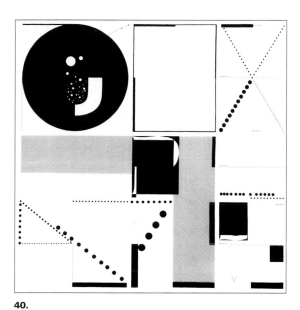

40.

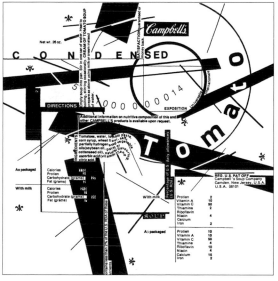

41.

42.

39–42
Designer: Ryoji Ohashi

Syntactic explorations
using onomatopoeic terms

Frank D'Astolfo

Rutgers University–Newark

An onomatopoeic term (a word that sounds like the thing or action denoted) was selected and used in syntactic explorations. The first level involved drawings exploring syntactic variations using a grid to create visual relationships. These studies evolved into complex type compositions expressing the term.

Level two saw an additional word added as a simple linear element. Unexpected yet meaningful relationships were sought. Visual relationships were created through alignment, balance, juxtaposition, and direction.

In level three, a photograph was added, completing the composition and forming a meaningful message. Unexpected, ironic, or complex associations were encouraged. A spectator or fan at a sporting event (Fig. **43**) adds a new dimension to the *ver* sound of a fan. Rabbit ears cause *schhh* (Fig. **44**) to denote the static of poor television reception. The meaning of the word *croak* (Fig. **45**) is changed by the gun. The *ding-dong* (Fig **46**) comes from the bell in a boxing match after a prize fighter is added to the design.

This project addresses a complex set of issues. Type style, size, and placement can express the meaning of words. Effective visual organization is achieved with the help of a grid. Words and pictures strengthen and even alter each other's meaning.

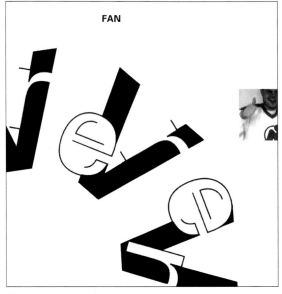

43.

44.

45.

46.

43.
Designer: Elisa Robels;
Ver, fan, and spectator.

44.
Designer: Kelly Olsen;
Schhh, static, and rabbit ears.

45.
Designer: Cheri Olsen;
Ribbitt, croak, and gun.

46.
Designer: Paris Jones;
Ding Dong, ready, and boxer.

Type chronology booklet

R. Roger Remington

Rochester Institute
of Technology

A comparative study of ten typefaces was made by each student. The information was organized chronologically in a booklet with four pages devoted to each typeface. In Figure **47**, the opening spread juxtaposes descriptive text and a complete font opposite a large letterform. The following spread contains a historical application of the type opposite a contemporary application created by the student.

This problem develops research skills, an understanding of typographic history, and an ability to work with different typefaces. Large amounts of complex data are organized; a consistent format is developed; diversity is created within this format.

47.

47.
Designer: Heinz Klinkon

Expressive typography: form amplifies message

Douglas Higgins

University of Cincinnati

Design students were introduced to computer typography in a project that explored the potential of computer techniques to intensify typographic messages. Content derived from scientific newsletters was used to create typographic identifiers that clearly summarize factual information contained in the article. By employing a source of subject matter that is usually designed routinely, the temptation to appropriate a solution was minimized.

Special attention was given to the role of visual hierarchy and typographic contrast while developing computer drafting skills useful in professional practice. The ease with which the computer generated variations facilitated visual refinements.

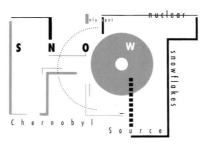

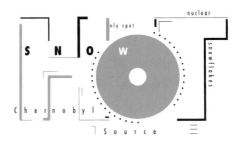

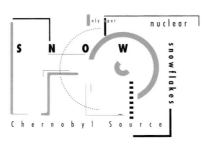

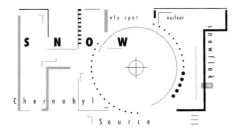

48.

49.

50.

48–50.
Designers: University of Cincinnati juniors

Computer improvisation and manipulation

Douglas Higgins

Ringling School
of Art and Design

Two letterforms in structural opposition were combined to create a "seed" configuration (Figs. **51** and **52**). Successive improvisations depart from the original while preserving the basic structural form, as basic computer operations are learned (Fig. **53**). Parallels are established between typographic concepts and computer techniques needed to explore them. Electronic page layout software was used to document the entire design process in book form.

Using a computer to deconstruct and manipulate digital type images allows students to hasten their understanding of letterform analysis and elemental structures governing each letter's legibility. Assignment goals include an understanding of letterform complexities and using forms inherent in a letter's design as points of departure for applied problem-solving.

51.
Designer: Michelle Carrier
52.
Designer: Teresa Leard
53.
Designer: Teresa Leard

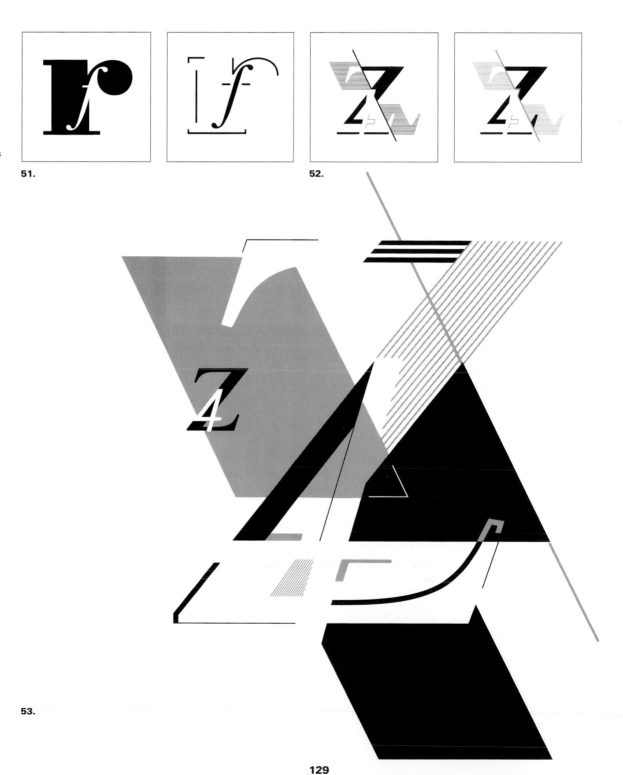

51.

52.

53.

Interpretive typography: exploring legibility and impact

Jan Conradi

Ball State University

Symphony poster series

David Colley

University of Illinois at Champaign-Urbana

Students design multiple solutions with the same content as a way to explore the relationship between legibility. Innovation is pursued while working within strict parameters and investigating the impact of typeface selection, size, leading, position, line length, tonal contrast, and tactile qualities. In the first of an eight-composition series, each student tries to maximize legibility while using a uniform type font, size, and weight, with no tonal variations. Subsequent compositions introduce geometric grids, then organic forms and multiple type weights and sizes (Figs. **54** and **55**). Images are added but remain subordinate to type. The final compositions emphasize texture and emotional impact rather than legibility (Figs. **56** and **57**).

Students are encouraged to reflect on the visual hierarchy of information and logical reading flow. The consequences of illegibility and people's emotional response to design are considered. Students learn that type can be as potent as images in achieving unique and identifiable communicative designs, and black and white can equal the visual impact of full color.

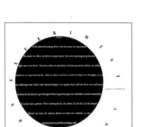

54.

55.

56.

57.

58.

A series of posters was designed to encourage local high school students to attend symphony concerts (Fig. **58**). Emphasis was placed on writing interpretive copy and selecting typefaces appropriate to that message. Diversity of expression to parallel the concert season was an important consideration. (These posters were printed by offset and donated to the symphony.)

This project introduces the student to the importance of the message in typographic communication. Language devices including metaphor, sound repetition, and rhyme were used to make the content memorable. The relationship of form and meaning was addressed; the nature of each composer's music was considered in the selection of typeface, size, placement, and color. In the examples shown, typographic dissonance in the Stockhausen poster parallels the composer's musical dissonance; word substitution occurs in the Brahms poster; and an auditory double meaning is found in the Bach poster.

58.
Designers: University of Illinois undergraduate students

54.
Designer: Dennis Good
55.
Designer: Dennis Good

56.
Designer: Autumn Musick
57.
Designer: Pam Lemming

Information design:
changing typographic parameters

Marcia Lausen

University of Illinois at Chicago

Selecting their own subject matter, students explore changing typographic parameters and the resulting effect of these changes upon communication in four exercises. Typographic variables change for each exercise: one size and one weight; two sizes or two weights; any number of sizes and weights; and incorporation of an image with any number of type sizes and weights.

Projects presented here are based upon a Chicago Transit Authority timetable (Figs. **59–62**), and statistical data for a student's vintage muscle car (Figs. **63–66**).

Related goals of the project include instructing students in the use of numeric figures in typography, the relationship of subject and data to visual presentation, the different forms of emphasis and hierarchy in typography, the interaction of type and image, and the basic systems of structure and alignment in typography.

Information design is a growing specialty of graphic design. The ability of designers to interpret, envision, and communicate information in typographical and graphical terms has become increasingly important. The Internet and other information media requiring nonlinear forms of communication are becoming increasingly important in the study and practice of visual communication.

59–62.
Designer: Eric Roth
63–66.
Designer: Tim Russow

59–62.

63–66.

R. Roger Remington

Rochester Institute
of Technology

Josef Godlewski

Indiana University

A visual presentation combining typography, images, and symbols was created as an extension of a self-assessment study by advanced design students (Figs. **67–69**). The students made a formal analysis of their past experiences and future goals. This part of the project stressed research and information gathering. The collected materials were evaluated for their communicative effectiveness in a complex design.

Transforming diverse information into a three-dimensional cube poses a complex design problem. Each side of the cube functions as part of a totality; the four contiguous sides are graphically and communicatively integrated.

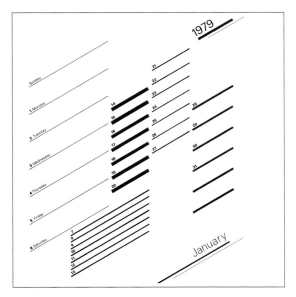

67.

68.　　　　**69.**

Calendar pages were designed using typographic elements to organize the space and direct eye movement on the page (Fig. **70**). Emphasis was placed upon experimentation, creating unity and movement on each page, and developing a visual elaboration over twelve pages. A grid structure was established and used to achieve diversity and order within a sequence of twelve designs. Graphic elements were limited to typography and rules.

This assignment enables students to explore interrelationships between graphic elements and the surrounding space.

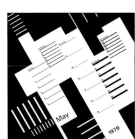

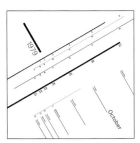

70.

67.
Designer: Beth April Smolev
68.
Designer: Katherine St. James
69.
Designer: Bruce Morgan

70.
Designer: Jean
Brueggenjohann

Unity of form
and communication

Christopher Ozubko

University of
Washington at Seattle

After selecting a historical
event as subject, students
were asked to develop a
typographic message using
the visual properties of type
and space to amplify content
(Figs. **71–74**). This project
develops an understanding of
the inventive potential of
typographic form. As a
message carrier, typography
can intensify and expand
content and meaning.

71.
Designer: Steve Cox
72.
Designer: Kyle Wiley
73.
Designer: Bill Jolley
74.
Designer: Susan Dewey

71.

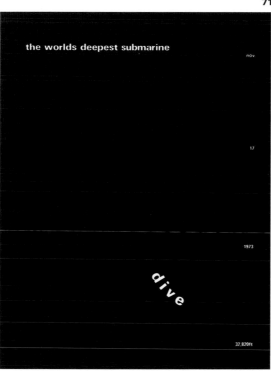

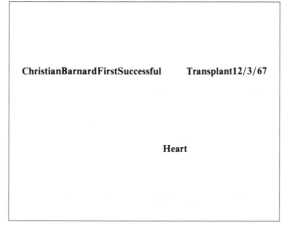

72.

73.

74.

Typeface history posters

Performance typography

Jan Baker

Rhode Island
School of Design

Paul Bruner

Rutgers University

Each student in the class was assigned a typeface to study and use in a poster design, communicating its essential characteristics (Figs. **75** and **76**). Letterforms that reveal the unique properties of the typeface were emphasized. The typeface name and entire alphabet were required components of the design

This project enables students to establish a visual hierarchy in a poster format, while introducing them to the visual characteristics of typefaces.

75.
Designer: Holly Hurwitz
76.
Designer: Luci Goodman

In this project, typography is defined as performance art – a personal form and expression actualized through the typographic medium. Each student wrote a personal poem, not by plan but by feeling. Through the process of typographic design, each student gave visual form to the felt content of the personal

poem. This process was conceived as the essence of performance. The poems and their typographic realization are conceived as art, so the project was conducted in an atmosphere of unconditional positive regard, with no attempt to make value judgments about student's typographic usage or feelings expressed in the poems.

The poems were assembled in handmade-boxed folios. Paul Bruner believes that, "this approach to feeling and reading stands in radical contrast to the information processing and sight-reading of so much attention-getting novelty-type-image displays in mass communications publications."

75.

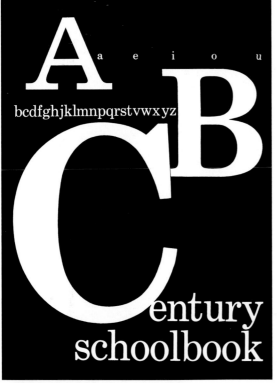

76.

77.

78.

79.

THE SATANISTIC THOUGHTS OF DOCTOR MCCALLISTER

77.
"Untitled." Author/designer: Jason Bass
78.
"PX." Author/designer: Kara Lukasik

79.
"The Satanic Thoughts of Dr. McCallister." Author/designer: John Jankowski

Typographic quotations

Richard D. Schuessler

University of Nebraska
at Kearney

Quotations about design are selected, and a large series of designs are developed emphasizing experimentation and expression. Students explore one of the following visual attributes to each of their designs: layering, separation, and fracture. The designs must evidence the assigned property.

Layering (Fig. **80**) is defined as achieving a sense of spatial depth by stacking forms in space.

Separation involves disconnecting elements by physical space, or by modifying their visual attributes such as size, color, or weight.

Fracturing is a break or rupture in the visual relationship between elements that creates an extreme contrast between them.

Further explorations (Figs. **81** and **82**) explore all three assigned properties as a stimulus for expressive typographic experiments.

80.
Designer: Sheraton Green
81.
Designer: Steve M. Hanson
82.
Designer: Nate Voss

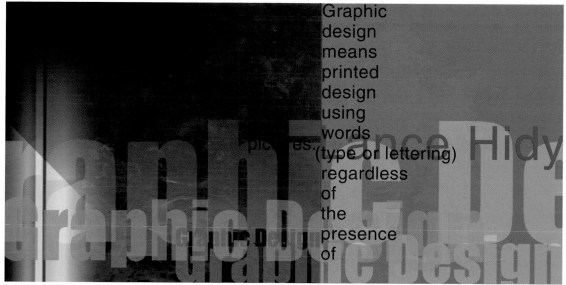

80.

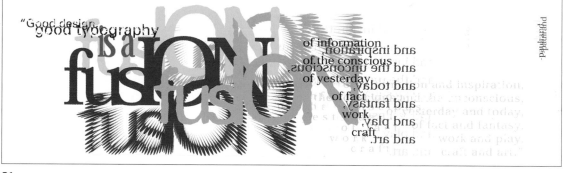

81.

82.

Type and image
in the third dimension

Marcia Lausen

University of Illinois
at Chicago

In 1952, Charles and Ray
Eames created the House of
Cards, a set of interlocking
playing cards for children and
adults. This project is an
adaptation of this now famous
design system.

The two-sided cards enable
students to study on opposite
sides of the twenty individual
cards the structural and
conceptual dualities (as
related to semiotics, color
theory, symbolism, etc.) of
their chosen subject matter.
The interlocking feature of the
cards allows for an exploration of type and image in
dimensional form and space.

Three excellent examples of
this project include *Fourteen
Generations,* the Holing family
lineage traced to the voyage
of the Mayflower (Fig. **83**);
Catalog of Building Materials
(Fig. **84**); and *Cards of
Mystery,* where type and
image are manipulated to
express different emotions
and sensations (Fig. **85**).

83.
Designer: Allison Holing
84.
Designer: Chul Kam
85.
Designer: Kyra Jacobs

83.

84.

85.

Comparative relationships: type and image

Jan Conradi

Ball State University

In this two-part project, students considered visual relationships between type and image. After selecting photographs, students chose typefaces and letterforms that related to the image through visual characteristics such as shape, weight, decorative embellishments, and other design attributes. Part one involved hand drawing the letterform in a side-by-side comparison of form (Figs. **86** and **87**).

In part two, the relationship was explored further by integrating the letterform into the image (Figs. **88** and **89**). Attention to typeface selection, scale, repetition, color, and balance allowed the merger of type and image into a single entity.

This project helps students who are innately image-oriented to understand how design characteristics of typefaces are individualized and distinctive. Selection of an appropriate font can enhance the communicative message, and type and image can be composed into a unified composition.

86.

87.

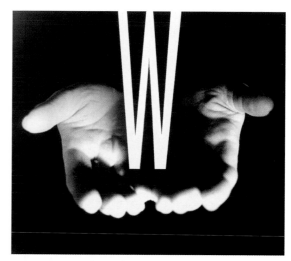

88.

89.

86.
Designer: Brandon Luhring
87.
Designer: Brandon Luhring
88.
Designer: Trina Denison
89.
Designer: Kara Holtzman

**Directional poster:
from your house to the university**

92.　　　　　93.

Malka E. Michelson

Philadelphia University

Typographic posters reveal the directional path between students' homes and the university. Message content, hierarchy, sequencing of letters, words, and lines of type were explored to enhance the development of a typographic landscape. Bumpy, smooth, straight, jagged, curvy, up, down, slow, traffic jams, smooth sailing, bumper to bumper, confusing, farmland, city, over water, and through tunnels are examples of concepts explored through typographic space to amplify and expand content, context, and meaning (Figs. **90–93**).

90.
Designer: Todd Duchynski
91.
Designer: Monique Maiorana
92.
Designer: Erin Roach
93.
Designer: Susan Ulsh

90.　　　　　91.

Graphic-design history posters and booklet

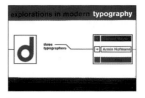

97.

Paul Nini

Ohio State University

Students create a series of three typographic history posters, each based upon one of the following structural themes: 1) orthogonal/grid, 2) diagonal/integral, and 3) combination of orthogonal and diagonal. An orthogonal/grid structure enables a composition consisting of flush-left typographic elements arranged within a grid structure (Fig. **94**). Compositions based on a diagonal/integral structure consist of flush-left typographic elements arranged upon a diagonal axis (Fig. **95**), and a combination structure provides students with an opportunity to explore in a fluid manner the interpretation of information (Fig. **96**).

Phase two of the project is the design of an accordion-fold booklet that profiles any three of the modern typographers appearing on the posters. Students conduct research about the typographers, gathering information and images for inclusion in the booklet. Shown here is a sample cover (Fig. **97**).

94–97.
Designer: Matthew Franco

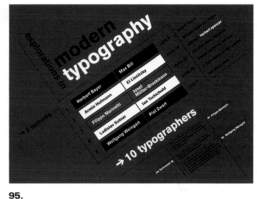

94.

95.

96.

Animated Web-site flash pages

Sandra Wheeler

Virginia Commonwealth University

Using only the letters of the alphabet and punctuation, students created a ten-second (120 frame) typographic narrative with an expressive aspect. After concepts were developed through preliminary sketches, storyboards were produced to explore the conversion of still images to sequential frames representing motion over time. The storyboards reveal and emphasize that type as a formal element is rooted not only in space but also in time. As such it offers endless possibilities for exploring rhythmic and sequential structures.

The storyboards provided the plan for the animated sequence using a 550 pixel x 400 pixel stage size and frame rate of twelve frames per second. Designing ten-second typographic animations develops an ability to create kinetic typographic splash pages for Web sites.

The animation of two "Gs and a Dot" brings energy to the screen (Fig. **98**). A large Ultra Bodoni capital *G* appears on the screen, then a Futura sans serif capital *G* enters from the left and moves in front of the bolder letter. A turquoise dot resting on the Ultra Bodoni *G* begins to roll through the circle of the Futura letter, while the two letters rotate in space, creating a series of dynamic shape configurations. At the end of the animated sequence, the turquoise dot

falls from the screen and the *G*s return to their normal position.

In "Little ä in Traffic" (Fig. **99**), an *ä* with an umlaut (German accent consisting of two dots over a vowel) looks to the left and right, then its "eyes" widen as a stampede of letters rushes past it. Finally, after the letters go by, the little *a*'s mother, a capital *A*, arrives to comfort and protect its child. Letters, motion, and color are used to tell a complex metaphorical story in a few seconds.

"Truth/Fiction" (Fig. **100**) explores the metamorphosis of the word *Truth* into the word *Fiction*. Starting as a horizontal word, the letters swing into a vertical position as they transform, ending with a stacked configuration of letters. Going from a five- to a seven-letter word is nicely resolved by treating the two *l*s as offshoots from the capital *T*.

98.
Designer: Bryan Keplesky

99.
Designer: Nancy Digman

100.
Designer: April Meyer

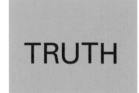

 98.
 **99.**   **100.**

Case Studies in Typographic Design

Many of the educational projects in the preceding chapter represent theoretical and exploratory investigations. They are structured to teach typographic history, theory, spatial concepts, form, and meaning. The goal of typographic education is to prepare young designers for the complexity of applied problem solving. The case studies presented in this chapter describe specific typographic design problems encountered in professional practice. The nature of each problem is analyzed, and the rationale for the solution is discussed.

These nine studies cover a wide range of typographic design: integrating type and image on posters, publication designs, environmental typography, CD-ROM and Web-site design, typographic motion-picture titles, and permutations of a title page.

Integrating type and image in poster design

1.

Alignment of the letterspaced type along the angled edges of the stars unifies word and image. (Designer: Jean-Benoît Lévy; photographer: Tom Wedell, Boston)

A remarkable integration of type with image is found in posters designed by Jean-Benoît Lévy, who has studios in Basel, Switzerland, and San Francisco, California. Lévy collaborates with photographers; he approaches their images as three-dimensional fields whose space is activated and extended by type. On the last day of class when Lévy was a student, teacher Armin Hofmann told him to place type *in* the photograph rather than *on* the photograph. Lévy says, "From that moment on, I knew what to do." In his inventive designs, words and images become a unified composition.

The large star in a "Happy New Year" poster (Fig. **1**) for the Basel studio AND (Trafic Grafic) conveys a sense of energy and motion through repetition on a diagonal axis. The background transition from orange to blue signifies earth to sky. *Happy* aligns with the two white stars, unifying the type and background. The sky is signified in three ways: symbolic stars; a photograph of clouds; and the lines and dots of a star chart. Subtle symbols of the world's major religions, and small type identifying each religion's deity or founder, date, and number of adherents, add another level of meaning in the bold celebratory message.

Grid structures for graphic designs are often implied, but in a poster (Fig. **2**) for the fashion store Inflagranti, the horizontal and vertical pattern of window blinds superimposed with a double portrait of a fashion model provides a visible structure of the placement of type. The translucency and graded tones of the vertical store name echo the translucent portrait and blended tones of the blinds, further uniting word and image.

The curved forms of watch parts, their shadows, and watch-face numerals were photographed in atmospheric space for a Montres et Bijouterie Bosch watch and jewelry store poster (Fig. **3**). Widely letterspaced type set in arcs reflects the curves in the photograph. Color is used to create harmony, for the yellow, white, and orange letters repeat the photograph's warm tones in contrast to the predominantly gray background. Lévy says the orange dots from the text signify seven planets, with the Sun in the exact center.

1.

2.

Three different sizes and amounts of tracking create variety, while using the same typeface brings unity to the design. (Designer: Jean-Benoît Lévy; photographer: Jean-Pascal Imsand)

3.

The simple geometry and spatial dispersion of the type echos these qualities in the photograph. (Designer: Jean-Benoît Lévy; photographer: Franz Werner)

2.

3.

4.

By making the x-height of the larger words the same height as the smaller words, a strong visual relationship is maintained. (Designer: Jean-Benoît Lévy; photographer: Jean-Pascal Imsand)

5.

Lévy carefully retained enough of the overlapped letters to ensure their legibility. (Designer: Jean-Benoît Lévy; photographer: Alexandre Genoud)

4.

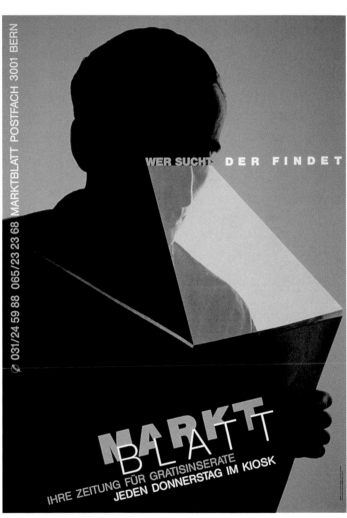

5.

For the Savoy Intercoiffure hair salon poster (Fig. **4**), Lévy used a photograph shot from a low viewpoint of a woman moving her head, causing her hair to fling about in a blurred shape. The photograph was carefully cropped to bleed on the right side and bottom, making a dynamic dark shape against the soft flat background. Two diagonal lines of condensed sans serif type are a sharp contrast to the blurred shape. One line links the top and bottom of the head, while the other links the top of the hair to the edge of the poster. The first word in each line is larger, and the tracking is increased for emphasis.

The *Markt Blatt* is a free newspaper of advertisements in Bern, Switzerland. A sidelit man (Fig. **5**) reads the paper against a warm yellow background. A trapezoid of light becomes a symbol for the process of reading, connecting the reader's eyes with the printed page. Alignment of the typography with the angles of the horizontal and vertical edges of the poster, and the diagonal of the newspaper page creates a structured relationship. By making the type on the photograph yellow and the type on the background white, further integration is achieved. The bold and light type, and overlapping of the two words of the title, produce an arresting visual element.

6.

Across the top, eight rows of modules are filled in with a darker pencil tone to spell the bookstore name in geometric letterforms. The condensed all-capital sans serif type at the bottom of the poster is two modules tall; this unifies with the labyrinth. (Designer and photographer: Jean-Benoît Lévy)

7.

The letters of the bookstore name were executed in outline slab-serif letterforms that are drawn to conform to the horizontal, vertical, and diagonal movements of the labyrinth image. (Designer and photographer: Jean-Benoît Lévy)

6.

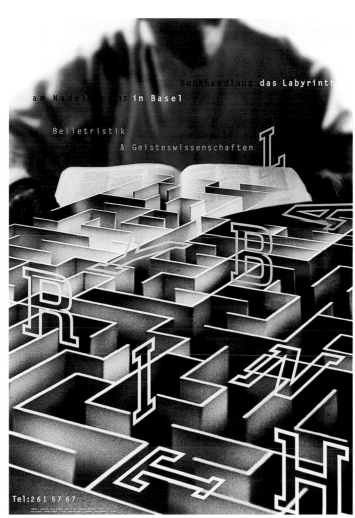

7.

In this poster (Fig. **6**) for the Labyrinth bookstore in Basel, the maze or labyrinth appearing on the poster reinforces the store's name. Lévy carefully drew his complex labyrinth in pencil on a modular grid. The soft pencil tones bring warmth to the rigid geometry. This labyrinth can actually be solved by a viewer standing at the poster kiosk. A photograph of a young man reading a book is superimposed over the labyrinth. "Reading," Lévy says, "is like entering a labyrinth." The organic properties of the human image provide contrast to the stark geometry of the labyrinth, softening and enriching the poster.

In a subsequent poster (Fig. **7**) for the Labyrinth bookstore, Lévy created an image of a three-dimensional labyrinth moving back into space. This compelling image fades back into an out-of-focus, tightly cropped photograph of a reader. These hover in space over the labyrinth; their openness and transparency echo its edges and open channels. A three-dimensional graphics program and Photoshop™ were used to execute this poster. As in Lévy's other posters, a dynamic integration of word and image is achieved through unexpected and original compositional relationships between pictorial and typographic forms.

The U.S. National Park Service Unigrid System

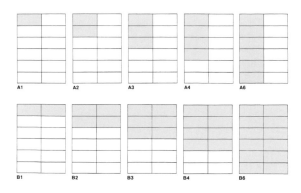

9.
Ten basic publication formats
are derived from the Unigrid
structure.

The United States National Park Service (NPS) developed the Unigrid System as a design system to unify the design of hundreds of site folders, while bringing harmony and economy to its publications program. Unigrid (Fig. **8**) is based on a sheet 965 by 1270 millimeters (about 16.5 by 23.5 inches), which folds into twelve panels that are 99 by 210 millimeters (about 4 by 8.25 inches). Ten basic formats (Fig. **9**) can be derived from the Unigrid ranging from one-panel leaflets to twelve-panel foldout broadsides. Each side of a folder is treated as a unified graphic surface that is completely unfolded by the user, just as one fully opens a map. The fold lines and the panels they create become background rather than a dominant structure, because the typical folder user quickly unfolds it to its full size; users rarely open a folder panel by panel. These standard formats permit great production economy because paper can be purchased in volume in two flat sizes or in web rolls. Most folders are printed in five of the available formats, further simplifying planning.

Grid modules for the folder formats measure 7 picas wide and 80 points high. Vertical spaces between modules are 1 pica wide; horizontal spaces between modules are 10 points high. Horizontal measurements are always made in picas, while vertical measurements are always made in 10-point units or modules. These spatial intervals provide a structure for organizing type, illustrations, photographs, and maps into an orderly whole.

Helvetica was selected as the type family for the Unigrid System because of "its crisp, clean details and typographic texture that make it aesthetically pleasing and easy to read." It was also determined that Helvetica would strengthen and unify the NPS map series that accompanies the folder program. Other considerations are Helvetica's clearly defined hierarchy of sizes and weights with predictable results, large x-height with good line strength and consistent color, and outstanding printing characteristics. Text type is usually set in 8/10 or 9/10 Helvetica or Helvetica Medium in columns two or three modules wide (15 or 23 picas wide, measuring two or three modules plus spatial intervals between them). Text type is often

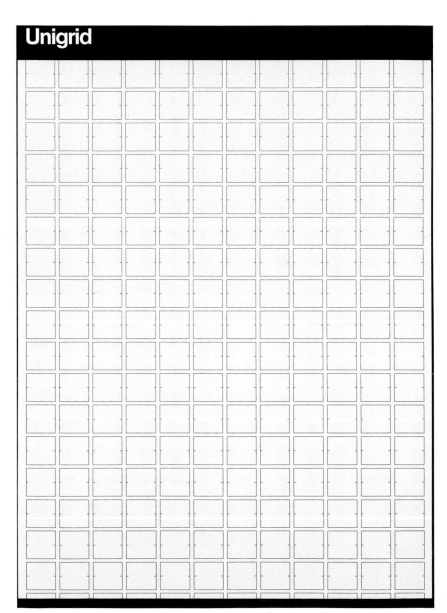

8.
The Unigrid was created by
Massimo Vignelli (consulting
designer), Vincent Gleason (art
director), and Dennis
McLaughlin (graphic
designer).

10 and **11.**
Copy the Unigrid on the preceding page onto transparent material and place it over these folders to study the underlying structure of the designs.

12.
The black bars and consistent typography on folder covers become a visual identification.

justified, and columns are aligned top and bottom to create horizontal movement. Sometimes the last column will run short. One line space, rather than indentations, is used to separate paragraphs.

Captions are set one or two modules wide (7 or 15 picas wide) in 7/7, 7/8, or 8/9 Helvetica Regular or Medium, and may be either roman or italic. This variety of weight, posture, and leading provides flexibility to create a value and texture that complements and contrasts with other typographic and pictorial elements. Captions are set rag right, and this helps create a strong separation between text and captions, as do contrasts between text and caption textures, weights, and line lengths.

Major display type can be set in 12-, 18-, or 24-point Helvetica Medium and is often positioned 10 points above the related text on a horizontal band of white space, frequently 40 points high, running above the text. The variety of display sizes gives the designer the flexibility needed to create appropriate scale relationships between display type, the size of the folder, image sizes, and density of text type. The margin below the text type is always a spatial interval at least 20 points high.

The cover panels of all folders have a 100-point black band that bleeds at the top and on both sides. Titles reverse from this bar and are set in standard sizes of Helvetica Medium for park names with fewer than twelve letters. When site designation and location appear reversed from the black bar, these are set in 12/14 or 8/9 Helvetica Medium and align on the seventh grid module. Service designations are the same size and align on the tenth grid module. Cover panel type is always positioned 10 points down from the top edge of the band. This horizontal black band with its standardized title type becomes a consistent visual identification device for the National Park Service. Horizontal movement is accentuated through the placement of the type, the horizontal margins, and internal bars that divide the space into zones of information. These bars correspond

10.

12.

to the title bar and may be complementary colors, contrasting colors, or black. These bars are 25 points wide, and one is always placed across the bottom of the folder. Display type is sometimes reversed from the bars.

The Unigrid System emphasizes clarity by clearly separating the elements. Type seldom overlaps images, and maps are not obscured by picture inserts or overlaps. Neutral grays and beiges, used to create backgrounds behind text areas or unify groups of images, are part of a standard palette of twenty-four colors, created from four-color process inks and a limited selection of secondary colors. This color palette creates continuity between various park publications.

Planning layouts are created using computer-generated typography, images, map windows, and the master grid sheets. A typesetter with a contract to set National Park Service typography uses electronic page makeup to format and position type, rules, and bars, providing repro-quality output for mechanicals.

Standardized formats and typographic specifications enable National Park Service designers to focus on content and design, rather than developing formats and specifications for each project. The Unigrid System is flexible, permitting unique solutions appropriate to specific messages, while leading to consistent graphic excellence and a unified visual identification.

Massimo Vignelli was the inventor and remains consulting designer for the Unigrid System. The program gained its vitality because the original design team remained intact over the first dozen years, and included Vincent Gleason (chief), Melissa Cronyn, Nicholas Kirilloff, Linda Meyers, Dennis McLaughlin, Phillip Musselwhite, and Mitchell Zetlin.

11.

**Design and typography
for *Interiors* magazine**

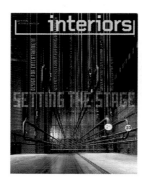

14.

15.

may 2001
US $7.00 | CAN $9.00

interiors

Peek Performance
New perspectives on the workplace

Amsterdam
Steven Holl's Het Oosten office
Vancouver
Francisco Kripacz's Lanyon Phillips office
Bay Area
Beige Design's Cahoots office
Manhattan
WalkerGroup/CNI's headquarters

While the National Park Service design program used standardized formats and typographic specifications to maintain consistency in hundreds of printed designs, the needs of *Interiors* magazine are very different. Art director Paul Carlos and editor Julie Lasky required a design system consistent enough to create an identity for the magazine, but with sufficient design flexibility to enable them to express a wide variety of interior design, architecture, and product design subjects.

The masthead (Fig. **13**) consists of the word *interiors* set in lowercase Gridnik, a bold geometric sans-serif font whose curved strokes are replaced by forty-five-degree diagonals. The junctions where diagonals join horizontals and verticals are softened by subtle curves. The name *interiors* is within an open-top, three-sided box. This becomes a subtle metaphor, as the word *interiors* sets in the interior of the box. This ruled-line device and typeface are used for the headers of regular departments to tie the editorial content together and reinforce the visual identity.

The masthead appears prominently on each cover in the same size and position, but its color changes for contrast or harmony with the photograph. Only one major article or theme is presented on each cover. Cover typeface style, size, and placement are selected to express content and/or become part of the photographic composition (Figs. **14–16**). Type colors are carefully chosen to complement the photograph's colors while having sufficient contrast for good legibility.

interiors

13.

13.
Interiors magazine masthead. The *r* and *t* were shortened to improve the spatial intervals inside the word. (Designer: Paul Carlos; typeface: Gridnik by Wim Crouwel)

14.
For a special issue on designing for the entertainment industry, a typeface evoking stage lights appears over a back-stage photograph. (Art director: Paul Carlos; photographer: KAN Photo Studio)

15.
A lengthy quotation from a panel discussion about the decline of hardwood forests in America engages the reader. (Art director: Paul Carlos; photographer: Graham McIndoe)

16.
To complement the understated elegance of a minimalist interior, small type in analogous colors is placed on the open space and aligned with the windows. (Art director: Paul Carlos; photographer: Paul Warchol)

17.

Page numbers on the contents page are in the margin, and a line-space interval separates type units. Titles are in large bold type, with italic authors' names and roman subheads. (Art director: Paul Carlos; photographer: KAN Photo Studio)

18.

A three-column grid, fine vertical rules separating items sharing a page, and silhouette photographs bring order and vitality to carefully balanced layouts. (Art director: Paul Carlos; photographer: supplied by manufacturers)

The double-page contents section (Fig. **17**) always uses the same format. The spread is divided horizontally, with photographs below and type above. Fine ruled lines separate elements, with departments on the left and features on the right. A clear and precise typographic plan enables readers to easily navigate the contents.

Design flexibility is achieved by using two-, three-, and four-column grids for various text settings in the magazine, reflecting a variety of content. The distinctive texture of the Quadraat Sans type family, used for all text settings, brings continuity to the pages. Other unifying factors are consistent use of type sizes, leading, and flush-left, ragged-right column alignment.

The "matter monthly" department (Fig. **18**) presents new furniture, wall coverings, and fabrics. The top two-thirds of each spread contains images of the products, handsomely composed with generous white space. Text type columns under each product are unified by a flow line. Captions are within fine ruled boxes placed close to the identified product, making figure numbers or directional words unnecessary.

The layout and typeface selection for editorial spreads opening each article reflect the subject matter and photography. A full-page photograph presents perforated metal panels, a vertical structure, and a luminous recessed window in a Dutch housing corporation pavilion (Fig. **19**) designed by Steven Holl. Carlos responded with a spatial echo effect. A black page (Fig. **20**) intensifies the glowing luminosity of the restored Hotel Burnham's terra-cotta facade.

The design of *Interiors* magazine represents a balance between a systematic approach using consistent text type, folios, margins, and flow lines for continuity, while other elements – notably feature article opening-spread display type and design elements – have great variety to express the visual and conceptual nature of the subject matter. There is sufficient consistency for easy navigation, and enough variety to delight and surprise readers.

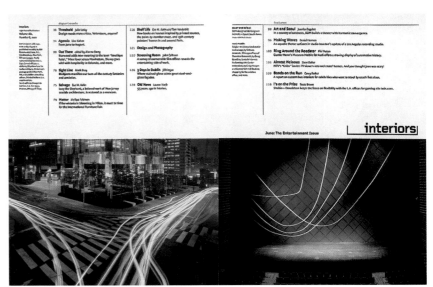

17.

18.

19.

A graphic structure with large title type and a repetitive texture of dots mimics the photograph. The green subtitle repeats the bright green color of the trees outside the window. (Art director: Paul Carlos; photographer: Paul Warchol)

20.

Text type set in the shape of the building, display type reflecting the palette of the hotel exterior, and use of color terra cotta to set the words *terra-cotta* complete the resonance between photography and typography. (Art director: Paul Carlos; photographer: Hedrich Blessing)

Holl Notes

Music and math inspired Steven Holl's pavilion for a housing corporation in the heart of Amsterdam. by Allard Jolles

19.

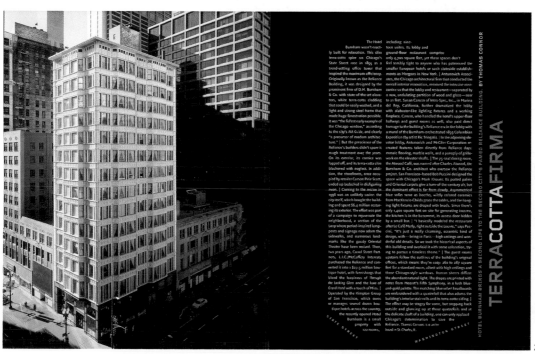

TERRACOTTAFIRMA

20.

Typographic film titles

Referring to a movie advertisement that used letterforms "painted by light," typographic historian Beatrice Warde wrote, "After forty centuries of the necessarily static Alphabet, I saw what its members could do in the fourth dimension of Time, 'flux,' movement. You may well say that I was electrified." Through advanced animation and computer graphics techniques, graphic designers are transforming typographic communication into kinetic sequences that might almost be called "visual music."

Richard Greenberg has distinguished himself as a leading innovator in graphic design for film titles, movie previews, special effects, and television commercials. He considers film titles to be a "visual metaphor" for the movie that follows, setting "the *tone* of the movie. You have to take the people who have just arrived at the theater and separate them from their ordinary reality – walking onto the street, waiting in line; you bring them *into* the movie. You want to tell them how to react: that it's all right to laugh, that they are going to be scared, or that something serious is going on."

In the titles for the Warner Brothers film *Superman – The Movie,* bright blue names and the Superman emblem streak through space like comets, stop for a moment, then evaporate into deep space (Fig. **21**). The speed and power of this film's fantasy superhero are evoked. This effect is accomplished by tracking rear-illuminated typography in front of an open camera lens. Each frame captures a streak of light that starts and stops slightly before the light streak recorded on the next frame. When shown at twenty-four frames per second, this series of still images is transformed into a dynamic expression of zooming energy.

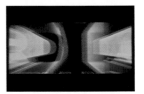

21.

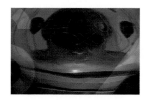

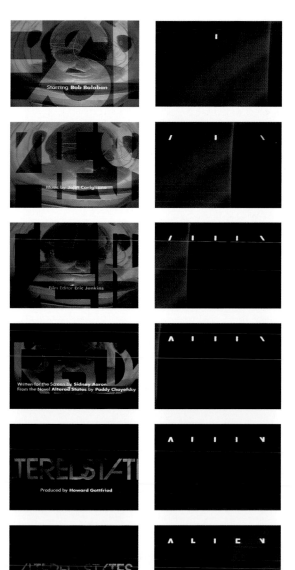

22.

23.

For the Warner Brothers movie *Altered States,* the title sequence opens with a wide-angle image of a researcher in an isolation tank (Fig. **22**). Superimposed over this image, the two words of the title – transparent, as if they are windows cut from a black background – overlap each other as they move slowly across the screen. The film credits are superimposed in white typography in front of this lively pattern of typographic forms and counterforms. Behind the title the background slowly darkens while the camera pulls away from it, causing the letterforms to become smaller and smaller. Finally, the complete title, *Altered States,* appears in its entirety before the totally black screen. In the title, set in Avant Garde Demi, the repetition of this unusual configuration unifies the two words and serves to make the title a unique and memorable signification.

An ominous mood is created in the title sequence for the Twentieth Century-Fox production *Alien* (Fig. **23**). Deep in outer space, the dark side of an immense planet (suggested by a sweeping curved edge) moves slowly onto the screen. Gradually, it passes from right to left, engulfs the screen in blackness, and then continues until it disappears from sight. As the planet passes, small white rectangles appear one by one, then undergo a metamorphosis to form a five-letter title letterspaced across the screen. An elevated sense of mystery is achieved by the harmonious juxtaposition of the passing planet and the typographical transformation. The impending arrival of aliens is evoked.

A striking three-dimensional effect is achieved in the seamless title sequences for *True Lies,* a film about a secret agent who learns about his wife's extramarital affair and pursues her using intelligence resources available in his profession, which is a job he kept secret from her. The title begins with four faint blue streaks that start to rotate in space (Fig. **24**). As the lines rotate, the flat, planar letters of the word *true* are revealed. These letterforms continue to rotate, appearing as independent cubelike structures, with the final sequence revealing the letters of the word *lies,* reversed and appearing in black on the adjacent surfaces of the structures. This simple and elegant visual transformation provides a surprising tension between the two opposing words of the film's title.

Martin Riggs, the lead character in the film *Lethal Weapon 3,* finally meets his match in Lorna Cole, a beautiful but tough policewoman. Together with his partner, Roger Murtaugh, the three attempt to expose the illegal arms racket of a fellow police officer. The heightened suspense of the film is established with the visceral image of fire licking the surface of a calm body of water. As the flames erupt from left to right along the screen, typography presenting the names of the film's stars follows their movement (Fig. **25**). In this film title, the synergistic relationship between type and image is fully developed as they move in time and space. This film title provides an excellent example of the integration of type into image, unlike many designs where type is merely added to, or placed upon, an image.

The time-space orientation of digital media enables the typographic designer to add motion, scale change, sequence, and metamorphosis to alphabet communication. As demonstrated by the work of Richard Greenberg, this opens new vistas of expressive communication.

24.

25.

Hancock Park: interpretive exhibit
for the La Brea Tar Pits

Hancock Park is a unique urban setting situated along Wilshire Boulevard in the Miracle Mile section of Los Angeles. Home to both the Los Angeles County Museum of Art and the Page Museum of La Brea Discoveries, Hancock Park is a natural historic site where both science and art are combined in a public setting. The park, which contains natural tar pits and fossils, dates back to the Miocene and Pliocene eras when the Los Angeles basin was covered by sea. In 1913, G. Alan Hancock gave the 23-acre tract of land to the County of Los Angeles for the purposes of preserving and exhibiting its scientific features.

Project director Paul Prejza, project manager Holly Hampton, and designer Niv Kasher teamed together on this project with the objective to enhance the social as well as the aesthetic value of Hancock Park as both a natural and cultural attraction.

From the offset, the didactic nature of the exhibits implied the importance of the role that typography would play. Consideration in the selection of type styles was given to legibility, color, and form as well as compatibility with existing typographic systems for museums located at this site. The final result was a system that combined the sans serif font Frutiger Roman with the serif font Fenice.

26.

27.

28.

Frutiger was the natural choice for the sans serif face. It not only provided exceptional legibility but also helped to establish a visual link to the Los Angeles County Museum of Art, which was also identified under the umbrella of Hancock Park. With this in mind the park itself needed an identity that would work well when combined with the sans serif font. To complement the clean strokes of Frutiger, the modern, somewhat condensed straight serif form Fenice was chosen and developed in combination with the Gingko leaf symbol as a vertical reading logotype for the park. Fenice was used for the body copy of the

29.

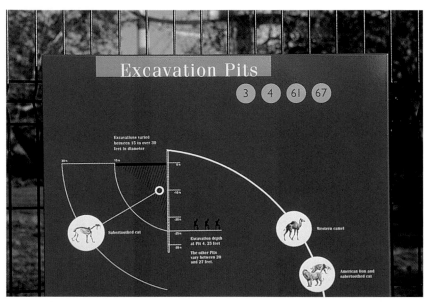

30.

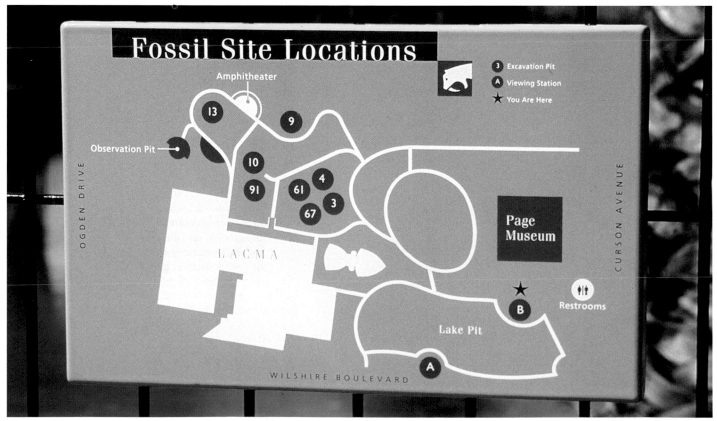

31.

33. **34.**

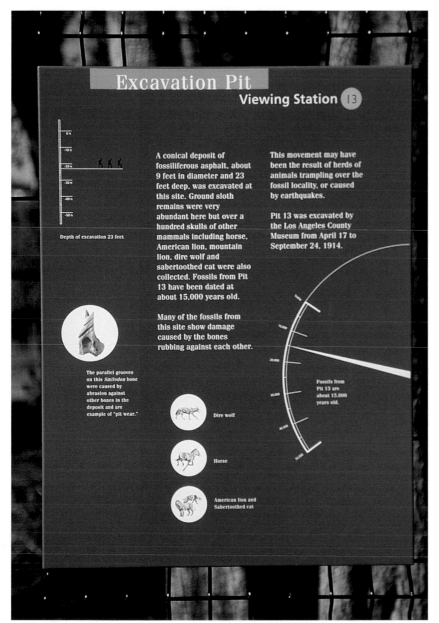

32.

exhibition portion of the project as well. A quarter-inch cap height with proper leading allowed for ease of legibility at a comfortable viewing distance.

Because of the expansive size of this outdoor exhibit environment, directional signage for optimal wayfinding was an important component of the system. To enable visitors to read signs from a distance, carefully letterspaced Frutiger was chosen for this task. Legibility was also strengthened by presenting black letters on yellow backgrounds (Figs. **26** and **27**). Note the unusual directional arrow. This form is visually consistent with the Gingko leaf symbol used as the park's logo (Fig. **28**).

This primary locator sign (Fig. **29**) introduces passersby to the park and identifies the Los Angeles County Museum of Art, Page Museum, and La Brea Tar Pits. The logotype and typographic units are sized and grouped for maximum clarity. Secondary locator signs within the park feature a logical hierarchy of type, images, diagrams, and maps to provide navigational clarity and give visitors the confidence to freely explore the area. The large numerals enclosed within circles on the locator signs clearly identify the park's various attractions (Figs. **30** and **31**).

The scientific interest in the tar pits is reflected in the written and visual history of the site. Porcelain enamel interpretive panels are located at the six major excavation sites within the park and identify the best view for each station. The content of the didactic panels combines typography, photography, and illustration. These elements are designed to visually display quantitative information including geologic time, animal life, and the preservation of the fossils excavated at Hancock Park. The interpretive panels reveal the compositional flexibility of the typographic system. While the treatment of the heads, text, captions, color, and asymmetrical organizational strategy remain constant, the panels exhibit a wide variety. For primary text, Fenice is set flush left, ragged right with generous interline spacing for ease of reading (Figs. **32–34**).

157

35.

36.

Nothing in the Hancock Park exhibit system is left to chance: differences in signage for womens' and mens' restrooms are established through variations in color, sign shape, figure, and plant icons (Fig. **35** and **36**); parking signs are identified with a large capital letter *P* to distinguish them from other park signs (Fig. **37**); the heights of graphic panels and rails are carefully determined to satisfy the needs of a wide-ranging audience (Fig. **38**), and exhibit components and signage are assigned different colors based on their given function: orange is for supplementary information, yellow for directional information, and red for interpretive information.

In designing environmental graphics at this major attraction for young and old alike, the researchers and designers gave every consideration to ensuring clear, concise communication. All elements, from the final installed height of the panels to the dynamics of color, typography, and composition, work together to signal the viewer from afar and draw them in for a closer look.

38.

37.

CD-ROM design for *Crank Call:*
a holiday typeface by MetaDesign

Multimedia is likely the most profound educational and entertainment tool to have been developed. It is powerful because, as its name suggests, it is capable of employing several media – video, animation, sound, text, and pictures – into a single highly engaging sensory experience. Because multimedia is also interactive, users travel from place to place, forward and backward at will. In such environments, typographical concerns have also changed. Unlike a book, where typography sits still on the page, typography on a screen is active; it is a kinetic element in a highly flexible environment, aiding in the navigational process of the user. While typography has traditionally been rooted in space only, in interactive environments it is also rooted in time: pacing, transition, and motion are important new facets that affect both legibility and aesthetics. Careful attention must be paid to how type appears on a screen (see Chapter Four), and how readers interact with it.

39.
The title page of the CD-ROM – saturated in holiday red – contains the title set in the *Crank Call* typeface. Secondary information is clearly presented in Meta. Anticipating what is to come, the architecture and primary graphic elements of the interactive experience are suggested in subtle, muted tones. A pulsating directional button in the form of an arrow cues the visitor to click it for entry into the presentation.

40.
In contrast to the expressive nature of the subject typeface, the introduction page, typeset in Meta, describes the project with clarity, restraint, and refinement. The text adheres also to legibility concerns specific to the world of the screen: type size, interletter and interline spacing, line length, and color contrast are carefully balanced.

41.
With another click of the mouse, visitors are taken to a page that provides entrance into the type-design process. A single click forward advances the user to the next letter of the alphabet; a single click backward retreats the user to the previous letterform.

39.

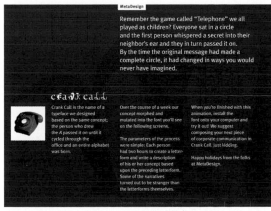

40.

41.

Crank Call, a holiday greeting and interactive CD-ROM designed and produced by MetaDesign, is based upon a familiar children's game. The game is described on the introductory page: "Remember the game called 'Telephone' we all played as children? Everyone sat in a circle, and the first person whispered a secret into their neighbor's ear and they in turn passed it on. By the time the original message had made a complete circle, it had changed in ways you would never have imagined."

The idea of the game was used by the designers at MetaDesign to create a new typeface: each person in the office "had two hours to create a letterform and write a description of his or her concept based upon the preceding letterform."

Upon clicking a directional button, the audience hears a dialing telephone and is taken to the next screen. Here, one clicks a "forward" button to advance to a page featuring the creation of the letter *A.* Each new click of the button advances the

42–47.
The design process is revealed by advancing through the "alphabet" pages. Each new page presents a design response to the previous letterform, a portrait photograph (or representational image) of each designer, and candid statements by the designers that provide entertaining insight into individual design criteria.

Visual consistency is achieved by providing a spatial zone for each of the diverse elements and placing them within a consistent structure.

42.

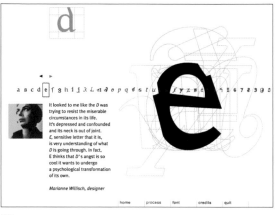

43.

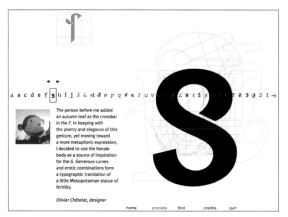

44.

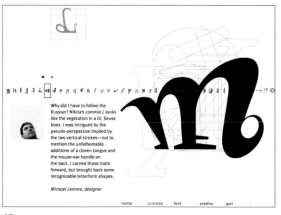

45.

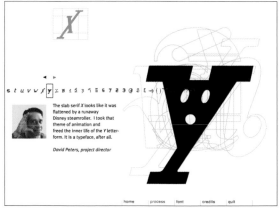

46.

47.

user to the next letter of the alphabet. It is possible to move forward or backward through the alphabet as desired. Each new page presents a new letterform, the previous letterform, a "portrait" photograph of the designer, and a designer's statement. Each click of a button is accompanied by a sound effect – the ring of a telephone, a busy signal.

The menu – consisting of the options, "home," "process," "font," "credits," and "quit," – appears at the bottom of every page, providing a clear and unencumbered navigational process for the user.

One of the most unique aspects of this CD-ROM is that not only is the interface itself interactive, but the gamelike process of designing the typeface *Crank Call* was an interaction of creative minds and a demonstration of team cooperation.

48–50.

Shown here are two process pages featuring the design of punctuation and a page showing the entire font, which consists of 26 letters, the numerals 0–9, and 12 characters of punctuation and symbols.

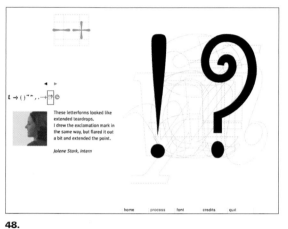

48.

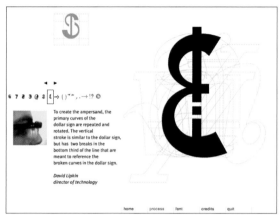

49.

50.

**Sonoma County Woodworkers
Association Web site**

51.
The title's dominant position in the visual hierarchy is established by its central high position and wide linespacing, rather than its size, weight, or color.

52.
When the cursor moves over the contents list, a subtitle appears at the lower center of the screen.

53.
The brown line becomes an important compositional device, linking elements into an open rectangle above the organic fish image.

In designing the Web site for the Sonoma County Woodworkers Association, designer Maureen Kringen of Kringen, Inc., in Sebastopol, California, sought to evoke an aesthetic response to the art and craft of woodworking. A clean, contemporary site was desired; but at the same time Kringen wanted to convey a feeling for the rich warmth of fine woods and the traditional heritage of excellent craftsmanship. Her final solution was based on a dark background, punctuated by understated, elegant typography and warm photographs of handmade objects designed and created by members of the association.

During the design process, important decisions about the site characteristics were made. The dark background was selected because Kringen felt it brought out the warmth of the wood in the photographs. She decided to make the type small and understated to focus the viewer's attention on the visual images rather than the typography. The opening page, often called the splash screen (Fig. **51**), establishes the design theme for the site. The organization's name is set in Classical Garamond BT, an elegant all-capital Old Style font that is highly readable on-screen. The five sections of the site are listed to the left in green letterspaced, all-capital Arial Black; a statement of the organization's purpose appears on the right in a Garamond Bold Italic. The color, texture, and spacing separate these three type elements into discrete units. They appear structured because they form a dynamic asymmetrical triangle. The green line between the contents list and title strengthens the vertical structure created by the flush edges.

Navigation is an important consideration in Web design. Kringen carefully developed visual cues to give the viewer easy access to information on the site. These include a warm brown bracket embracing a section title when the cursor moves over it (Fig. **52**), and the addition of "Home" to the contents list (Fig. **53**) so visitors can return to the opening page from any section of the Web site.

51.

52.

53.

54.

The title page for the "Gallery" section of the site contains a second contents list of artists whose works are on display. Web-site content is set in Arial; initial caps are Arial Bold.

55.

Clicking on an artist's name takes one to a scrolling portfolio, shown here in its entirety, of images by that artist.

56.

Clicking on any image on the scrolling portfolio opens a window with a larger photograph of the art object.

57.

Clicking on "Contact the artist" brings up a screen with contact information; the navigational device "Back to Portfolio" is important in preventing viewers from becoming trapped in a dead end.

54.

56.

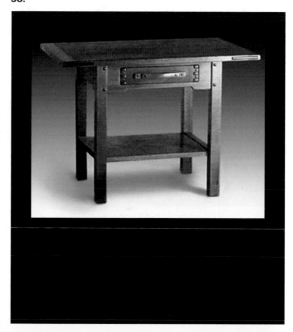

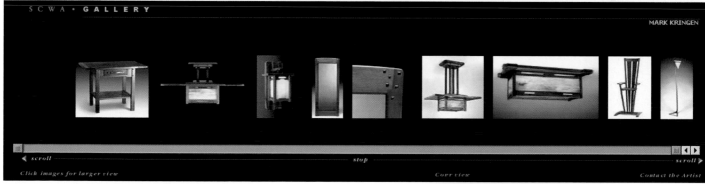

55.

Section title pages have subtle background images depicting details of woodwork. Some of these fade softly into the background. Smaller images also showing woodwork details animate the screen by appearing and changing while each page is viewed. The screens are carefully composed to achieve a lively asymmetrical balance.

This site evidences how careful planning, consistent visual characteristics, and superb images can be used with understated type to create an effective and engaging Web site.

57.

58.

The "Resources" page uses fine brown lines as visual punctuation to separate and structure a long scrolling list of available videotapes.

59 and 60.

The "Newsletter" and "Membership" title pages use a subtle color change and underlining to emphasize type with links to other information.

By changing the placement and horizontal or vertical orientation of the background images, and the location of the small photographs, variety is achieved within the unified site.

58.

59.

60.

Book design for
Listen Up: The Lives of Quincy Jones

61.
Type was expanded and condensed by computer to form a column, but the designers were very careful to minimize awkward optical distortions.

62.
Quincy Jones's friends call him "Q"; this inspired the large red *Q* on the cover, which is repeated on the title page.

The release of a major motion picture about musician and composer Quincy Jones was accompanied by an oversize book. Design director Kent Hunter and designers Thomas Bricker, Riki Sethiadi, and Johan Vipper of the Frankfurt Gips Balkind design office responded to the structure and content of the movie, which had a syncopated rhythm of rapid cuts, musical performances, and interviews. This inspired a lively design approach using typography for expression and interpretation. The background material for this 192-page montage included hundreds of photographs, long and short quotations gleaned from the film sound track, and 800 pages of transcripts, and a lengthy essay by jazz journalist George Nelson.

Jazz albums from the 1950s and 1960s influenced the use of the sans serif Franklin Gothic type family, especially its condensed versions, for display type. This was combined with Sabon old style for the running text. A lively dissonance resulted from the contrast between Franklin Gothic's bold verticality and Sabon's lighter, more organic forms. On the book jacket (Fig. **61**), a vertical column of type was printed in red over a photograph of Jones. This typographic configuration was also used on the sound-track packaging and movie publicity to unify graphics for the book, film, and recording.

Upon opening the book (Fig. **62**), the reader experiences dynamic typographic scale, including informational copy on the brown-and-black jacket flap; the blue-and-black shapes of the words *Quincy Jones* printed on the inside of the jacket; and a large red *Q* that wraps around the front and back book cover.

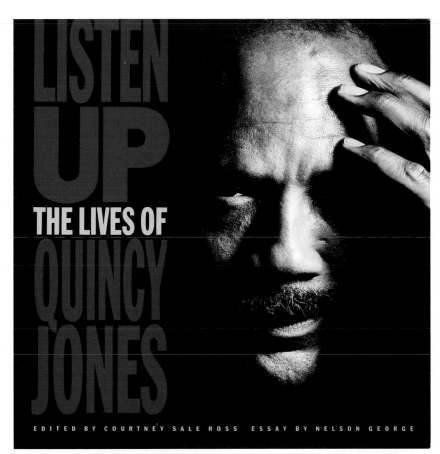

61.

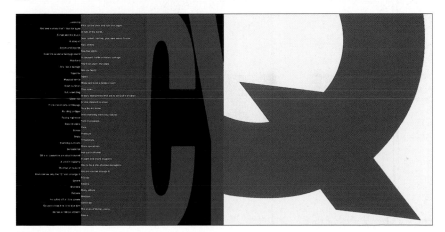

62.

64.
Large outline letters were freely arranged on the computer screen to create an electronic collage using a drawing program. The areas were then filled with colors.

63.
Layering, overlapping, and extreme scale changes were qualities generated using the capabilities of electronic page design.

63.

The back cover (Fig. **63**) is a typographic montage of words expressing music and life. This typographic montage reappeared in animated form for the film titles, further tying the two works together. Typographic experimentation to express content and a thorough understanding of electronic page design enabled the design team to make *Listen Up: The Lives of Quincy Jones* an outstanding example of innovative typography

The book is divided into seven chapters representing periods of Quincy Jones's life and work, entitled "Early years," "Player," "Film scorer," and so on. Each section opens with a large typographic design (Fig. **64**) of overlapping letters in black, gray and a bright color, such as red in the first title page shown here, opposite a full-page photograph. Quiet pages (Fig. **65**) are introduced periodically as calm areas after more complex, energetic pages to bring variety to the visual flow; that is, sequential movement, repetition, and rhythm from spread to spread. Unity within tremendous diversity is achieved through the repetition of several themes throughout the book. These include a series of full-page bleed photographs of musicians accompanied by Quincy Jones's remembrances (Fig. **66**), and pages combining one or more small photographs with quotations from the movie as well as other sources (Fig. **67**).

The essay takes about one-fourth of the book's pages. The running text was placed on gray rectangles (Fig. **68**). These rectangles containing text type help the reader find the essay after it skips several pages. The essay becomes a thread running throughout the book, contributing to the visual flow. The content suggested typographic themes to the designers. A double-page spread (Fig. **69**) uses type to express the cadence and dissonance of rap music.

If Ray had followed the strict commercial line, he may have had more hits, but he would have had less meaning. People buy an armful of Ray Charles cassettes or discs, and what they're buying is an armful of **integrity.** –Jesse Jackson

"*Every music has its soul. And if you really are sincere and surrender to it and explore it, it's all soulful.*" –*Ray Charles*

*When he became the vice president in charge of **A**rtists & **R**epertoire of Mercury Records, the first black person to reach that level, I absolutely was so proud, it was just unbelievable. And then he says, "I'm going out to Hollywood!!"*–*Lloyd Jones*

I just dropped everything and just took that chance. I said, "Maybe I won't make it out there, but **I'm going!**" –Quincy

65.

66.

67.

Quotations from the movie expressing contradictory opinions about Jones's trumpet-playing skills are asymmetrically composed around a centrally placed photograph.

Scale, weight, and color are used to emphasize key words in the comments.

68.

Negative leading was specified on the computer, squeezing interline space from between the lines to create a rhythmical cadence.

69.

Typography becomes a visual metaphor for the auditory intensity of rap music. The text type's alignment and structure are influenced by the large letters and words.

67.

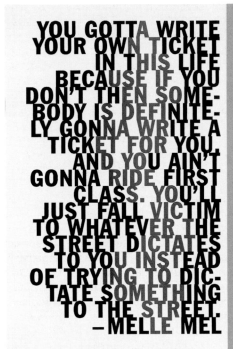

68.

69.

Permutations in a title-page design

The range of potential solutions to a typographic problem is seemingly infinite. Variations, permutations, and transformations can be developed, exploring changes in both fundamental aspects and subtle details. In this case study, designer Thomas Detrie has developed a sequence of solutions for a title-page design. Detrie's approach to the design process is based on his beliefs that "solutions come from within the problem" and "ideas come from working with the material and are not supplied or preconceived."

The problem-solving sequence is a three-stage design process: preliminary exploration, message investigation, and visualization of solutions. In his preliminary exploration, Detrie considered the nature and content of the problem and made sketches to explore possible directions. Typographic information (title, subtitle, authors, and publisher) was assigned priority. Detrie raised the question, "For the book *Basic Typography,* what is basic to typography that can be signified in a visual solution?" His answer established parameters appropriate to the given problem: a right-angled system, black on white, printed and unprinted areas, and a clear message. These considerations became the criteria for the investigation.

To investigate the range of typographic possibilities for the clear presentation of the manuscript, actual type was set and used in the initial visualizations for accuracy. A sans-serif face was chosen, and the message was printed in three sizes and two weights for use as raw material in these typographic studies. While maintaining the message priorities determined in the first stage, a variety of visual solutions were executed. Decisions were made through subtle comparisons of type sizes and weights to select those that provided the best visual balance and message conveyance. Detrie did not place the type upon a predetermined grid; rather, he allowed the organizational structure to evolve from the process of working with the type proofs. Selecting the basic typographic arrangement was an intermediate step in the design process (Fig. **70**).

Next, Detrie developed a series of variations of this arrangement by investigating the application of horizontal and vertical lines, positive and negative shapes with positive type, and positive and negative shapes with positive and reversed type. Figure **71** shows nine permutations with the application of vertical lines to the basic typographic schema. Permutations range from type alone to the addition of linear and rectilinear elements to a solid black page with reversed type (Fig. **72**). A graded arrangement of twenty-four of the many solutions is shown in Figure **73**. Observe the horizontal and vertical sequencing.

Unlimited solutions are possible in typographic design, and selection becomes an integral part of the design process. Not every possible solution is appropriate; the designer must continually evaluate each one against the problem criteria. The significance of Detrie's investigations lay in the workings of the design process.

70.

This project commenced in the postgraduate program in graphic design at the Basel School of Design, Switzerland. The encouragement and criticism of Wolfgang Weingart are gratefully acknowledged.

71.

72.

Ruedi Rüegg/Godi Fröhlich

ABC Verlag Zürich — Handbuch für Technik und Gestaltung
Typografische Grundlagen

Editions ABC Zurich — Manual pour technique et conception
Bases Typographiques

ABC Edition Zurich — Handbook for technique and design
Basic Typography

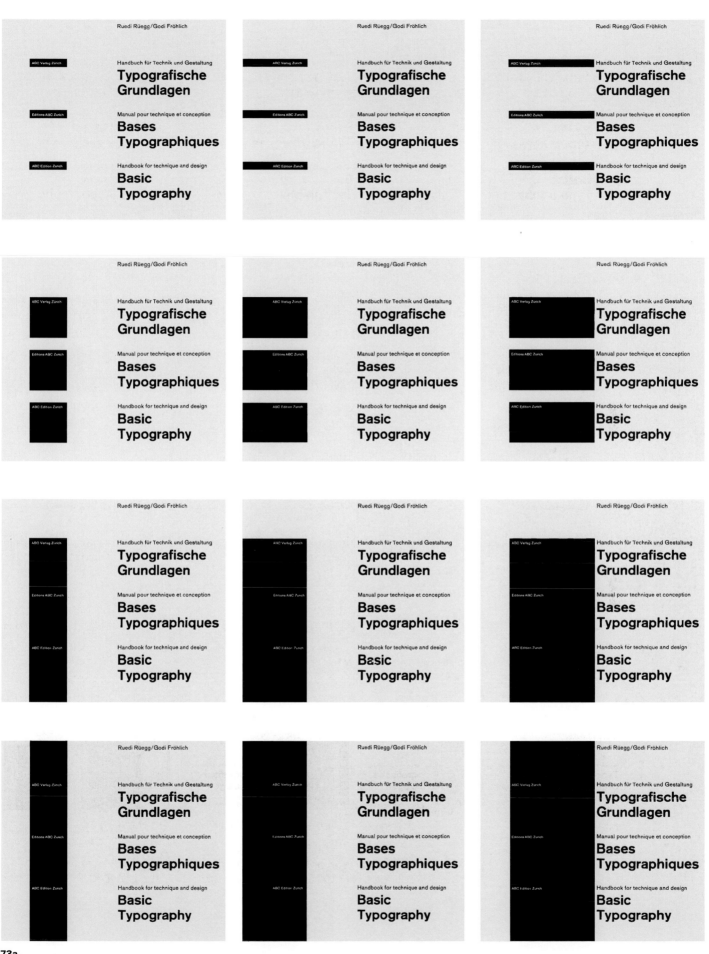

73a.

73b.

The uses of typographic specimens by graphic designers have changed dramatically in the age of digital technology. Earlier generations of designers used specimens to determine which fonts and sizes to specify and order from typesetting companies, and for reference or tracing purposes when drawing layouts. A limited range of sizes were manufactured, and specimen sheets or books showed all available sizes.

Digital computers make an infinite range of sizes and style variations available, and designers can study and purchase fonts from digital type foundry Web sites. Today printed specimens are used for study and comparison purposes. The typeface specimens in this chapter were selected from outstanding type families to provide examples of the major historical classifications: Old Style, Transitional, Modern, Egyptian, and Sans Serif. More extensive specimens of Old Style and Sans Serif fonts are included, for these are the most widely used categories.

A bewildering number of typeface variations are available today, including versions originally designed for hand-, machine-, or phototype composition. Excellent newer varieties have been designed specifically for digital media. Designers need to study the subtlety of form and spacing in fonts, because their quality can vary widely.

ORONTII FINEI

DELPHINATIS, REGII MATHEMA-
TICARVM PROFESSORIS, DE
ARITHMETICA PRACTICA
LIBRI QVATVOR.

LIBER PRIMVS, DE INTEGRIS: HOC EST,
eiusdem speciei, siue denominationis tractat numeris.

De fructu, atq; dignitate ipsius Arithmeticæ: Prooemium.

1 NTER LIBERALES MA-
thematicas, quæ solæ disciplinæ vocátur,
Arithmeticam primum locum sibi vendi-
casse: nemo sanæ mentis ignorat. Est enim
Arithmetica omnium aliarum disciplina-
rum mater, & nutrix antiquissima: numerorū qualitates, vim, & naturam, ac id genus alia demonstrans, quæ absolutum vi-
dentur respicere numerum. Cuius prin-
cipia tanta excellunt simplicitate, vt nul-
lius artis videatur indigere suffragio: sed cunctis opituletur artibus. Ad
cuius puritatem illud etiam plurimum facit: quoniam nulla diuinitati
adeò cónexa est disciplina, quantùm Arithmetica. Nam vnitas omniū
numerorū radix & origo, in se, à se, ac circum seipsam vnica vel impar-
tibilis permanet: ex cuius tamen coaceruatione, omnis cósurgit & ge-
neratur, omnísque tandem in eam resoluitur numerus. Quemadmo-
dum cuncta quæ seu discreta, siue composita inspectentur Vniuerso, à
summo rerum conditore in definitum digesta, redactáve sunt, & demū
2 resoluenda numerum. Quot autem vtilitates cognita, quótve laby-
rinthos ignota præbeat Arithmetica: conspicere facile est. Numerorū
etenim ratione sublata, tollitur & musicarum modulationū intelligen-
tia: geometricorum, cælestiúmve arcanorum subtilis aufertur ingres-
sio: tollitur & vniuersa Philosophia, siue quæ diuina, seu quæ contem-
platur humana: imperfecta relinquitur legū administratio, vtpote, quæ

Dignitas arithmeticç.

Fructus arithmeticç.

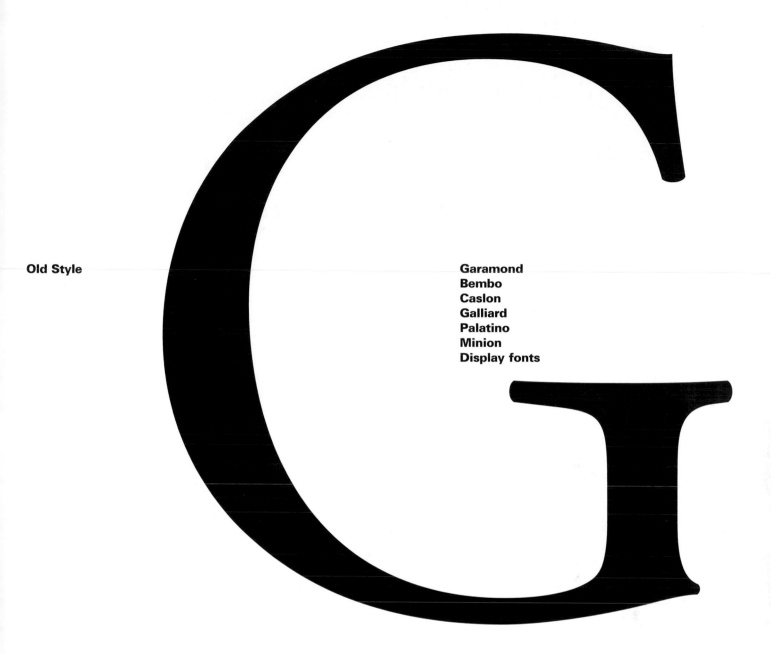

Old Style

1.

Page three of the French Renaissance book *Arithmetica* by Oronce Fine, printed by Simon de Colines in Paris, 1535.

Although Old Style typefaces trace their heritage to the printers of the Italian Renaissance, their heritage extends to an earlier time, for Roman inscriptional letterforms (see Chapter One, Fig. **18**) inspired their capital-letter design. The Caroline Minuscules (see Chapter One, Fig. **27**) from medieval manuscripts inspired writing styles during the fifteenth century, and these became the model for Old Style lowercase letters.

Many Old Style typefaces bear the name of Claude Garamond, a leading typeface designer and punchcutter working in Paris when the book *Arithmetica* (Fig. **1**) was published. In the heading material, the designer has used bold capitals for the author's name, two sizes of capitals for the title, and italics for the subhead. The spatial intervals between these units have been established with great care. Fleurons (printer's flowers), paragraph marks, a woodcut headpiece, and a large initial letter *I* intricately carved on a woodblock bring vibrancy to this elegant example of French Renaissance book design and letterpress printing.

For over five hundreds years, designers have created lively typeface variations inspired by Italian and French Old Style fonts of the fifteenth and sixteenth centuries. The specimens in this section display digitized versions of traditional typefaces with distinctive design attributes.

A digital version designed by
Robert Slimbach for Adobe
Systems and released in 1992.

abcdefghij
klmnopq
rstuvwxyz
$1234567
890(.,'''-;:)!?

140 point

ABCDEF
GHIJKL
MNOPQ
RSTUV
WXYZ&

140 point

abcdefghijklmnopqrstuvwxyz
ABCDEFGHIJKLMNOPQR
STUVWXYZ$1234567890
(.,'"-;:)!?&

26 point

abcdefghijklmn

opqrstuvwxyz

ABCDEFGHIJK

LMNOPQRSTU

VWXYZ$12345

67890(.,'"-;:)!?&

81 point

abcdefghijklmnopqrstuvwxyz
ABCDEFGHIJKLMNOPQRS
TUVWXYZ1234567890
(.,'"-;:)!?&

26 point

abcdefghijklmno
pqrstuvwxyz
ABCDEFGHIJK
LMNOPQRSTU
VWXYZ$12345
67890(.,'"-;:)!?&

81 point

abcdefghijklmnopqrstuvwxyzA
BCDEFGHIJKLMNOPQRS
TUVWXYZ$1234567890
(.,'"-;:)!?&

26 point

abcdefghijklmno
pqrstuvwxyz
ABCDEFGHIJK
LMNOPQRST
UVWXYZ$1234
567890(.,'"-;:)!?&

81 point

Adobe Garamond

abcdefghijklmnopqrstuvwxyz
ABCDEFGHIJKLMNOPQRSTUVWXYZ
$1234567890(.,'"-;:!)?&
abcdefghijklmnopqrstuvwxyz
ABCDEFGHIJKLMNOPQRSTUVWXYZ
8 point $1234567890(.,'"-;:)!?&

abcdefghijklmnopqrstuvwxyz
ABCDEFGHIJKLMNOPQRSTUVWXYZ
$1234567890(.,'"-;:)!?&
abcdefghijklmnopqrstuvwxyz
ABCDEFGHIJKLMNOPQRSTUVWXYZ
9 point $1234567890(.,'"-;:)!?&

abcdefghijklmnopqrstuvwxyz
ABCDEFGHIJKLMNOPQRSTUVWXYZ
$1234567890(.,'"-;:)!?&
abcdefghijklmnopqrstuvwxyz
ABCDEFGHIJKLMNOPQRSTUVWXYZ
10 point $1234567890(.,'"-;:)!?&

abcdefghijklmnopqrstuvwxyz
ABCDEFGHIJKLMNOPQRSTUVWXYZ
$1234567890(.,'"-;:)!?&
abcdefghijklmnopqrstuvwxyz
ABCDEFGHIJKLMNOPQRSTUVWXYZ
12 point $1234567890(.,'"-;:)!?&

The whole duty of typography, *as with calligraphy,* is to communicate to the imagination, without loss by the way, the thought or image intended to be communicated by the author. And the whole duty of beautiful typography is not to substitute for the beauty or interest of the thing thought and intended to be conveyed by the symbol, a beauty or interest of its own, but, on the one hand, to win access for that communication by the clearness and beauty of the vehicle, and on the other hand, to take advantage of every pause or stage in that communication to interpose some characteristic & restful beauty in its own art. We thus have a reason for the clearness and beauty of the first and introductory page and of the title, and for the especial beauty of the headings of chapters, capital or initial letters, and so on, and an opening for the illustrator as we shall see by and by. Further, in the case of poetry, verse, in my opinion, appeals by its form to the eye, as well as to the
8/10

The whole duty of typography, *as with calligraphy,* is to communicate to the imagination, without loss by the way, the thought or image intended to be communicated by the author. And the whole duty of beautiful typography is not to substitute for the beauty or interest of the thing thought and intended to be conveyed by the symbol, a beauty or interest of its own, but, on the one hand, to win access for that communication by the clearness and beauty of the vehicle, and on the other hand, to take advantage of every pause or stage in that communication to interpose some characteristic & restful beauty in its own art. We thus have a reason for the clearness and beauty of the first and introductory page and of the title, and for the especial beauty of the headings of chapters, capital or initial letters, and
8/12

The whole duty of typography, *as with calligraphy,* is to communicate to the imagination, without loss by the way, the thought or image intended to be communicated by the author. And the whole duty of beautiful typography is not to substitute for the beauty or interest of the thing thought and intended to be conveyed by the symbol, a beauty or interest of its own, but, on the one hand, to win access for that communication by the clearness and beauty of the vehicle, and on the other hand, to take advantage of every pause or stage in that communication to interpose some characteristic & restful beauty in its own art. We thus have a reason for the clearness and beauty of the first and introductory page and of the title, and for the especial beauty of the headings of chapters, capital or initial letters,
9/11

The whole duty of typography, *as with calligraphy,* is to communicate to the imagination, without loss by the way, the thought or image intended to be communicated by the author. And the whole duty of beautiful typography is not to substitute for the beauty or interest of the thing thought and intended to be conveyed by the symbol, a beauty or interest of its own, but, on the one hand, to win access for that communication by the clearness and beauty of the vehicle, and on the other hand, to take advantage of every pause or stage in that communication to interpose some characteristic & restful beauty in its own art. We thus have a reason for the
9/13

The whole duty of typography, *as with calligraphy,* is to communicate to the imagination, without loss by the way, the thought or image intended to be communicated by the author. And the whole duty of beautiful typography is not to substitute for the beauty or interest of the thing thought and intended to be conveyed by the symbol, a beauty or interest of its own, but, on the one hand, to win access for that communication by the clearness and beauty of the vehicle, and on the other hand, to take advantage of every pause or stage in that communication to interpose some characteristic & restful beauty in its own art. We thus have a reason
10/12

The whole duty of typography, *as with calligraphy,* is to communicate to the imagination, without loss by the way, the thought or image intended to be communicated by the author. And the whole duty of beautiful typography is not to substitute for the beauty or interest of the thing thought and intended to be conveyed by the symbol, a beauty or interest of its own, but, on the one hand, to win access for that communication by the clearness and beauty of the vehicle, and on the other hand, to take advantage of every pause or stage in that communication to interpose some
10/14

The whole duty of typography, *as with calligraphy,* is to communicate to the imagination, without loss by the way, the thought or image intended to be communicated by the author. And the whole duty of beautiful typography is not to substitute for the beauty or interest of the thing thought and intended to be conveyed by the symbol, a beauty or interest of its own, but, on the one hand, to win access for that communication by the
12/14

The whole duty of typography, *as with calligraphy,* is to communicate to the imagination, without loss by the way, the thought or image intended to be communicated by the author. And the whole duty of beautiful typography is not to substitute for the beauty or interest of the thing thought and intended to be conveyed by the symbol, a beauty or interest of its own,
12/16

Bembo Regular

Bembo was released in 1929
by the Lanston Monotype
Corporation, based on 1495
fonts by Francesco Griffo.

abcdefghij

klmnopqr

stuvwxyz

$1234567

890(,'"–,:)!?

140 point

ABCDEF GHIJKL MNOPQ RSTUV WXYZ&

140 point

Bembo Regular

abcdefghijklmnopqrstuvwxyz
ABCDFGHIJKLMNOPQRS
TUVWXYZ$1234567890
(.,'''-;:)!?&

26 point

abcdefghijklmn

opqrstuvwxyz

ABCDEFGHIJK

LMNOPQRST

UVWXYZ$123

4567890(.,'''-;:)!?&

81 point

abcdefghijklmnopqrstuvwxyz
ABCDFGHIJKLMNOPQRS
TUVWXYZ1234567890
(.,'"-;:!)?&

26 point

abcdefghijklmno

pqrstuvwxyz

ABCDEFGHIJK

LMNOPQRST

UVWXYZ$1234

567890(.,'"-;:)!?&

81 point

abcdefghijklmnopqrstuv
wxyzABCDFGHIJKLMN
OPQRSTUVWXYZ
$1234567890(.,’”-;:)!?&
26 point

abcdefghijklmn
opqrstuvwxyz
ABCDEFGHIJK
LMNOPQRST
UVWXYZ$1234
567890(.,’”-;:)!?&

77 point

Bembo Regular

abcdefghijklmnopqrstuvwxyz
ABCDEFGHIJKLMNOPQRSTUVWXYZ
$1234567890(.,'"-;:!)?&
abcdefghijklmnopqrstuvwxyz
ABCDEFGHIJKLMNOPQRSTUVWXYZ
8 point *$1234567890(.,'"-;:)!?&*

abcdefghijklmnopqrstuvwxyz
ABCDEFGHIJKLMNOPQRSTUVWXYZ
$1234567890(.,'"-;:)!?&
abcdefghijklmnopqrstuvwxyz
ABCDEFGHIJKLMNOPQRSTUVWXYZ
9 point *$1234567890(.,'"-;:)!?&*

abcdefghijklmnopqrstuvwxyz
ABCDEFGHIJKLMNOPQRSTUVWXYZ
$1234567890(.,'"-;:)!?&
abcdefghijklmnopqrstuvwxyz
ABCDEFGHIJKLMNOPQRSTUVWXYZ
10 point *$1234567890(.,'"-;:)!?&*

abcdefghijklmnopqrstuvwxyz
ABCDEFGHIJKLMNOPQRSTUVWXYZ
$1234567890(.,'"-;:)!?&
abcdefghijklmnopqrstuvwxyz
ABCDEFGHIJKLMNOPQRSTUVWXYZ
12 point *$1234567890(.,'"-;:)!?&*

The whole duty of typography, *as with calligraphy,* is to communicate to the imagination, without loss by the way, the thought or image intended to be communicated by the author. And the whole duty of beautiful typography is not to substitute for the beauty or interest of the thing thought and intended to be conveyed by the symbol, a beauty or interest of its own, but, on the one hand, to win access for that communication by the clearness and beauty of the vehicle, and on the other hand, to take advantage of every pause or stage in that communication to interpose some characteristic & restful beauty in its own art. We thus have a reason for the clearness and beauty of the first and introductory page and of the title, and for the especial beauty of the headings of chapters, capital or initial letters, and so on, and an opening for the illustrator as we shall see by and by. Further, in the case of poetry, verse, in my opinion, appeals by its form to the eye, as well as to the ear,

8/10

The whole duty of typography, *as with calligraphy,* is to communicate to the imagination, without loss by the way, the thought or image intended to be communicated by the author. And the whole duty of beautiful typography is not to substitute for the beauty or interest of the thing thought and intended to be conveyed by the symbol, a beauty or interest of its own, but, on the one hand, to win access for that communication by the clearness and beauty of the vehicle, and on the other hand, to take advantage of every pause or stage in that communication to interpose some characteristic & restful beauty in its own art. We thus have a reason for the clearness and beauty of the first and introductory page and of the title, and for the especial beauty of the

9/11

The whole duty of typography, *as with calligraphy,* is to communicate to the imagination, without loss by the way, the thought or image intended to be communicated by the author. And the whole duty of beautiful typography is not to substitute for the beauty or interest of the thing thought and intended to be conveyed by the symbol, a beauty or interest of its own, but, on the one hand, to win access for that communication by the clearness and beauty of the vehicle, and on the other hand, to take advantage of every pause or stage in that communication to interpose some characteristic & restful beauty in its own art. We thus have a reason

10/12

The whole duty of typography, *as with calligraphy,* is to communicate to the imagination, without loss by the way, the thought or image intended to be communicated by the author. And the whole duty of beautiful typography is not to substitute for the beauty or interest of the thing thought and intended to be conveyed by the symbol, a beauty or interest of its own, but, on the one hand, to win access for that communication by the

12/14

The whole duty of typography, *as with calligraphy,* is to communicate to the imagination, without loss by the way, the thought or image intended to be communicated by the author. And the whole duty of beautiful typography is not to substitute for the beauty or interest of the thing thought and intended to be conveyed by the symbol, a beauty or interest of its own, but, on the one hand, to win access for that communication by the clearness and beauty of the vehicle, and on the other hand, to take advantage of every pause or stage in that communication to interpose some characteristic & restful beauty in its own art. We thus have a reason for the clearness and beauty of the first and introductory page and of the title, and for the especial beauty of the headings of chapters, capital or initial

8/12

The whole duty of typography, *as with calligraphy,* is to communicate to the imagination, without loss by the way, the thought or image intended to be communicated by the author. And the whole duty of beautiful typography is not to substitute for the beauty or interest of the thing thought and intended to be conveyed by the symbol, a beauty or interest of its own, but, on the one hand, to win access for that communication by the clearness and beauty of the vehicle, and on the other hand, to take advantage of every pause or stage in that communication to interpose some characteristic & restful beauty in its own art. We thus have a reason

9/13

The whole duty of typography, *as with calligraphy,* is to communicate to the imagination, without loss by the way, the thought or image intended to be communicated by the author. And the whole duty of beautiful typography is not to substitute for the beauty or interest of the thing thought and intended to be conveyed by the symbol, a beauty or interest of its own, but, on the one hand, to win access for that communication by the clearness and beauty of the vehicle, and on the other hand, to take advantage of every pause or stage in that communication to interpose

10 /14

The whole duty of typography, *as with calligraphy,* is to communicate to the imagination, without loss by the way, the thought or image intended to be communicated by the author. And the whole duty of beautiful typography is not to substitute for the beauty or interest of the thing thought and intended to be conveyed by the symbol, a beauty or interest of its own, but, on

12 /16

The earliest Caslon Old Style fonts were designed by William Caslon in 1725. The digital display specimens shown here are in Big Caslon CC, designed by Matthew Carter.

abcdefghij

klmnopqr

stuvwxyz

1234567

90(,"''-;:)!?&

120 point

ABCDE
FGHIJK
LMNOP
QRSTU
VWXYZ

120 point

This version of Caslon with
short descenders was
originally designed by
American Type Founders
for display headlines.

abcdefghijklmnopqrstuvwxyz
ABCDFGHIJKLMNOPQ
RSTUVWXYZ$1234567890
(.,'''-;:)!?&

26 point

abcdefghijklmn

opqrstuvwxyz

ABCDEFGHIJK

LMNOPQRST

UVWXYZ$1234

567890(.,'''-;:)!?&

76 point

190

abcdefghijklmnopqrstuvwxyz
ABCDFGHIJKLMNOPQRS
TUVWXYZ1234567890
(.,'''-;:)!?&

26 point

abcdefghijklmno

pqrstuvwxyz

ABCDEFGHIJK

LMNOPQRSTU

VWXYZ$123456

7890(.,'''-;:)!?&

76 point

Big Caslon CC

Inspired by William Caslon's large display types, Big Caslon CC is recommended for display settings only.

abcdefghijklmnopqrstuv
wxyzABCDFGHIJKLMN
OPQRSTUVWXYZ
$1234567890(.,'"-;:)!?&

abcdefghijklmno

pqrstuvwxyz

ABCDEFGHIJ

KLMNOPQRS

TUVWXYZ$123

4567890(.,'"-;:)!?&

Adobe Caslon Regular

A digital version designed by Carol Twombly and recommended for text in sizes ranging from 6- to 14-point.

8 point

abcdefghijklmnopqrstuvwxyz
ABCDEFGHIJKLMNOPQRSTUVWXYZ
$1234567890(.,'"-;:!)?&
abcdefghijklmnopqrstuvwxyz
ABCDEFGHIJKLMNOPQRSTUVWXYZ
$1234567890(.,'"-;:)!?&

9 point

abcdefghijklmnopqrstuvwxyz
ABCDEFGHIJKLMNOPQRSTUVWXYZ
$1234567890(.,'"-;:)!?&
abcdefghijklmnopqrstuvwxyz
ABCDEFGHIJKLMNOPQRSTUVWXYZ
$1234567890(.,'"-;:)!?&

10 point

abcdefghijklmnopqrstuvwxyz
ABCDEFGHIJKLMNOPQRSTUVWXYZ
$1234567890(.,'"-;:)!?&
abcdefghijklmnopqrstuvwxyz
ABCDEFGHIJKLMNOPQRSTUVWXYZ
$1234567890(.,'"-;:)!?&

12 point

abcdefghijklmnopqrstuvwxyz
ABCDEFGHIJKLMNOPQRSTUVWXYZ
$1234567890(.,'"-;:)!?&
abcdefghijklmnopqrstuvwxyz
ABCDEFGHIJKLMNOPQRSTUVWXYZ
$1234567890(.,'"-;:)!?&

The whole duty of typography, *as with calligraphy,* is to communicate to the imagination, without loss by the way, the thought or image intended to be communicated by the author. And the whole duty of beautiful typography is not to substitute for the beauty or interest of the thing thought and intended to be conveyed by the symbol, a beauty or interest of its own, but, on the one hand, to win access for that communication by the clearness and beauty of the vehicle, and on the other hand, to take advantage of every pause or stage in that communication to interpose some characteristic & restful beauty in its own art. We thus have a reason for the clearness and beauty of the first and introductory page and of the title, and for the especial beauty of the headings of chapters, capital or initial letters, and so on, and an opening for the illustrator as we shall see by and by. Further, in the case of poetry, verse, in my opinion, appeals by its

8/10

The whole duty of typography, *as with calligraphy,* is to communicate to the imagination, without loss by the way, the thought or image intended to be communicated by the author. And the whole duty of beautiful typography is not to substitute for the beauty or interest of the thing thought and intended to be conveyed by the symbol, a beauty or interest of its own, but, on the one hand, to win access for that communication by the clearness and beauty of the vehicle, and on the other hand, to take advantage of every pause or stage in that communication to interpose some characteristic & restful beauty in its own art. We thus have a reason for the clearness and beauty of the first and introductory page and of the title, and for the especial beauty of the headings of chapters, capital or

8/12

The whole duty of typography, *as with calligraphy,* is to communicate to the imagination, without loss by the way, the thought or image intended to be communicated by the author. And the whole duty of beautiful typography is not to substitute for the beauty or interest of the thing thought and intended to be conveyed by the symbol, a beauty or interest of its own, but, on the one hand, to win access for that communication by the clearness and beauty of the vehicle, and on the other hand, to take advantage of every pause or stage in that communication to interpose some characteristic & restful beauty in its own art. We thus have a reason for the clearness and beauty of the first and introductory page and of the title, and for the especial beauty of the

9/11

The whole duty of typography, *as with calligraphy,* is to communicate to the imagination, without loss by the way, the thought or image intended to be communicated by the author. And the whole duty of beautiful typography is not to substitute for the beauty or interest of the thing thought and intended to be conveyed by the symbol, a beauty or interest of its own, but, on the one hand, to win access for that communication by the clearness and beauty of the vehicle, and on the other hand, to take advantage of every pause or stage in that communication to interpose some characteristic & restful beauty in its

9/13

The whole duty of typography, *as with calligraphy,* is to communicate to the imagination, without loss by the way, the thought or image intended to be communicated by the author. And the whole duty of beautiful typography is not to substitute for the beauty or interest of the thing thought and intended to be conveyed by the symbol, a beauty or interest of its own, but, on the one hand, to win access for that communication by the clearness and beauty of the vehicle, and on the other hand, to take advantage of every pause or stage in that communication to interpose some characteristic & restful beauty in its own art. We

10/12

The whole duty of typography, *as with calligraphy,* is to communicate to the imagination, without loss by the way, the thought or image intended to be communicated by the author. And the whole duty of beautiful typography is not to substitute for the beauty or interest of the thing thought and intended to be conveyed by the symbol, a beauty or interest of its own, but, on the one hand, to win access for that communication by the clearness and beauty of the vehicle, and on the other hand, to take advantage of every pause or stage in that communication to

10/14

The whole duty of typography, *as with calligraphy,* is to communicate to the imagination, without loss by the way, the thought or image intended to be communicated by the author. And the whole duty of beautiful typography is not to substitute for the beauty or interest of the thing thought and intended to be conveyed by the symbol, a beauty or interest of its own, but, on the one hand, to win access for that communication by

12/14

The whole duty of typography, *as with calligraphy,* is to communicate to the imagination, without loss by the way, the thought or image intended to be communicated by the author. And the whole duty of beautiful typography is not to substitute for the beauty or interest of the thing thought and intended to be conveyed by the symbol, a beauty or interest of its own, but, on

12/16

Galliard Regular

Galliard, designed by Matthew Carter based on sixteenth-century fonts by Robert Grandjon, was first released in 1982.

abcdefghij

klmnopqr

stuvwxyz

$1234567

890(,'"",-;:)!?

ABCDEF
GHIJKL
MNOPQ
RSTUV
WXYZ&

Galliard Regular

abcdefghijklmnopqrstuvwxyz
ABCDFGHIJKLMNOPQRS
TUVWXYZ$1234567890
(.,'"-;:)!?&

25 point

abcdefghijklmn

opqrstuvwxyz

ABCDEFGHIJK

LMNOPQRSTU

VWXYZ$123456

7890(.,'"-;:)!?&

73 point

196

abcdefghijklmnopqrstuvwxyz
ABCDFGHIJKLMNOPQRS
TUVWXYZ1234567890
(.,'''-;:!)?&

25 point

abcdefghijklmno
pqrstuvwxyz
ABCDEFGHIJK
LMNOPQRSTU
VWXYZ$123456
7890(.,'''-;:-)!?&

73 point

Galliard Bold

abcdefghijklmnopqrstuv
wxyzABCDFGHIJKLMN
OPQRSTUVWXYZ
$1234567890(.,'''-;:)!?&

25 point

abcdefghijklmno
pqrstuvwxyzAB
CDEFGHIJKL
MNOPQRSTU
VWXYZ$12345
67890(.,'''-;:)!?&

73 point

Galliard Regular

abcdefghijklmnopqrstuvwxyz
ABCDEFGHIJKLMNOPQRSTUVWXYZ
$1234567890(.,'"-;:!)?&
abcdefghijklmnopqrstuvwxyz
ABCDEFGHIJKLMNOPQRSTUVWXYZ
8 point *$1234567890(.,'"-;:)!?&*

abcdefghijklmnopqrstuvwxyz
ABCDEFGHIJKLMNOPQRSTUVWXYZ
$1234567890(.,'"-;:)!?&
abcdefghijklmnopqrstuvwxyz
ABCDEFGHIJKLMNOPQRSTUVWXYZ
9 point *$1234567890(.,'"-;:)!?&*

abcdefghijklmnopqrstuvwxyz
ABCDEFGHIJKLMNOPQRSTUVWXYZ
$1234567890(.,'"-;:)!?&
abcdefghijklmnopqrstuvwxyz
ABCDEFGHIJKLMNOPQRSTUVWXYZ
10 point *$1234567890(.,'"-;:)!?&*

abcdefghijklmnopqrstuvwxyz
ABCDEFGHIJKLMNOPQRSTUVW
XYZ$1234567890(.,'"-;:)!?&
abcdefghijklmnopqrstuvwxyz
ABCDEFGHIJKLMNOPQRSTUVW
12 point *XYZ$1234567890(.,'"-;:)!?&*

The whole duty of typography, *as with calligraphy,* is to communicate to the imagination, without loss by the way, the thought or image intended to be communicated by the author. And the whole duty of beautiful typography is not to substitute for the beauty or interest of the thing thought and intended to be conveyed by the symbol, a beauty or interest of its own, but, on the one hand, to win access for that communication by the clearness and beauty of the vehicle, and on the other hand, to take advantage of every pause or stage in that communication to interpose some characteristic & restful beauty in its own art. We thus have a reason for the clearness and beauty of the first and introductory page and of the title, and for the especial beauty of the headings of chapters, capital or initial letters, and so on, and an opening for the illustrator as we shall see by and by.
8/10

The whole duty of typography, *as with calligraphy,* is to communicate to the imagination, without loss by the way, the thought or image intended to be communicated by the author. And the whole duty of beautiful typography is not to substitute for the beauty or interest of the thing thought and intended to be conveyed by the symbol, a beauty or interest of its own, but, on the one hand, to win access for that communication by the clearness and beauty of the vehicle, and on the other hand, to take advantage of every pause or stage in that communication to interpose some characteristic & restful beauty in its own art. We thus have a reason for the clearness and beauty of the first and introductory page and of the title, and
8/12

The whole duty of typography, *as with calligraphy,* is to commnicate to the imagination, without loss by the way, the thought or image intended to be communicated by the author. And the whole duty of beautiful typography is not to substitute for the beauty or interest of the thing thought and intended to be conveyed by the symbol, a beauty or interest of its own, but, on the one hand, to win access for that communication by the clearness and beauty of the vehicle, and on the other hand, to take advantage of every pause or stage in that communication to interpose some characteristic & restful beauty in its own art. We thus have a reason for the clearness and beauty of the first and introductory page and
9/11

The whole duty of typography, *as with calligraphy,* is to communicate to the imagination, without loss by the way, the thought or image intended to be communicated by the author. And the whole duty of beautiful typography is not to substitute for the beauty or interest of the thing thought and intended to be conveyed by the symbol, a beauty or interest of its own, but, on the one hand, to win access for that communication by the clearness and beauty of the vehicle, and on the other hand, to take advantage of every pause or stage in that communication to interpose some characteristic &
9/13

The whole duty of typography, *as with calligraphy,* is to communicate to the imagination, without loss by the way, the thought or image intended to be communicated by the author. And the whole duty of beautiful typography is not to substitute for the beauty or interest of the thing thought and intended to be conveyed by the symbol, a beauty or interest of its own, but, on the one hand, to win access for that communication by the clearness and beauty of the vehicle, and on the other hand, to take advantage of every pause or stage in that communication to interpose some characteristic
10/12

The whole duty of typography, *as with calligraphy,* is to communicate to the imagination, without loss by the way, the thought or image intended to be communicated by the author. And the whole duty of beautiful typography is not to substitute for the beauty or interest of the thing thought and intended to be conveyed by the symbol, a beauty or interest of its own, but, on the one hand, to win access for that communication by the clearness and beauty of the vehicle, and on the other hand, to take advantage of every pause or
10/14

The whole duty of typography, *as with calligraphy,* is to communicate to the imagination, without loss by the way, the thought or image intended to be communicated by the author. And the whole duty of beautiful typography is not to substitute for the beauty or interest of the thing thought and intended to be conveyed by the symbol, a beauty or interest of its own, but, on the
12/14

The whole duty of typography, *as with calligraphy,* is to communicate to the imagination, without loss by the way, the thought or image intended to be communicated by the author. And the whole duty of beautiful typography is not to substitute for the beauty or interest of the thing thought and intended to be conveyed by the
12/16

Palatino was designed
by Hermann Zapf and first
released by the Stempel
foundry in 1950.

abcdefghij

klmnopqr

stuvwxyz

$12345678

90(.,'""-;:)!?

120 point

ABCDEF
GHIJKL
MNOPQ
RSTUV
WXYZ&

abcdefghijklmnopqrstuvwxyz
ABCDFGHIJKLMNOPQRST
UVWXYZ$1234567890
(.,'"-;:)!?&

abcdefghijklmn

opqrstuvwxyz

ABCDEFGHIJKL

MNOPQRSTU

VWXYZ$123456

7890(.,'"-;:)!?&

abcdefghijklmnopqrstuvwxyz
ABCDFGHIJKLMNOPQRST
UVWXYZ$1234567890
(.,'"-;:!)?&

24 point

abcdefghijklmno
pqrstuvwxyz
ABCDEFGHIJKL
MNOPQRSTU
VWXYZ$123456
7890(.,'"-;:!)?&

abcdefghijklmnopqrstuvwxyz
ABCDFGHIJKLMNOPQ
RSTUVWXYZ$1234567890
(.,'"-;:)!?&

23 point

abcdefghijklmn

opqrstuvwxyz

ABCDEFGHIJK

LMNOPQRSTU

VWXYZ$123456

7890(.,'"-;:)!?&

72 point

Palatino Regular

The whole duty of typography, *as with calligraphy,* is to communicate to the imagination, without loss by the way, the thought or image intended to be communicated by the author. And the whole duty of beautiful typography is not to substitute for the beauty or interest of the thing thought and intended to be conveyed by the symbol, a beauty or interest of its own, but, on the one hand, to win access for that communication by the clearness and beauty of the vehicle, and on the other hand, to take advantage of every pause or stage in that communication to interpose some characteristic & restful beauty in its own art. We thus have a reason for the clearness and beauty of the first and introductory page and of the title, and for the especial beauty of the headings of chapters, capital or initial letters, and so on, and an opening for the illustrator as we shall see

8/10

The whole duty of typography, *as with calligraphy,* is to communicate to the imagination, without loss by the way, the thought or image intended to be communicated by the author. And the whole duty of beautiful typography is not to substitute for the beauty or interest of the thing thought and intended to be conveyed by the symbol, a beauty or interest of its own, but, on the one hand, to win access for that communication by the clearness and beauty of the vehicle, and on the other hand, to take advantage of every pause or stage in that communication to interpose some characteristic & restful beauty in its own art. We thus have a reason for the clearness and beauty of the first and introductory page and of the

8/12

The whole duty of typography, *as with calligraphy,* is to communicate to the imagination, without loss by the way, the thought or image intended to be communicated by the author. And the whole duty of beautiful typography is not to substitute for the beauty or interest of the thing thought and intended to be conveyed by the symbol, a beauty or interest of its own, but, on the one hand, to win access for that communication by the clearness and beauty of the vehicle, and on the other hand, to take advantage of every pause or stage in that communication to interpose some characteristic & restful beauty in its own art. We thus have a reason for the clearness and beauty of the first and

9/11

The whole duty of typography, *as with calligraphy,* is to communicate to the imagination, without loss by the way, the thought or image intended to be communicated by the author. And the whole duty of beautiful typography is not to substitute for the beauty or interest of the thing thought and intended to be conveyed by the symbol, a beauty or interest of its own, but, on the one hand, to win access for that communication by the clearness and beauty of the vehicle, and on the other hand, to take advantage of every pause or stage in that communication to interpose

9/13

The whole duty of typography, *as with calligraphy,* is to communicate to the imagination, without loss by the way, the thought or image intended to be communicated by the author. And the whole duty of beautiful typography is not to substitute for the beauty or interest of the thing thought and intended to be conveyed by the symbol, a beauty or interest of its own, but, on the one hand, to win access for that communication by the clearness and beauty of the vehicle, and on the other hand, to take advantage of every pause or stage in that communication to interpose some

10/12

The whole duty of typography, *as with calligraphy,* is to communicate to the imagination, without loss by the way, the thought or image intended to be communicated by the author. And the whole duty of beautiful typography is not to substitute for the beauty or interest of the thing thought and intended to be conveyed by the symbol, a beauty or interest of its own, but, on the one hand, to win access for that communication by the clearness and beauty of the vehicle, and on the other hand, to take advantage of every

10/14

The whole duty of typography, *as with calligraphy,* is to communicate to the imagination, without loss by the way, the thought or image intended to be communicated by the author. And the whole duty of beautiful typography is not to substitute for the beauty or interest of the thing thought and intended to be conveyed by the symbol, a beauty or interest of its own, but, on

12/14

The whole duty of typography, *as with calligraphy,* is to communicate to the imagination, without loss by the way, the thought or image intended to be communicated by the author. And the whole duty of beautiful typography is not to substitute for the beauty or interest of the thing thought and intended to be conveyed by the symbol, a

12/16

**Adobe Minion
Display Regular**

The Minion type family was
designed by Robert Slimbach
for Adobe Systems in 1990.

abcdefghij

klmnopqr

stuvwxyz

$12345678

90(.,'"-;:)!?

ABCDEF
GHIJKL
MNOPQ
RSTUV
WXYZ&

120 point

abcdefghijklmnopqrstuvwxyz
ABCDFGHIJKLMNOPQRSTU
VWXYZ$1234567890
(.,'''-;:)!?&

25 point

abcdefghijklmn

opqrstuvwxyz

ABCDEFGHIJKL

MNOPQRSTU

VWXYZ$12345

67890(.,'''-;:)!?&

75 point

abcdefghijklmnopqrstuvwxyz
ABCDFGHIJKLMNOPQRSTU
VWXYZ$1234567890
(.,'"-;:)!?&

25 point

abcdefghijklmno

pqrstuvwxyz

ABCDEFGHIJKL

MNOPQRSTU

VWXYZ$1234567

890(.,'"-;:)!?&

75 point

abcdefghijklmnopqrstuvwxyz
ABCDFGHIJKLMNOPQ
RSTUVWXYZ$1234567890
(.,'"-;:)!?&

25 point

abcdefghijklmn

opqrstuvwxyz

ABCDEFGHIJKL

MNOPQRSTU

VWXYZ$12345

67890(.,'"-;:)!?&

74 point

Adobe Minion Regular

abcdefghijklmnopqrstuvwxyz
ABCDEFGHIJKLMNOPQRSTUVWXYZ
$1234567890(.,'"-;:!)?&
abcdefghijklmnopqrstuvwxyz
ABCDEFGHIJKLMNOPQRSTUVWXYZ
8 point *$1234567890(.,'"-;:)!?&*

abcdefghijklmnopqrstuvwxyz
ABCDEFGHIJKLMNOPQRSTUVWXYZ
$1234567890(.,'"-;:)!?&
abcdefghijklmnopqrstuvwxyz
ABCDEFGHIJKLMNOPQRSTUVWXYZ
9 point *$1234567890(.,'"-;:)!?&*

abcdefghijklmnopqrstuvwxyz
ABCDEFGHIJKLMNOPQRSTUVWXYZ
$1234567890(.,'"-;:)!?&
abcdefghijklmnopqrstuvwxyz
ABCDEFGHIJKLMNOPQRSTUVWXYZ
10 point *$1234567890(.,'"-;:)!?&*

abcdefghijklmnopqrstuvwxyz
ABCDEFGHIJKLMNOPQRSTUVWXYZ
$1234567890(.,'"-;:)!?&
abcdefghijklmnopqrstuvwxyz
ABCDEFGHIJKLMNOPQRSTUVWXYZ
12 point *$1234567890(.,'"-;:)!?&ß*

The whole duty of typography, *as with calligraphy,* is to communicate to the imagination, without loss by the way, the thought or image intended to be com municated by the author. And the whole duty of beautiful typography is not to substitute for the beauty or interest of the thing thought and intended to be conveyed by the symbol, a beauty or interest of its own, but, on the one hand, to win access for that communication by the clearness and beauty of the vehicle, and on the other hand, to take advantage of every pause or stage in that communication to interpose some characteristic & restful beauty in its own art. We thus have a reason for the clearness and beauty of the first and introductory page and of the title, and for the especial beauty of the headings of chapters, capital or initial letters, and so on, and an opening for the illustrator as we shall see by and by. Further, in the case of poetry, verse, in my opinion, appeals by its
8/10

The whole duty of typography, *as with calligraphy,* is to communicate to the imagination, without loss by the way, the thought or image intended to be communicated by the author. And the whole duty of beautiful typography is not to substitute for the beauty or interest of the thing thought and intended to be conveyed by the symbol, a beauty or interest of its own, but, on the one hand, to win access for that communication by the clearness and beauty of the vehicle, and on the other hand, to take advantage of every pause or stage in that communication to interpose some characteristic & restful beauty in its own art. We thus have a reason for the clearness and beauty of the first and introductory page and of the title, and for the especial beauty of the
9/11

The whole duty of typography, *as with calligraphy,* is to commu nicate to the imagination, without loss by the way, the thought or image intended to be communicated by the author. And the whole duty of beautiful typography is not to substitute for the beauty or interest of the thing thought and intended to be con veyed by the symbol, a beauty or interest of its own, but, on the one hand, to win access for that communication by the clearness and beauty of the vehicle, and on the other hand, to take advan tage of every pause or stage in that communication to interpose some characteristic & restful beauty in its own art. We thus have
10/12

The whole duty of typography, *as with calligraphy,* is to communicate to the imagination, without loss by the way, the thought or image intended to be commu nicated by the author. And the whole duty of beautiful typography is not to substitute for the beauty or inter est of the thing thought and intended to be conveyed by the symbol, a beauty or interest of its own, but, on the one hand, to win access for that communication
12/14

The whole duty of typography, *as with calligraphy,* is to communicate to the imagination, without loss by the way, the thought or image intended to be com municated by the author. And the whole duty of beautiful typography is not to substitute for the beauty or interest of the thing thought and intended to be conveyed by the symbol, a beauty or interest of its own, but, on the one hand, to win access for that communication by the clearness and beauty of the vehicle, and on the other hand, to take advantage of every pause or stage in that commu nication to interpose some characteristic & restful beauty in its own art. We thus have a reason for the clearness and beauty of the first and introductory page and of the title, and for the especial beauty of the headings of chapters, capital or
8/12

The whole duty of typography, *as with calligraphy,* is to communicate to the imagination, without loss by the way, the thought or image intended to be communicated by the author. And the whole duty of beautiful typography is not to substitute for the beauty or interest of the thing thought and intended to be conveyed by the symbol, a beauty or interest of its own, but, on the one hand, to win access for that communication by the clearness and beauty of the vehicle, and on the other hand, to take advantage of every pause or stage in that communication to interpose some characteristic & restful beauty in its own art. We thus have a reason
9/13

The whole duty of typography, *as with calligraphy,* is to commu nicate to the imagination, without loss by the way, the thought or image intended to be communicated by the author. And the whole duty of beautiful typography is not to substitute for the beauty or interest of the thing thought and intended to be con veyed by the symbol, a beauty or interest of its own, but, on the one hand, to win access for that communication by the clearness and beauty of the vehicle, and on the other hand, to take advan tage of every pause or stage in that communication to interpose
10/14

The whole duty of typography, *as with calligraphy,* is to communicate to the imagination, without loss by the way, the thought or image intended to be commu nicated by the author. And the whole duty of beautiful typography is not to substitute for the beauty or inter est of the thing thought and intended to be conveyed by the symbol, a beauty or interest of its own, but, on
12/16

Centaur

abcdefghijklmnopqrstuvwxyz
ABCDEFGHIJKLMNOPQRSTUVW
XYZ$1234567890(.,'"-;:)!?&

ITC Garamond Book

abcdefghijklmnopqrstuvwxyz
ABCDEFGHIJKLMNOPQRSTUVW
XYZ$1234567890(.,'"-;:)!?&

ITC Garamond Book Italic

abcdefghijklmnopqrstuvwxyz
ABCDEFGHIJKLMNOPQRSTUVW
XYZ$1234567890(.,'"-;:)!?&

ITC Garamond Bold Condensed

abcdefghijklmnopqrstuvwxyz
ABCDEFGHIJKLMNOPQRSTUVW
XYZ$1234567890(.,'"-;:)!?&

ITC Garamond Bold Condensed Italic

abcdefghijklmnopqrstuvwxyz
ABCDEFGHIJKLMNOPQRSTUVW
XYZ$1234567890(.,'"-;:)!?&

abcdefghijklmnopqrstuvwxyz
ABCDEFGHIJKLMNOPQRSTUVW
XYZ$1234567890(.,'"-;:)!?&

abcdefghijklmnopqrstuvwxyz
ABCDEFGHIJKLMNOPQRSTUVW
XYZ$1234567890(.,'"-;:)!?&

abcdefghijklmnopqrstuvwxyz
ABCDEFGHIJKLMNOPQRSTUV
WXYZ$1234567890(.,'"-;:)!?&

abcdefghijklmnopqrstuvwxyz
ABCDEFGHIJKLMNOPQRSTUV
WXYZ$1234567890(.,'"-;:)!?&

abcdefghijklmnopqrstuvwxyz
ABCDEFGHIJKLMNOPQRSTVW
XYZ$1234567890(.,'"-;:)!?&

Im VERLAG DES BILDUNGSVERBANDES der Deutschen Buchdrucker,
Berlin SW 61, Dreibundstr. 5, erscheint demnächst:

JAN TSCHICHOLD
Lehrer an der Meisterschule für Deutschlands Buchdrucker in München

DIE NEUE TYPOGRAPHIE

**Handbuch für die gesamte Fachwelt
und die drucksachenverbrauchenden Kreise**

Das Problem der neuen gestaltenden Typographie hat eine lebhafte
Diskussion bei allen Beteiligten hervorgerufen. Wir glauben dem Bedürf-
nis, die aufgeworfenen Fragen ausführlich behandelt zu sehen, zu ent-
sprechen, wenn wir jetzt ein Handbuch der **NEUEN TYPOGRAPHIE**
herausbringen.

Es kam dem Verfasser, einem ihrer bekanntesten Vertreter, in diesem
Buche zunächst darauf an, den engen Zusammenhang der neuen
Typographie mit dem **Gesamtkomplex heutigen Lebens** aufzuzei-
gen und zu beweisen, daß die neue Typographie ein ebenso notwendi-
ger Ausdruck einer neuen Gesinnung ist wie die neue Baukunst und
alles Neue, das mit unserer Zeit anbricht. Diese geschichtliche Notwen-
digkeit der neuen Typographie belegt weiterhin eine kritische Dar-
stellung der **alten Typographie**. Die Entwicklung der **neuen Male-
rei**, die für alles Neue unserer Zeit geistig bahnbrechend gewesen ist,
wird in einem reich illustrierten Aufsatz des Buches leicht faßlich dar-
gestellt. Ein kurzer Abschnitt „**Zur Geschichte der neuen Typographie**" leitet zu dem wichtigsten Teile des Buches, den **Grundbegriffen
der neuen Typographie** über. Diese werden klar herausgeschält,
richtige und falsche Beispiele einander gegenübergestellt. Zwei wei-
tere Artikel behandeln „**Photographie und Typographie**" und
„**Neue Typographie und Normung**".

Der Hauptwert des Buches für den Praktiker besteht in dem zweiten
Teil „**Typographische Hauptformen**" (siehe das nebenstehende
Inhaltsverzeichnis). Es fehlte bisher an einem Werke, das wie dieses Buch
die schon bei einfachen Satzaufgaben auftauchenden gestalterischen
Fragen in gebührender Ausführlichkeit behandelte. Jeder Teilabschnitt
enthält neben **allgemeinen typographischen Regeln** vor allem die
Abbildungen aller in Betracht kommenden **Normblätter** des Deutschen
Normenausschusses, alle andern (z. B. postalischen) **Vorschriften** und
zahlreiche Beispiele, Gegenbeispiele und Schemen.

Für jeden Buchdrucker, insbesondere jeden Akzidenzsetzer, wird „Die
neue Typographie" ein **unentbehrliches Handbuch** sein. Von nicht
geringerer Bedeutung ist es für Reklamefachleute, Gebrauchsgraphiker,
Kaufleute, Photographen, Architekten, Ingenieure und Schriftsteller,
also für alle, die mit dem Buchdruck in Berührung kommen.

INHALT DES BUCHES

Werden und Wesen der neuen Typographie
Das neue Weltbild
Die alte Typographie (Rückblick und Kritik)
Die neue Kunst
Zur Geschichte der neuen Typographie
Die Grundbegriffe der neuen Typographie
Photographie und Typographie
Neue Typographie und Normung

Typographische Hauptformen

Das Typosignet
Der Geschäftsbrief
Der Halbbrief
Briefhüllen ohne Fenster
Fensterbriefhüllen
Die Postkarte
Die Postkarte mit Klappe
Die Geschäftskarte
Die Besuchskarte
Werbsachen (Karten, Blätter, Prospekte, Kataloge)
Das Typoplakat
Das Bildplakat
Schildformate, Tafeln und Rahmen
Inserate
Die Zeitschrift
Die Tageszeitung
Die illustrierte Zeitung
Tabellensatz
Das neue Buch

Bibliographie
Verzeichnis der Abbildungen
Register

typ. tschichold

**Das Buch enthält über 125 Abbildungen, von
denen etwa ein Viertel zweifarbig gedruckt ist,
und umfaßt gegen 200 Seiten auf gutem Kunst-
druckpapier. Es erscheint im Format DIN A5 (148×
210 mm) und ist biegsam in Ganzleinen gebunden.**

Preis bei Vorbestellung bis 1. Juni 1928:   **5.00** RM
durch den Buchhandel nur zum Preise von   **6.50** RM

Bestellschein umstehend ➡

Sans Serif

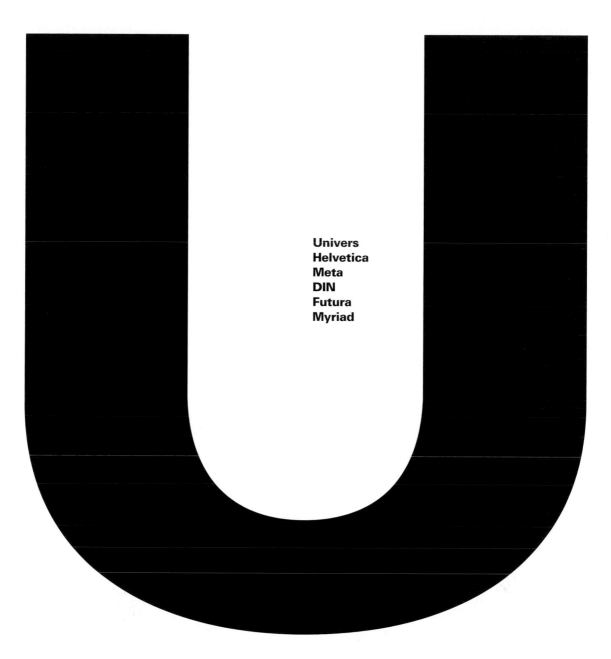

Univers
Helvetica
Meta
DIN
Futura
Myriad

2.

Prospectus designed by Jan Tschichold for his book *Die Neue Typographie,* 1928.

Sans serif typefaces have elemental letterforms stripped of serifs and decorations. Although sans serifs first appeared early in the nineteenth century, their use accelerated during the 1920s. "Form follows function" became the design dictum, and the functional simplicity of sans serif typefaces led many designers to look upon them as the ideal typographic expression of a scientific and technological century.

In Jan Tschichold's influential book *Die Neue Typographie,* he advocated a new functional style for a rational era. In the prospectus for the book, he used sans serif type as an expression of the age (Fig. **2**). The page also demonstrates asymmetrical balancing of elements on a grid

system, visual contrasts of type size and weight, and the importance of spatial intervals and white space as design elements.

During the 1950s, Univers and Helvetica were both designed as more contemporary versions of Akzidenz Grotesque, a German turn-of-the-century sans serif. Compare the text setting and the display specimens of Helvetica with their Univers counterparts. There are subtle differences in the drawing of many letterforms. The Univers family is renowned for its remarkable graphic unity, which enables the typographic designer to use all twenty-one fonts together as a flexible, integrated typographic system.

Univers was designed by
Adrian Frutiger and released
in 1957.

abcdefgh
ijklmnop
qrstuvwx
yz$12345
67890!?

124 point

ABCDEF

GHIJKLM

NOPQRS

TUVWX

YZ&(,'"";:)

abcdefghijklmnopqrstuv
wxyzABCDEFGHIJKLMN
OPQRSTUVWXYZ$12345
67890(.,'"-;:)!?&

26 point

abcdefghijklmn

opqrstuvwxyz

ABCDEFGHIJKL

MNOPQRSTUV

WXYZ$12345678

90(.,'"-;:)!?&

72 point

abcdefghijklmnopqrstuv
wxyzABCDEFGHIJKLMN
OPQRSTUVWXYZ123456
7890(.,'"-;:)!?&

26 point

abcdefghijklmn

opqrstuvwxyz

ABCDEFGHIJKL

MNOPQRSTUV

WXYZ$1234567

890(.,'"-;:)!?&

72 point

abcdefghijklmnopqrstuv
wxyzABCDEFGHIJKLMN
OPQRSTUVWXYZ$12345
67890(.,'"-;:)!?&

26 point

abcdefghijklmn
opqrstuvwxyz
ABCDEFGHIJKL
MNOPQRSTUV
WXYZ$1234567
890(.,'"-;:)!?&

72 point

abcdefghijklmnopqrstuv
wxyzABCDEFGHIJKLMN
OPQRSTUVWXYZ123456
7890(.,'"-;:)!?&

26 point

abcdefghijklmn
opqrstuvwxyz
ABCDEFGHIJKL
MNOPQRSTUV
WXYZ$1234567
890(.,'"-;:)!?&

72 point

abcdefghijklmnopqrst
uvwxyzABCDEFGHIJKL
MNOPQRSTUVWXYZ$
1234567890(.,'"-;:)!?&

26 point

abcdefghijklm
nopqrstuvwx
yzABCDEFG
HIJKLMNOPQ
RSTUVWXYZ
$1234567890
(.,'"-;:)!?&

72 point

abcdefghijklmnopqrst
uvwxyzABCDEFGHIJK
LMNOPQRSTUVWXYZ
1234567890(.,'"-;:)!?&

26 point

abcdefghijklm
nopqrstuvwx
yzABCDEFG
HIJKLMNOPQ
RSTUVWXYZ
$1234567890
(.,'"-;:)!?&

72 point

223

abcdefghijklmnopqrstuvwxyzAB
CDEFGHIJKLMNOPQRSTUVWXY
Z$1234567890(.,'"-;:)!?&

26 point

abcdefghijklmnopqr
stuvwxyzABCDEFGHI
JKLMNOPQRSTUV
WXYZ$1234567890
(.,'"-;:)!?&

72 point

Univers 55

The whole duty of typography, *as with calligraphy,* is to communicate to the imagination, without loss by the way, the thought or image intended to be communicated by the author. And the whole duty of beautiful typography is not to substitute for the beauty or interest of the thing thought and intended to be conveyed by the symbol, a beauty or interest of its own, but, on the one hand, to win access for that communication by the clearness and beauty of the vehicle, and on the other hand, to take advantage of every pause or stage in that communication to interpose some characteristic & restful beauty in its own art. We thus have a reason for the clearness and beauty of the first and introductory page and of the title, and for the especial beauty of the headings of chapters, capital or initial letters, and so on, and an opening for the illustrator as

8/10

The whole duty of typography, *as with calligraphy,* is to communicate to the imagination, without loss by the way, the thought or image intended to be communicated by the author. And the whole duty of beautiful typography is not to substitute for the beauty or interest of the thing thought and intended to be conveyed by the symbol, a beauty or interest of its own, but, on the one hand, to win access for that communication by the clearness and beauty of the vehicle, and on the other hand, to take advantage of every pause or stage in that communication to interpose some characteristic & restful beauty in its own art. We thus have a reason for the clearness and beauty of the first and introductory page and of the

8/12

The whole duty of typography, *as with calligraphy,* is to communicate to the imagination, without loss by the way, the thought or image intended to be communicated by the author. And the whole duty of beautiful typography is not to substitute for the beauty or interest of the thing thought and intended to be conveyed by the symbol, a beauty or interest of its own, but, on the one hand, to win access for that communication by the clearness and beauty of the vehicle, and on the other hand, to take advantage of every pause or stage in that communication to interpose some characteristic & restful beauty in its own art. We thus have a reason for the clearness and beauty of the first

9/11

The whole duty of typography, *as with calligraphy,* is to communicate to the imagination, without loss by the way, the thought or image intended to be communicated by the author. And the whole duty of beautiful typography is not to substitute for the beauty or interest of the thing thought and intended to be conveyed by the symbol, a beauty or interest of its own, but, on the one hand, to win access for that communication by the clearness and beauty of the vehicle, and on the other hand, to take advantage of every pause or stage in that communication to

9/13

The whole duty of typography, *as with calligraphy,* is to communicate to the imagination, without loss by the way, the thought or image intended to be communicated by the author. And the whole duty of beautiful typography is not to substitute for the beauty or interest of the thing thought and intended to be conveyed by the symbol, a beauty or interest of its own, but, on the one hand, to win access for that communication by the clearness and beauty of the vehicle, and on the other hand, to take advantage of every pause or stage in that communication

10/12

The whole duty of typography, *as with calligraphy,* is to communicate to the imagination, without loss by the way, the thought or image intended to be communicated by the author. And the whole duty of beautiful typography is not to substitute for the beauty or interest of the thing thought and intended to be conveyed by the symbol, a beauty or interest of its own, but, on the one hand, to win access for that communication by the clearness and beauty of the vehicle, and on the other hand, to take advantage of every

10 /14

The whole duty of typography, *as with calligraphy,* is to communicate to the imagination, without loss by the way, the thought or image intended to be communicated by the author. And the whole duty of beautiful typography is not to substitute for the beauty or interest of the thing thought and intended to be conveyed by the symbol, a beauty or interest of its own, but, on the one hand, to win

12 /14

The whole duty of typography, *as with calligraphy,* is to communicate to the imagination, without loss by the way, the thought or image intended to be communicated by the author. And the whole duty of beautiful typography is not to substitute for the beauty or interest of the thing thought and intended to be conveyed by the symbol, a beauty

12 /16

Helvetica 55 Roman

Helvetica was designed by
Max Miedinger around 1957;
Neue Helvetica is a digital
family designed by Linotype
Design Studio in 1983.

abcdefghi
jklmnopqr
stuvwxyz
$1234567
890!?

120 point

ABCDEF
GHIJKLM
NOPQRS
TUVWXY
Z&(.,'"-;:)

abcdefghijklmnopqrstuvw
xyzABCDFGHIJKLMNOP
QRSTUVWXYZ$12345678
90(.,'"-;:)!?&

26 point

abcdefghijklmn

opqrstuvwxyz

ABCDEFGHIJKL

MNOPQRSTUV

WXYZ$1234567

890(.,'"-;:)!?&

72 point

abcdefghijklmnopqrstuvw
xyzABCDFGHIJKLMNOPQ
RSTUVWXYZ1234567890
(.,'''-;:)!?&

26 point

abcdefghijklmno
pqrstuvwxyz
ABCDEFGHIJKL
MNOPQRSTUV
WXYZ$1234567
890(,'''-;:)!?&

72 point

abcdefghijklmnopqrstuvw
xyzABCDFGHIJKLMNOP
QRSTUVWXYZ$12345678
90(.,'"-;:)!?&

abcdefghijklmno
pqrstuvwxyz
ABCDEFGHIJKL
MNOPQRSTUV
WXYZ$1234567
890(.,'"-;:)!?&

Helvetica 55 Roman

abcdefghijklmnopqrstuvwxyz
ABCDEFGHIJKLMNOPQRSTUVWXYZ
$1234567890(.,'"-;:)!?&
abcdefghijklmnopqrstuvwxyz
ABCDEFGHIJKLMNOPQRSTUVWXYZ
8 point   *$1234567890(.,'"-;:)!?&*

abcdefghijklmnopqrstuvwxyz
ABCDEFGHIJKLMNOPQRSTUVWXYZ
$1234567890(.,'"-;:)!?&
abcdefghijklmnopqrstuvwxyz
ABCDEFGHIJKLMNOPQRSTUVWXYZ
9 point   *$1234567890(.,'"-;:)!?&*

abcdefghijklmnopqrstuvwxyz
ABCDEFGHIJKLMNOPQRSTUVWXYZ
$1234567890(.,'"-;:)!?&
abcdefghijklmnopqrstuvwxyz
ABCDEFGHIJKLMNOPQRSTUVWXYZ
10 point   *$1234567890(.,'"-;:)!?&*

abcdefghijklmnopqrstuvwxyz
ABCDEFGHIJKLMNOPQRSTUVWXYZ
$1234567890(.,'"-;:)!?&
abcdefghijklmnopqrstuvwxyz
ABCDEFGHIJKLMNOPQRSTUVWXYZ
12 point   *$1234567890(.,'"-;:)!?&*

The whole duty of typography, *as with calligraphy,* is to communicate to the imagination, without loss by the way, the thought or image intended to be communicated by the author. And the whole duty of beautiful typography is not to substitute for the beauty or interest of the thing thought and intended to be conveyed by the symbol, a beauty or interest of its own, but, on the one hand, to win access for that communication by the clearness and beauty of the vehicle, and on the other hand, to take advantage of every pause or stage in that communication to interpose some characteristic & restful beauty in its own art. We thus have a reason for the clearness and beauty of the first and introductory page and of the title, and for the especial beauty of the headings of chapters, capital or initial letters, and so on, and an opening
8/10

The whole duty of typography, *as with calligraphy,* is to communicate to the imagination, without loss by the way, the thought or image intended to be communicated by the author. And the whole duty of beautiful typography is not to substitute for the beauty or interest of the thing thought and intended to be conveyed by the symbol, a beauty or interest of its own, but, on the one hand, to win access for that communication by the clearness and beauty of the vehicle, and on the other hand, to take advantage of every pause or stage in that communication to interpose some characteristic & restful beauty in its own art. We thus have a reason for the clearness and beauty of the first
8/12

The whole duty of typography, *as with calligraphy,* is to communicate to the imagination, without loss by the way, the thought or image intended to be communicated by the author. And the whole duty of beautiful typography is not to substitute for the beauty or interest of the thing thought and intended to be conveyed by the symbol, a beauty or interest of its own, but, on the one hand, to win access for that communication by the clearness and beauty of the vehicle, and on the other hand, to take advantage of every pause or stage in that communication to interpose some characteristic & restful beauty in its own art. We thus have a reason for the clearness and beauty of the first
9/11

The whole duty of typography, as with calligraphy, *is to* communicate to the imagination, without loss by the way, the thought or image intended to be communicated by the author. And the whole duty of beautiful typography is not to substitute for the beauty or interest of the thing thought and intended to be conveyed by the symbol, a beauty or interest of its own, but, on the one hand, to win access for that communication by the clearness and beauty of the vehicle, and on the other hand, to take advantage of every pause or stage in that communication to
9/13

The whole duty of typography, *as with calligraphy,* is to communicate to the imagination, without loss by the way, the thought or image intended to be communicated by the author. And the whole duty of beautiful typography is not to substitute for the beauty or interest of the thing thought and intended to be conveyed by the symbol, a beauty or interest of its own, but, on the one hand, to win access for that communication by the clearness and beauty of the vehicle, and on the other hand, to take advantage of every pause or stage in that communication
10/12

The whole duty of typography, *as with calligraphy,* is to communicate to the imagination, without loss by the way, the thought or image intended to be communicated by the author. And the whole duty of beautiful typography is not to substitute for the beauty or interest of the thing thought and intended to be conveyed by the symbol, a beauty or interest of its own, but, on the one hand, to win access for that communication by the clearness and beauty of the vehicle, and on the other hand, to take advantage of every
10 /14

The whole duty of typography, *as with calligraphy,* is to communicate to the imagination, without loss by the way, the thought or image intended to be communicated by the author. And the whole duty of beautiful typography is not to substitute for the beauty or interest of the thing thought and intended to be conveyed by the symbol, a beauty or interest of its own, but, on the one hand, to win access for
12 /14

The whole duty of typography, *as with calligraphy,* is to communicate to the imagination, without loss by the way, the thought or image intended to be communicated by the author. And the whole duty of beautiful typography is not to substitute for the beauty or interest of the thing thought and intended to be conveyed by the symbol, a beauty or interest
12 /16

Meta Normal

Meta was designed by Erik
Spiekermann and released by
Fontshop in 1991.

abcdefghij
klmnopq
rstuvwxyz
$1234567
890!?

ABCDEF
GHIJKLMN
OPQRSTU
VWXYZ&
(,'',",-,;;)

abcdefghijklmnopqrstuvwxy
zABCDFGHIJKLMNOPQRS
TUVWXYZ$1234567890
(.,'""-;:)!?&

26 point

abcdefghijklmnop
qrstuvwxyzABCDE
FGHIJKLMNOPQRS
TUVWXYZ$123456
7890(.,'""-;:)!?&

abcdefghijklmnopqrstuvwxy
zABCDFGHIJKLMNOPQRS
TUVWXYZ1234567890
(.,'""-;:)!?&

26 point

abcdefghijklmnop
qrstuvwxyzABCDE
FGHIJKLMNOPQRS
TUVWXYZ$123456
7890(.,'"";:)!?&

72 point

abcdefghijklmnopqrstuvw
xyzABCDEFGHIJKLMNOPQRS
TUVWXYZ$1234567890
(.,'"'-;:)!?&

26 point

abcdefghijklmnop
qrstuvwxyzABCD
EFGHIJKLMNOPQ
RSTUVWXYZ$123
4567890(.,'";:)!?&

72 point

Meta Normal

The whole duty of typography, *as with calligraphy,* is to communicate to the imagination, without loss by the way, the thought or image intended to be communicated by the author. And the whole duty of beautiful typography is not to substitute for the beauty or interest of the thing thought and intended to be conveyed by the symbol, a beauty or interest of its own, but, on the one hand, to win access for that communication by the clearness and beauty of the vehicle, and on the other hand, to take advantage of every pause or stage in that communication to interpose some characteristic & restful beauty in its own art. We thus have a reason for the clearness and beauty of the first and introductory page and of the title, and for the especial beauty of the headings of chapters, capital or initial letters, and so on, and an opening for the illustrator as we shall see

8/10

The whole duty of typography, *as with calligraphy,* is to communicate to the imagination, without loss by the way, the thought or image intended to be communicated by the author. And the whole duty of beautiful typography is not to substitute for the beauty or interest of the thing thought and intended to be conveyed by the symbol, a beauty or interest of its own, but, on the one hand, to win access for that communication by the clearness and beauty of the vehicle, and on the other hand, to take advantage of every pause or stage in that communication to interpose some characteristic & restful beauty in its own art. We thus have a reason for the clearness and beauty of the first and

9/11

The whole duty of typography, as with calligraphy, is to communicate to the imagination, without loss by the way, the thought or image intended to be communicated by the author. And the whole duty of beautiful typography is not to substitute for the beauty or interest of the thing thought and intended to be conveyed by the symbol, a beauty or interest of its own, but, on the one hand, to win access for that communication by the clearness and beauty of the vehicle, and on the other hand, to take advantage of every pause or stage in that communication to interpose some

10/12

The whole duty of typography, *as with calligraphy,* is to communicate to the imagination, without loss by the way, the thought or image intended to be communicated by the author. And the whole duty of beautiful typography is not to substitute for the beauty or interest of the thing thought and intended to be conveyed by the symbol, a beauty or interest of its own, but, on the one hand, to win access for

12/14

The whole duty of typography, *as with calligraphy,* is to communicate to the imagination, without loss by the way, the thought or image intended to be communicated by the author. And the whole duty of beautiful typography is not to substitute for the beauty or interest of the thing thought and intended to be conveyed by the symbol, a beauty or interest of its own, but, on the one hand, to win access for that communication by the clearness and beauty of the vehicle, and on the other hand, to take advantage of every pause or stage in that communication to interpose some characteristic & restful beauty in its own art. We thus have a reason for the clearness and beauty of the first and introductory page and of the

8/12

The whole duty of typography, *as with calligraphy,* is to communicate to the imagination, without loss by the way, the thought or image intended to be communicated by the author. And the whole duty of beautiful typography is not to substitute for the beauty or interest of the thing thought and intended to be conveyed by the symbol, a beauty or interest of its own, but, on the one hand, to win access for that communication by the clearness and beauty of the vehicle, and on the other hand, to take advantage of every pause or stage in that communication to

9/13

The whole duty of typography, *as with calligraphy,* is to communicate to the imagination, without loss by the way, the thought or image intended to be communicated by the author. And the whole duty of beautiful typography is not to substitute for the beauty or interest of the thing thought and intended to be conveyed by the symbol, a beauty or interest of its own, but, on the one hand, to win access for that communication by the clearness and beauty of the vehicle, and on the other hand, to take advantage of every pause or

10/14

The whole duty of typography, *as with calligraphy,* is to communicate to the imagination, without loss by the way, the thought or image intended to be communicated by the author. And the whole duty of beautiful typography is not to substitute for the beauty or interest of the thing thought and intended to be conveyed by the symbol, a beauty or interest

12/16

DIN, designed by H. Berthold
AG in 1936, stands for
Deutsche Industrienorm
(German Industrial Standard).

abcdefghij
klmnopqr
stuvwxyz
$12345678
90!?

130 point

ABCDEF
GHIJKLM
NOPQRST
UVWXYZ
&(.,'""–:;)

abcdefghijklmnopqrstuvwx
yzABCDFGHIJKLMNOPQR
STUVWXYZ$1234567890
(.,'"-;:)!?&

26 point

abcdefghijklmnop
qrstuvwxyz
ABCDEFGHIJKLM
NOPQRSTUVWX
YZ$1234567890
(.,'"-;:)!?&

72 point

240

abcdefghijklmnopqrstuvw
xyzABCDFGHIJKLMNOPQR
STUVWXYZ1234567890
(.,'"-;:)!?&

26 point

abcdefghijklmnop
qrstuvwxyz
ABCDEFGHIJKLM
NOPQRSTUVWX
YZ$1234567890
(.,'"-;:)!?&

72 point

241

abcdefghijklmnopqrstuvw
xyzABCDEFGHIJKLMNOPQ
RSTUVWXYZ$1234567890
(.,'"-;:)!?&

26 point

abcdefghijklmn
opqrstuvwxyz
ABCDEFGHIJKL
MNOPQRSTUVW
XYZ$123456789
o(.,'"-;:)!?&

72 point

DIN Regular

The whole duty of typography, as with calligraphy, is to communicate to the imagination, without loss by the way, the thought or image intended to be communicated by the author. And the whole duty of beautiful typography is not to substitute for the beauty or interest of the thing thought and intended to be conveyed by the symbol, a beauty or interest of its own, but, on the one hand, to win access for that communication by the clearness and beauty of the vehicle, and on the other hand, to take advantage of every pause or stage in that communication to interpose some characteristic & restful beauty in its own art. We thus have a reason for the clearness and beauty of the first and introductory page and of the title, and for the especial beauty of the headings of chapters, capital or initial letters, and so on, and an opening for the illustrator as we shall see

8/10

The whole duty of typography, as with calligraphy, is to communicate to the imagination, without loss by the way, the thought or image intended to be communicated by the author. And the whole duty of beautiful typography is not to substitute for the beauty or interest of the thing thought and intended to be conveyed by the symbol, a beauty or interest of its own, but, on the one hand, to win access for that communication by the clearness and beauty of the vehicle, and on the other hand, to take advantage of every pause or stage in that communication to interpose some characteristic & restful beauty in its own art. We thus have a reason for the clearness and beauty of the first and

9/11

The whole duty of typography, as with calligraphy, is to communicate to the imagination, without loss by the way, the thought or image intended to be communicated by the author. And the whole duty of beautiful typography is not to substitute for the beauty or interest of the thing thought and intended to be conveyed by the symbol, a beauty or interest of its own, but, on the one hand, to win access for that communication by the clearness and beauty of the vehicle, and on the other hand, to take advantage of every pause or stage in that communication to interpose some

10/12

The whole duty of typography, as with calligraphy, is to communicate to the imagination, without loss by the way, the thought or image intended to be communicated by the author. And the whole duty of beautiful typography is not to substitute for the beauty or interest of the thing thought and intended to be conveyed by the symbol, a beauty or interest of its own, but, on the one hand, to win

12/14

The whole duty of typography, as with calligraphy, is to communicate to the imagination, without loss by the way, the thought or image intended to be communicated by the author. And the whole duty of beautiful typography is not to substitute for the beauty or interest of the thing thought and intended to be conveyed by the symbol, a beauty or interest of its own, but, on the one hand, to win access for that communication by the clearness and beauty of the vehicle, and on the other hand, to take advantage of every pause or stage in that communication to interpose some characteristic & restful beauty in its own art. We thus have a reason for the clearness and beauty of the first and introductory page and of the

8/12

The whole duty of typography, as with calligraphy, is to communicate to the imagination, without loss by the way, the thought or image intended to be communicated by the author. And the whole duty of beautiful typography is not to substitute for the beauty or interest of the thing thought and intended to be conveyed by the symbol, a beauty or interest of its own, but, on the one hand, to win access for that communication by the clearness and beauty of the vehicle, and on the other hand, to take advantage of every pause or stage in that communication to

9/13

The whole duty of typography, as with calligraphy, is to communicate to the imagination, without loss by the way, the thought or image intended to be communicated by the author. And the whole duty of beautiful typography is not to substitute for the beauty or interest of the thing thought and intended to be conveyed by the symbol, a beauty or interest of its own, but, on the one hand, to win access for that communication by the clearness and beauty of the vehicle, and on the other hand, to take advantage of every

10/14

The whole duty of typography, as with calligraphy, is to communicate to the imagination, without loss by the way, the thought or image intended to be communicated by the author. And the whole duty of beautiful typography is not to substitute for the beauty or interest of the thing thought and intended to be conveyed by the symbol, a beauty or

12/16

Futura Regular

Futura was designed Paul Renner; the first fonts were released in 1927.

abcdefghi
jklmnopqr
stuvwxyz
$1234567
890!?

130 point

ABCDEF
GHIJKLM
NOPQRS
TUVWXY
Z&(,'""-;:)

abcdefghijklmnopqrstuvwxy
zABCDFGHIJKLMNOPQRS
TUVWXYZ$1234567890
(.,'"-;:)!?&

26 point

abcdefghijklmno
pqrstuvwxyz
ABCDEFGHIJKL
MNOPQRSTUV
WXYZ$1234567
890(.,'"-;:)!?&

72 point

abcdefghijklmnopqrstuvwxy
zABCDFGHIJKLMNOPQRS
TUVWXYZ1234567890
(.,'"-;:)!?&

26 point

abcdefghijklmno
pqrstuvwxyzABC
DEFGHIJKLMNO
PQRSTUVWXYZ
$1234567890
(.,'"-;:)!?&

72 point

Futura Bold

abcdefghijklmnopqrstu
vwxyzABCDEFGHIJKLM
NOPQRSTUVWXYZ$12
34567890(.,'"-;:)!?&

abcdefghijklmn
opqrstuvwxyz
ABCDEFGHIJKL
MNOPQRSTUV
WXYZ$123456
7890(.,'"-;:)!?&

Futura Regular

abcdefghijklmnopqrstuvwxyz
ABCDEFGHIJKLMNOPQRSTUVWXYZ
$1234567890(.,'"-;:)!?&
abcdefghijklmnopqrstuvwxyz
ABCDEFGHIJKLMNOPQRSTUVWXYZ
8 point *$1234567890(.,'"-;:)!?&*

abcdefghijklmnopqrstuvwxyz
ABCDEFGHIJKLMNOPQRSTUVWXYZ
$1234567890(.,'"-;:)!?&
abcdefghijklmnopqrstuvwxyz
ABCDEFGHIJKLMNOPQRSTUVWXYZ
9 point *$1234567890(.,'"-;:)!?&*

abcdefghijklmnopqrstuvwxyz
ABCDEFGHIJKLMNOPQRSTUVWXYZ
$1234567890(.,'"-;:)!?&
abcdefghijklmnopqrstuvwxyz
ABCDEFGHIJKLMNOPQRSTUVWXYZ
10 point *$1234567890(.,'"-;:)!?&*

abcdefghijklmnopqrstuvwxyz
ABCDEFGHIJKLMNOPQRSTUVWXYZ
$1234567890(.,'"-;:)!?&
abcdefghijklmnopqrstuvwxyz
ABCDEFGHIJKLMNOPQRSTUVWXYZ
12 point *$1234567890(.,'"-;:)!?&*

The whole duty of typography, *as with calligraphy,* is to communicate to the imagination, without loss by the way, the thought or image intended to be communicated by the author. And the whole duty of beautiful typography is not to substitute for the beauty or interest of the thing thought and intended to be conveyed by the symbol, a beauty or interest of its own, but, on the one hand, to win access for that communication by the clearness and beauty of the vehicle, and on the other hand, to take advantage of every pause or stage in that communication to interpose some characteristic & restful beauty in its own art. We thus have a reason for the clearness and beauty of the first and introductory page and of the title, and for the especial beauty of the headings of chapters, capital or initial letters, and so on, and an opening for the illustrator as we shall see by and by. Further, in the case of poetry, verse, in

8/10

The whole duty of typography, *as with calligraphy,* is to communicate to the imagination, without loss by the way, the thought or image intended to be communicated by the author. And the whole duty of beautiful typography is not to substitute for the beauty or interest of the thing thought and intended to be conveyed by the symbol, a beauty or interest of its own, but, on the one hand, to win access for that communication by the clearness and beauty of the vehicle, and on the other hand, to take advantage of every pause or stage in that communication to interpose some characteristic & restful beauty in its own art. We thus have a reason for the clearness and beauty of the first and introductory page and of the title, and for the especial beauty of the headings

8/12

The whole duty of typography, *as with calligraphy,* is to communicate to the imagination, without loss by the way, the thought or image intended to be communicated by the author. And the whole duty of beautiful typography is not to substitute for the beauty or interest of the thing thought and intended to be conveyed by the symbol, a beauty or interest of its own, but, on the one hand, to win access for that communication by the clearness and beauty of the vehicle, and on the other hand, to take advantage of every pause or stage in that communication to interpose some characteristic & restful beauty in its own art. We thus have a reason for the clearness and beauty of the first and introductory page and of the title, and for

9/11

The whole duty of typography, *as with calligraphy,* is to communicate to the imagination, without loss by the way, the thought or image intended to be communicated by the author. And the whole duty of beautiful typography is not to substitute for the beauty or interest of the thing thought and intended to be conveyed by the symbol, a beauty or interest of its own, but, on the one hand, to win access for that communication by the clearness and beauty of the vehicle, and on the other hand, to take advantage of every pause or stage in that communication to interpose some characteristic & restful

9/13

The whole duty of typography, *as with calligraphy,* is to communicate to the imagination, without loss by the way, the thought or image intended to be communicated by the author. And the whole duty of beautiful typography is not to substitute for the beauty or interest of the thing thought and intended to be conveyed by the symbol, a beauty or interest of its own, but, on the one hand, to win access for that communication by the clearness and beauty of the vehicle, and on the other hand, to take advantage of every pause or stage in that communication to interpose some characteristic

10/12

The whole duty of typography, *as with calligraphy,* is to communicate to the imagination, without loss by the way, the thought or image intended to be communicated by the author. And the whole duty of beautiful typography is not to substitute for the beauty or interest of the thing thought and intended to be conveyed by the symbol, a beauty or interest of its own, but, on the one hand, to win access for that communication by the clearness and beauty of the vehicle, and on the other hand, to take advantage of every pause or

10/14

The whole duty of typography, *as with calligraphy,* is to communicate to the imagination, without loss by the way, the thought or image intended to be communicated by the author. And the whole duty of beautiful typography is not to substitute for the beauty or interest of the thing thought and intended to be conveyed by the symbol, a beauty or interest of its own, but, on the one hand,

12/14

The whole duty of typography, *as with calligraphy,* is to communicate to the imagination, without loss by the way, the thought or image intended to be communicated by the author. And the whole duty of beautiful typography is not to substitute for the beauty or interest of the thing thought and intended to be conveyed by the symbol, a beauty or

12/16

Myriad Regular

Myriad, designed by Carol Twombly and Robert Slimbach, was relased by Adobe in 1992.

abcdefgh
ijklmnop
qrstuvwx
yz$12345
67890!?

140 point

ABCDEF
GHIJKLM
NOPQRS
TUVWXY
Z&(.,'"–;;)

abcdefghijklmnopqrstuvwx
yzABCDEFGHIJKLMNOPQRS
TUVWXYZ$1234567890
(.,'"-;:)!?&

26 point

abcdefghijklmno
pqrstuvwxyz
ABCDEFGHIJKLM
NOPQRSTUVWXY
Z$1234567890
(.,'"-;:)!?&

72 point

abcdefghijklmnopqrstuvwxyz
ABCDEFGHIJKLMNOPQRSTUV
WXYZ1234567890 (.,'"-;:)!?&

26 point

abcdefghijklmno
pqrstuvwxyz
ABCDEFGHIJKLMN
OPQRSTUVWXYZ$
1234567890
(.,'"-;:)!?&

72 point

abcdefghijklmnopqrstuvw
xyzABCDEFGHIJKLMNOPQ
RSTUVWXYZ$1234567890
(.,'"-;:)!?&

26 point

abcdefghijklmno
pqrstuvwxyz
ABCDEFGHIJKLM
NOPQRSTUVWX
YZ$1234567890
(.,'"-;:!)?&

72 point

Myriad Regular

abcdefghijklmnopqrstuvwxyz
ABCDEFGHIJKLMNOPQRSTUVWXYZ
$1234567890(.,'"-;:)!?&
abcdefghijklmnopqrstuvwxyz
ABCDEFGHIJKLMNOPQRSTUVWXYZ
8 point $1234567890(.,'"-;:)!?&

abcdefghijklmnopqrstuvwxyz
ABCDEFGHIJKLMNOPQRSTUVWXYZ
$1234567890(.,'"-;:)!?&
abcdefghijklmnopqrstuvwxyz
ABCDEFGHIJKLMNOPQRSTUVWXYZ
9 point $1234567890(.,'"-;:)!?&

abcdefghijklmnopqrstuvwxyz
ABCDEFGHIJKLMNOPQRSTUVWXYZ
$1234567890(.,'"-;:)!?&
abcdefghijklmnopqrstuvwxyz
ABCDEFGHIJKLMNOPQRSTUVWXYZ
10 point $1234567890(.,'"-;:)!?&

abcdefghijklmnopqrstuvwxyz
ABCDEFGHIJKLMNOPQRSTUVWXYZ
$1234567890(.,'"-;:)!?&
abcdefghijklmnopqrstuvwxyz
ABCDEFGHIJKLMNOPQRSTUVWXYZ
12 point $1234567890(.,'"-;:)!?&

The whole duty of typography, *as with calligraphy,* is to communicate to the imagination, without loss by the way, the thought or image intended to be communicated by the author. And the whole duty of beautiful typography is not to substitute for the beauty or interest of the thing thought and intended to be conveyed by the symbol, a beauty or interest of its own, but, on the one hand, to win access for that communication by the clearness and beauty of the vehicle, and on the other hand, to take advantage of every pause or stage in that communication to interpose some characteristic & restful beauty in its own art. We thus have a reason for the clearness and beauty of the first and introductory page and of the title, and for the especial beauty of the headings of chapters, capital or initial letters, and so on, and an opening for the illustrator as we shall see by and by. Further, in the case of poetry, verse, in my
8/10

The whole duty of typography, *as with calligraphy,* is to communicate to the imagination, without loss by the way, the thought or image intended to be communicated by the author. And the whole duty of beautiful typography is not to substitute for the beauty or interest of the thing thought and intended to be conveyed by the symbol, a beauty or interest of its own, but, on the one hand, to win access for that communication by the clearness and beauty of the vehicle, and on the other hand, to take advantage of every pause or stage in that communication to interpose some characteristic & restful beauty in its own art. We thus have a reason for the clearness and beauty of the first and introductory page and of the title, and for
9/11

The whole duty of typography, *as with calligraphy,* is to communicate to the imagination, without loss by the way, the thought or image intended to be communicated by the author. And the whole duty of beautiful typography is not to substitute for the beauty or interest of the thing thought and intended to be conveyed by the symbol, a beauty or interest of its own, but, on the one hand, to win access for that communication by the clearness and beauty of the vehicle, and on the other hand, to take advantage of every pause or stage in that communication to interpose some characteristic
10/12

The whole duty of typography, *as with calligraphy,* is to communicate to the imagination, without loss by the way, the thought or image intended to be communicated by the author. And the whole duty of beautiful typography is not to substitute for the beauty or interest of the thing thought and intended to be conveyed by the symbol, a beauty or interest of its own, but, on the one hand, to win
12/14

The whole duty of typography, *as with calligraphy,* is to communicate to the imagination, without loss by the way, the thought or image intended to be communicated by the author. And the whole duty of beautiful typography is not to substitute for the beauty or interest of the thing thought and intended to be conveyed by the symbol, a beauty or interest of its own, but, on the one hand, to win access for that communication by the clearness and beauty of the vehicle, and on the other hand, to take advantage of every pause or stage in that communication to interpose some characteristic & restful beauty in its own art. We thus have a reason for the clearness and beauty of the first and introductory page and of the title, and for the especial beauty of the headings
8/12

The whole duty of typography, *as with calligraphy,* is to communicate to the imagination, without loss by the way, the thought or image intended to be communicated by the author. And the whole duty of beautiful typography is not to substitute for the beauty or interest of the thing thought and intended to be conveyed by the symbol, a beauty or interest of its own, but, on the one hand, to win access for that communication by the clearness and beauty of the vehicle, and on the other hand, to take advantage of every pause or stage in that communication to interpose some characteristic &
9/13

The whole duty of typography, *as with calligraphy,* is to communicate to the imagination, without loss by the way, the thought or image intended to be communicated by the author. And the whole duty of beautiful typography is not to substitute for the beauty or interest of the thing thought and intended to be conveyed by the symbol, a beauty or interest of its own, but, on the one hand, to win access for that communication by the clearness and beauty of the vehicle, and on the other hand, to take advantage of every pause or
10/14

The whole duty of typography, *as with calligraphy,* is to communicate to the imagination, without loss by the way, the thought or image intended to be communicated by the author. And the whole duty of beautiful typography is not to substitute for the beauty or interest of the thing thought and intended to be conveyed by the symbol, a beauty or
12/16

GEORGICON.

LIBER SECUNDUS.

HActenus arvorum cultus, et fidera cœli:
Nunc te, Bacche, canam, nec non filveftria tecum
Virgulta, et prolem tarde crefcentis olivæ.
Huc, pater o Lenæe; (tuis hic omnia plena
5 Muneribus: tibi pampineo gravidus autumno
Floret ager; fpumat plenis vindemia labris)
Huc, pater o Lenæe, veni; nudataque mufto
Tinge novo mecum direptis crura cothurnis.
   Principio arboribus varia eft natura creandis:
10 Namque aliæ, nullis hominum cogentibus, ipfæ
Sponte fua veniunt, campofque et flumina late
Curva tenent: ut molle filer, lentæque geniftæ,
Populus, et glauca canentia fronde falicta.
Pars autem pofito furgunt de femine: ut altæ
15 Caftaneæ, nemorumque Jovi quæ maxima frondet
Aefculus, atque habitæ Graiis oracula quercus.
Pullulat ab radice aliis denfiffima filva:
Ut cerafis, ulmifque: etiam Parnaffia laurus
Parva fub ingenti matris fe fubjicit umbra.
20 Hos natura modos primum dedit: his genus omne
Silvarum, fruticumque viret, nemorumque facrorum.
Sunt alii, quos ipfe via fibi repperit ufus.
Hic plantas tenero abfcindens de corpore matrum

Depofuit

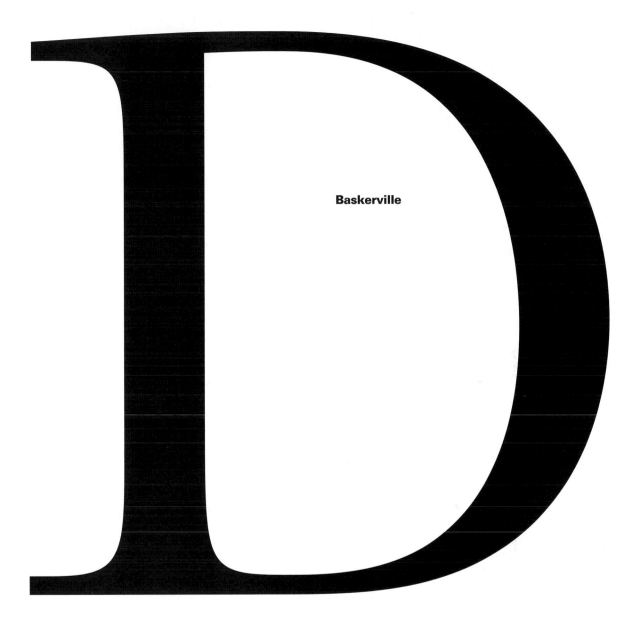

Transitional

Baskerville

Transitional type appeared during the eighteenth
century, a period of typographic evolution.
Steady technical advances allowed more refined
punches, matrices, and typecasting. Designers
were able to gradually increase the contrast
between thick and thin strokes, apply sharper and
more horizontal serifs to their characters, and
make the stress of rounded letterforms more
vertical. By the century's end, Old Style typefaces
had evolved into the Modern styles with hairline
serifs and geometric proportions: typefaces
designed during the middle of this period of
evolving designs were *transitional.*

Simplicity and understated elegance were
achieved through the use of John Baskerville's
masterful Transitional typefaces, seen in the title

page of Virgil's *Georgics* (Fig. **3**). Generous
margins, careful letterspacing of display type, and
thoughtfully considered interline and wordspacing
are present. The great Roman poet is presented
to the reader with clarity and dignity in a book that
"went forth to astonish all the librarians of
Europe."

If the words *Transitional* and *Baskerville* have
become interwoven in the lexicon of typography,
it is because the Transitional typefaces produced
by John Baskerville of Birmingham, England, have
an unsurpassed beauty and harmony. Many
Transitional typefaces in use today, including most
of the specimens in this section, are inspired by
the exquisite beauty of Baskerville's work.

Early twentieth-century adaptations were released by American Type Founders, Linotype, and Monotype.

abcdefghi

jklmnopq

rstuvwxyz

$1234567

890(,'"-;:)!?

130 point

ABCDEF
GHIJKL
MNOPQ
RSTUV
WXYZ&

130 point

abcdefghijklmnopqrstuvw
xyzABCDFGHIJKLMNO
PQRSTUVWXYZ
$1234567890(.,'''-;:)!?&

27 point

abcdefghijklmn

opqrstuvwxyz

ABCDEFGHIJK

LMNOPQRSTU

VWXYZ$123456

7890(.,'''-;:)!?&

78 point

abcdefghijklmnopqrstuvwxyz
ABCDEFGHIJKLMNOPQ
RSTUVWXYZ$123456
7890(.,'''-;:)!?&

27 point

abcdefghijklmnop

qrstuvwxyz

ABCDEFGHIJKL

MNOPQRSTU

VWXYZ$123456

7890(.,'''-;:)!?&

78 point

abcdefghijklmnopqrst
uvwxyzABCDFGHIJKL
MNOPQRSTUVWXYZ
$1234567890(.,'''-;:)!?&

abcdefghijklmn

opqrstuvwxyz

ABCDEFGHIJK

LMNOPQRSTU

VWXYZ$123456

7890(.,'''-;:!)?&

Baskerville Regular

abcdefghijklmnopqrstuvwxyz
ABCDEFGHIJKLMNOPQRSTUVWXYZ
$1234567890(.,'"-;:)!?&
abcdefghijklmnopqrstuvwxyz
ABCDEFGHIJKLMNOPQRSTUVWXYZ
8 Point $1234567890(.,'"-;:)!?&

abcdefghijklmnopqrstuvwxyz
ABCDEFGHIJKLMNOPQRSTUVWXYZ
$1234567890(.,'"-;:)!?&
abcdefghijklmnopqrstuvwxyz
ABCDEFGHIJKLMNOPQRSTUVWXYZ
9 Point $1234567890(.,'"-;:)!?&

abcdefghijklmnopqrstuvwxyz
ABCDEFGHIJKLMNOPQRSTUVWXYZ
$1234567890(.,'"-;:)!?&
abcdefghijklmnopqrstuvwxyz
ABCDEFGHIJKLMNOPQRSTUVWXYZ
10 Point $1234567890(.,'"-;:)!?&

abcdefghijklmnopqrstuvwxyz
ABCDEFGHIJKLMNOPQRSTUVW
XYZ$1234567890(.,'"-;:)!?&
abcdefghijklmnopqrstuvwxyz
ABCDEFGHIJKLMNOPQRSTUVW
12 Point *XYZ$1234567890(.,'"-;:)!?&*

The whole duty of typography, *as with calligraphy,* is to communicate to the imagination, without loss by the way, the thought or image intended to be communicated by the author. And the whole duty of beautiful typography is not to substitute for the beauty or interest of the thing thought and intended to be conveyed by the symbol, a beauty or interest of its own, but, on the one hand, to win access for that communication by the clearness and beauty of the vehicle, and on the other hand, to take advantage of every pause or stage in that communication to interpose some characteristic & restful beauty in its own art. We thus have a reason for the clearness and beauty of the first and introductory page and of the title, and for the especial beauty of the headings of chapters, capital or initial letters, and so on, and an opening for the illustrator as we shall see by and by. Further, in the case of poetry, verse, in my opinion, appeals by its
8/10

The whole duty of typography, *as with calligraphy,* is to communicate to the imagination, without loss by the way, the thought or image intended to be communicated by the author. And the whole duty of beautiful typography is not to substitute for the beauty or interest of the thing thought and intended to be conveyed by the symbol, a beauty or interest of its own, but, on the one hand, to win access for that communication by the clearness and beauty of the vehicle, and on the other hand, to take advantage of every pause or stage in that communication to interpose some characteristic & restful beauty in its own art. We thus have a reason for the clearness and beauty of the first and introductory page and of the title, and for the especial beauty of the headings of chapters,
8/12

The whole duty of typography, *as with calligraphy,* is to communicate to the imagination, without loss by the way, the thought or image intended to be communicated by the author. And the whole duty of beautiful typography is not to substitute for the beauty or interest of the thing thought and intended to be conveyed by the symbol, a beauty or interest of its own, but, on the one hand, to win access for that communication by the clearness and beauty of the vehicle, and on the other hand, to take advantage of every pause or stage in that communication to interpose some characteristic & restful beauty in its own art. We thus have a reason for the clearness and beauty of the first and introductory page and of the title, and for the especial
9/11

The whole duty of typography, *as with calligraphy,* is to communicate to the imagination, without loss by the way, the thought or image intended to be communicated by the author. And the whole duty of beautiful typography is not to substitute for the beauty or interest of the thing thought and intended to be conveyed by the symbol, a beauty or interest of its own, but, on the one hand, to win access for that commu nication by the clearness and beauty of the vehicle, and on the other hand, to take advantage of every pause or stage in that communication to interpose some characteristic & restful beauty in its own art. We thus
9/13

The whole duty of typography, *as with calligraphy,* is to com municate to the imagination, without loss by the way, the thought or image intended to be communicated by the author. And the whole duty of beautiful typography is not to substitute for the beauty or interest of the thing thought and intended to be con veyed by the symbol, a beauty or interest of its own, but, on the one hand, to win access for that communication by the clearness and beauty of the vehicle, and on the other hand, to take advan tage of every pause or stage in that communication to interpose some characteristic & restful beauty in its own art. We thus have
10/12

The whole duty of typography, *as with calligraphy,* is to com municate to the imagination, without loss by the way, the thought or image intended to be communicated by the author. And the whole duty of beautiful typography is not to substitute for the beauty or interest of the thing thought and intended to be con veyed by the symbol, a beauty or interest of its own, but, on the one hand, to win access for that communication by the clearness and beauty of the vehicle, and on the other hand, to take advan tage of every pause or stage in that communication to interpose
10/14

The whole duty of typography, *as with calligraphy,* is to communicate to the imagination, without loss by the way, the thought or image intended to be commu nicated by the author. And the whole duty of beau tiful typography is not to substitute for the beauty or interest typographyof the thing thought and intended to be conveyed by the symbol, a beauty or interest of its own, but, on the one hand, to win access for that
12/14

The whole duty of typography, *as with calligraphy,* is to communicate to the imagination, without loss by the way, the thought or image intended to be commu nicated by the author. And the whole duty of beau tiful typography is not to substitute for the beauty or interest of the thing thought and intended to be con veyed by the symbol, a beauty or interest of its own,
12/16

Times Roman

abcdefghijklmnopqrstuvwxyz
ABCDEFGHIJKLMNOPQRSTUVWXY
Z$1234567890(.,'"-;:)!?&

Times Roman Italic

abcdefghijklmnopqrstuvwxyz
ABCDEFGHIJKLMNOPQRSTUVW
XYZ$1234567890(.,'"-;:)!?&

Times Roman Bold

abcdefghijklmnopqrstuvwxyz
ABCDEFGHIJKLMNOPQRSTUV
WXYZ$1234567890(.,'"-;:)!?&

Times Roman Bold Italic

abcdefghijklmnopqrstuvwxyz
ABCDEFGHIJKLMNOPQRSTUVW
XYZ$1234567890(.,'"-;:)!?&

Stone Serif

abcdefghijklmnopqrstuvwxyz
ABCDEFGHIJKLMNOPQRSTUVWXY
Z$1234567890(.,'"-;:)!?&

Plantin Regular

abcdefghijklmnopqrstuvwxyz
ABCDEFGHIJKLMNOPQRSTU
VWXYZ$1234567890(.,'"-;:)!?&

Plantin Italic

abcdefghijklmnopqrstuvwxyz
ABCDEFGHIJKLMNOPQRSTUV
WXYZ$1234567890(.,'"-;:)!?&

Plantin Light

abcdefghijklmnopqrstuvwxyz
ABCDEFGHIJKLMNOPQRSTUV
WXYZ$1234567890(.,'"-;:)!?&

Plantin Bold

abcdefghijklmnopqrstuvwxyz
ABCDEFGHIJKLMNOPQRSTU
VWXYZ$1234567890(.,'"-;:)!?&

Plantin Bold Condensed

abcdefghijklmnopqrstuvwxyz
ABCDEFGHIJKLMNOPQRSTVWXYZ
$1234567890(.,'"-;:)!?&

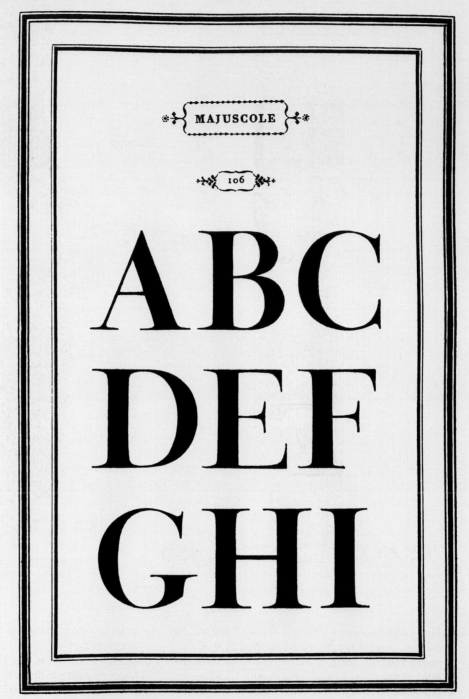

MAJUSCOLE

106

ABC
DEF
GHI

Modern　　　　　　　　　　**Bodoni**

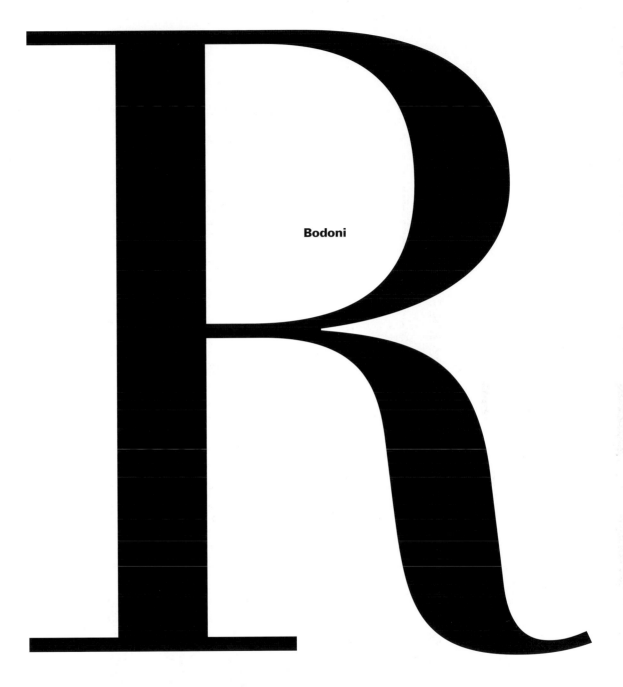

4.
Page 250 from the *Manuale Tipographico*, 1818.

The word *modern* is a relative term. Often, we use it interchangeably with the term *contemporary;* sometimes it is used to identify movements in the arts representing a radical break with tradition. In typographic design, *Modern* identifies typefaces of the late 1700s with flat, unbracketed serifs, extreme contrasts between thick-and-thin strokes, and geometric construction. The influence of writing and calligraphy upon type design was replaced by mathematical measurement and the use of mechanical instruments to construct letterforms.

After the death of type designer and printer Giambattista Bodoni, his widow and foreman published the *Manuale Tipographico,* displaying specimens of the approximately three hundred

type fonts designed by Bodoni. The page reproduced here in its actual size shows the dazzling contrasts and vigorous proportions found in Modern-style typefaces (Fig. **4**). Thick-and-thin oxford or scotch rules (see Fig. **17**, Chapter Three) echo and complement the letters' stroke weight.

Modern-style typefaces were widely used for book text type during the nineteenth century and have enjoyed continued acceptance for over two centuries. Numerous variations – from extreme fineline versions to ultrabolds; and from very narrow, condensed fonts to wide, expanded letterforms – have been designed. Many contemporary fonts bear the names of eighteenth-century designers: Bodoni, Didot, and Walbaum.

**Bauer Bodoni
Regular**

This version was released
by the Bauer type foundry
in Germany in 1926.

abcdefghij

klmnopq

rstuvwxyz

$1234567

890(.,'"'"-;:)!?

ABCDEF
GHIJKL
MNOPQR
STUV
WXYZ&

130 point

abcdefghijklmnopqrstuvw
xyzABCDFGHIJKLMNO
PQRSTUVWXYZ$12345
67890(.,'''-;:)!?&

27 point

abcdefghijklmn

opqrstuvwxyz

ABCDEFGHIJK

LMNOPQRSTU

VWXYZ$1234

567890(.,'''-;:)!?&

81 point

Bauer Bodoni Italic

abcdefghijklmnopqrstuvw
xyzABCDEFGHIJKLMNO
PQRSTUVWXYZ1234567
890(.,'"-;:)!?&

27 point

abcdefghijklmno

pqrstuvwxyz

ABCDEFGHIJK

LMNOPQRSTU

VWXYZ$12345

67890(.,'"-;:)!?&

81 point

abcdefghijklmnopqrstuvw
xyzABCDFGHIJKLMNOP
QRSTUVWXYZ$12345678
90(.,'"-;:)!?&

abcdefghijklmn

opqrstuvwxyz

ABCDEFGHIJK

LMNOPQRSTU

VWXYZ$12345

67890(.,'"-;:!)?&

**Bauer Bodoni
Regular**

8 point
abcdefghijklmnopqrstuvwxyz
ABCDEFGHIJKLMNOPQRSTUVWXYZ
$1234567890(.,'"-:;!)?&
abcdefghijklmnopqrstuvwxyz
ABCDEFGHIJKLMNOPQRSTUVWXYZ
$1234567890(.,'"-:;)!?&

9 point
abcdefghijklmnopqrstuvwxyz
ABCDEFGHIJKLMNOPQRSTUVWXYZ
$1234567890(.,'"-:;)!?&
abcdefghijklmnopqrstuvwxyz
ABCDEFGHIJKLMNOPQRSTUVWXYZ
$1234567890(.,'"-:;)!?&

10 point
abcdefghijklmnopqrstuvwxyz
ABCDEFGHIJKLMNOPQRSTUVWXYZ
$1234567890(.,'"-:;)!?&
abcdefghijklmnopqrstuvwxyz
ABCDEFGHIJKLMNOPQRSTUVWXYZ
$1234567890(.,'"-:;)!?&

12 point
abcdefghijklmnopqrstuvwxyz
ABCDEFGHIJKLMNOPQRSTUVWXYZ
$1234567890(.,'"-:;)!?&
abcdefghijklmnopqrstuvwxyz
ABCDEFGHIJKLMNOPQRSTUVWXYZ
$1234567890(.,'"-:;)!?&

The whole duty of typography, *as with calligraphy,* is to communicate to the imagination, without loss by the way, the thought or image intended to be communicated by the author. And the whole duty of beautiful typography is not to substitute for the beauty or interest of the thing thought and intended to be conveyed by the symbol, a beauty or interest of its own, but, on the one hand, to win access for that communication by the clearness and beauty of the vehicle, and on the other hand, to take advantage of every pause or stage in that communication to interpose some characteristic & restful beauty in its own art. We thus have a reason for the clearness and beauty of the first and introductory page and of the title, and for the especial beauty of the headings of chapters, capital or initial letters, and so on, and an opening for the illustrator as we shall see by and by.
8/10

The whole duty of typography, *as with calligraphy,* is to communicate to the imagination, without loss by the way, the thought or image intended to be communicated by the author. And the whole duty of beautiful typography is not to substitute for the beauty or interest of the thing thought and intended to be conveyed by the symbol, a beauty or interest of its own, but, on the one hand, to win access for that communication by the clearness and beauty of the vehicle, and on the other hand, to take advantage of every pause or stage in that communication to interpose some characteristic & restful beauty in its own art. We thus have a reason for the clearness and beauty of the first and introductory page and of the title, and for the especial
8/12

The whole duty of typography, *as with calligraphy,* is to commu nicate to the imagination, without loss by the way, the thought or image intended to be communicated by the author. And the whole duty of beautiful typography is not to substitute for the beauty or interest of the thing thought and intended to be conveyed by the symbol, a beauty or interest of its own, but, on the one hand, to win access for that communication by the clearness and beauty of the vehicle, and on the other hand, to take advantage of every pause or stage in that communication to interpose some characteristic & restful beauty in its own art. We thus have a reason for the clearness and beauty of the first and introductory page and of the title, and
9/11

The whole duty of typography, *as with calligraphy,* is to commu nicate to the imagination, without loss by the way, the thought or image intended to be communicated by the author. And the whole duty of beautiful typography is not to substitute for the beauty or interest of the thing thought and intended to be conveyed by the symbol, a beauty or interest of its own, but, on the one hand, to win access for that communication by the clearness and beauty of the vehicle, and on the other hand, to take advantage of every pause or stage in that communication to interpose some characteristic &
9/13

The whole duty of typography, *as with calligraphy,* is to communicate to the imagination, without loss by the way, the thought or image intended to be communicated by the author. And the whole duty of beautiful typography is not to substitute for the beauty or interest of the thing thought and intended to be conveyed by the symbol, a beauty or interest of its own, but, on the one hand, to win access for that communication by the clearness and beauty of the vehicle, and on the other hand, to take advantage of every pause or stage in that communication to interpose some characteristic
10/12

The whole duty of typography, *as with calligraphy,* is to communicate to the imagination, without loss by the way, the thought or image intended to be communicated by the author. And the whole duty of beautiful typography is not to substitute for the beauty or interest of the thing thought and intended to be conveyed by the symbol, a beauty or interest of its own, but, on the one hand, to win access for that communication by the clearness and beauty of the vehicle, and on the other hand, to take advantage of every pause or
10 /14

The whole duty of typography, *as with calligraphy,* is to communicate to the imagination, without loss by the way, the thought or image intended to be com municated by the author. And the whole duty of beautiful typography is not to substitute for the beau ty or interest of the thing thought and intended to be conveyed by the symbol, a beauty or interest of its own, but, on the one hand, to win access for that
12 /14

The whole duty of typography, *as with calligraphy,* is to communicate to the imagination, without loss by the way, the thought or image intended to be com municated by the author. And the whole duty of beautiful typography is not to substitute for the beau ty or interest of the thing thought and intended to be conveyed by the symbol, a beauty or interest of its own, but, on the one hand, to win access for that
12 /16

Bauer Bodoni Bold

abcdefghijklmnopqrstuvwxyz
ABCDEFGHIJKLMNOPQRSTUVWX
YZ$1234567890(.,'"-;:)!?&

Bauer Bodoni Bold Italic

abcdefghijklmnopqrstuvwxyz
ABCDEFGHIJKLMNOPQRSTUVW
XYZ$1234567890(.,'"-;:)!?&

Bauer Bodoni Black

abcdefghijklmnopqrstuvwxyz
ABCDEFGHIJKLMNOPQRSTUV
WXYZ$1234567890(.,'"-;:)!?&

Bauer Bodoni Black Condensed

abcdefghijklmnopqrstuvwxyz
ABCDEFGHIJKLMNOPQRSTUVWXYZ
$1234567890(.,'"-;:)!?&

Ultra Bodoni

abcdefghijklmnopqrstuvwxyz
ABCDEFGHIJKLMNOPQRSTUV
WXYZ$1234567890(.,'"-;:)!?&

Filosofia Grand

abcdefghijklmnopqrstuvwxyz
ABCDEFGHIJKLMNOPQRSTUVWXYZ
$1234567890(.,'"-;:)!?&

Didot Roman

abcdefghijklmnopqrstuvwxyz
ABCDEFGHIJKLMNOPQRSTUV
WXYZ$1234567890(.,'"-;:)!?&

Didot Italic

abcdefghijklmnopqrstuvwxyz
ABCDEFGHIJKLMNOPQRSTUV
WXYZ$1234567890(.,'"-;:)!?&

Didot Bold

abcdefghijklmnopqrstuvwxyz
ABCDEFGHIJKLMNOPQRSTU
VWXYZ$1234567890(.,'"-;:)!?&

Onyx

abcdefghijklmnopqrstuvwxyz
ABCDEFGHIJKLMNOPQRSTVWXYZ
$1234567890(.,'"-;:)!?&

NEW LINE BETWEEN
ALBANY & NEWBURG

LANDING AT

Hamburgh, Marlborough, Milton, Poughkeepsie, Hyde Park, Kingston, Rhinebeck, Barrytown, Redhook, Bristol, Westcamp Catskill, Hudson, Coxsackie, Stuyvesant, Baltimore & Coeymans.

On and after MONDAY, October 15th,

The Superior Low Pressure Steame

ST. NICHOLAS

CAPTAIN WILSON,

Will run as a Passage and Freight Boat between Newburgh and Albany, leaving Newburgh

MONDAYS, WEDNESDAYS & FRIDAYS

AT SEVEN O'CLOCK A.M.,

And ALBANY on Tuesdays, Thursdays & Saturdays, at half-past 9 o'clock A.M.

Albany, Oct. 9th, 1849.

Egyptian

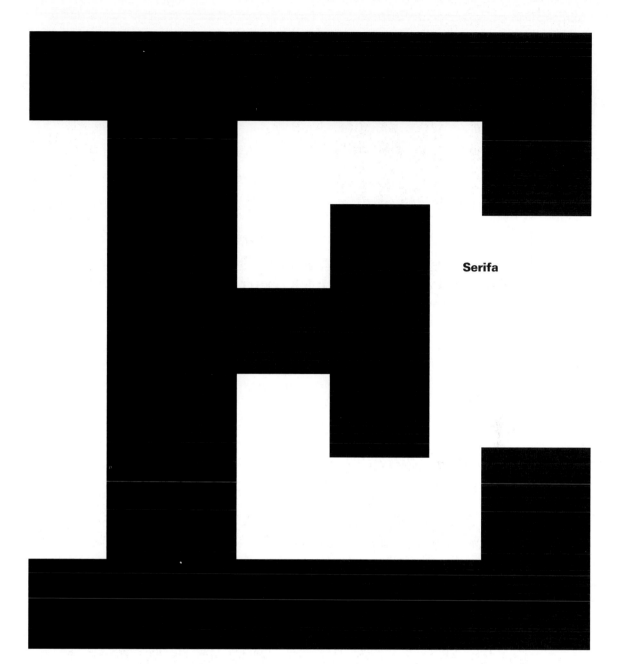

Serifa

5.
Broadsheet, 1849. This slab-serif display type has been lightly inked, and the textured grain of the wooden type is clearly visible, as in the words *St. Nicholas.*

Egyptian or slab-serif typefaces first appeared in the early nineteenth century and enjoyed great popularity. Their bold, machinelike qualities offered a dynamic expression of the industrial age. During the Industrial Revolution, letterpress printers delighted in using bold slab-serif display fonts to give their messages graphic impact (Fig. **5**). Rectangular serifs, uniform or almost uniform stroke weight, and geometric letterform construction give Egyptian typefaces a bold, abstract quality. Egyptian styles whose abrupt right-angle joinery is tempered by curved bracketing include the Clarendon, Century, and Cheltenham type families.

Serifa was designed Adrian
Frutiger in 1966.

abcdefghi

jklmnopqr

stuvwxyz

$12345678

90(,'"-;:)!?

120 point

ABCDEF
GHIJKL
MNOPQR
STUVWX
YZ&&

120 point

abcdefghijklmnopqrstuvw
xyzABCDEFGHIJKLMNO
PQRSTUVWXYZ$1234567
890(.,'"-;:)!?&

26 point

abcdefghijklmn
opqrstuvwxyz
ABCDEFGHIJK
LMNOPQRSTU
VWXYZ$123456
7890(.,'"-;:)!?&

72 point

abcdefghijklmnopqrstuvw
xyzABCDEFGHIJKLMNO
PQRSTUVWXYZ12345678
90(.,'"-;:)!?&

26 point

abcdefghijklmn
opqrstuvwxyz
ABCDEFGHIJKL
MNOPQRSTUV
WXYZ$12345
67890(.,'"-;:)!?&

abcdefghijklmnopqrstu
vwxyzABCDEFGHIJKL
MNOPQRSTUVWXYZ
$1234567890(.,'''-;:)!?&

26 point

abcdefghijklmn

opqrstuvwxyz

ABCDEFGHIJK

LMNOPQRSTU

VWXYZ$123456

7890(.,'''-;:)!?&

68 point

Serifa Roman

8 point
abcdefghijklmnopqrstuvwxyz
ABCDEFGHIJKLMNOPQRSTUVWXYZ
$1234567890(.,'"-;:)!?&
abcdefghijklmnopqrstuvwxyz
ABCDEFGHIJKLMNOPQRSTUVWXYZ
$1234567890(.,'"-;:)!?&

9 point
abcdefghijklmnopqrstuvwxyz
ABCDEFGHIJKLMNOPQRSTUVWXYZ$
1234567890(.,'"-;:)!?&
abcdefghijklmnopqrstuvwxyz
ABCDEFGHIJKLMNOPQRSTUVWXYZ$
1234567890(.,'"-;:)!?&

10 point
abcdefghijklmnopqrstuvwxyz
ABCDEFGHIJKLMNOPQRSTUVWXYZ
$1234567890(.,'"-;:)!?&
abcdefghijklmnopqrstuvwxyz
ABCDEFGHIJKLMNOPQRSTUVWXYZ
$1234567890(.,'"-;:)!?&

12 point
abcdefghijklmnopqrstuvwxyz
ABCDEFGHIJKLMNOPQRSTUVWXY
Z$1234567890(.,'"-;:)!?&
abcdefghijklmnopqrstuvwxyz
ABCDEFGHIJKLMNOPQRSTUVWXY
Z$1234567890(.,'"-;:)!?&

The whole duty of typography, *as with calligraphy,* is to communicate to the imagination, without loss by the way, the thought or image intended to be communicated by the author. And the whole duty of beautiful typography is not to substitute for the beauty or interest of the thing thought and intended to be conveyed by the symbol, a beauty or interest of its own, but, on the one hand, to win access for that communication by the clearness and beauty of the vehicle, and on the other hand, to take advantage of every pause or stage in that communication to interpose some characteristic & restful beauty in its own art. We thus have a reason for the clearness and beauty of the first and introductory page and of the title, and for the especial beauty of the headings of chapters,

8/10

The whole duty of typography, *as with calligraphy,* is to communicate to the imagination, without loss by the way, the thought or image intended to be communicated by the author. And the whole duty of beautiful typography is not to substitute for the beauty or interest of the thing thought and intended to be conveyed by the symbol, a beauty or interest of its own, but, on the one hand, to win access for that communication by the clearness and beauty of the vehicle, and on the other hand, to take advantage of every pause or stage in that communication to interpose some characteristic & restful beauty in its own art. We thus have a reason for the clearness

8/12

The whole duty of typography, *as with calligraphy,* is to communicate to the imagination, without loss by the way, the thought or image intended to be communicated by the author. And the whole duty of beautiful typography is not to substitute for the beauty or interest of the thing thought and intended to be conveyed by the symbol, a beauty or interest of its own, but, on the one hand, to win access for that communication by the clearness and beauty of the vehicle, and on the other hand, to take advantage of every pause or stage in that communication to interpose some characteristic & restful beauty in its own art. We thus have

9/11

The whole duty of typography, *as with calligraphy,* is to communicate to the imagination, without loss by the way, the thought or image intended to be communicated by the author. And the whole duty of beautiful typography is not to substitute for the beauty or interest of the thing thought and intended to be conveyed by the symbol, a beauty or interest of its own, but, on the one hand, to win access for that communication by the clearness and beauty of the vehicle, and on the other hand, to take advantage of every pause or

9/13

The whole duty of typography, *as with calligraphy,* is to communicate to the imagination, without loss by the way, the thought or image intended to be communicated by the author. And the whole duty of beautiful typography is not to substitute for the beauty or interest of the thing thought and intended to be conveyed by the symbol, a beauty or interest of its own, but, on the one hand, to win access for that communication by the clearness and beauty of the vehicle, and on the other hand, to take advantage of

10/12

The whole duty of typography, *as with calligraphy,* is to communicate to the imagination, without loss by the way, the thought or image intended to be communicated by the author. And the whole duty of beautiful typography is not to substitute for the beauty or interest of the thing thought and intended to be conveyed by the symbol, a beauty or interest of its own, but, on the one hand, to win access for that communication by the clearness and beauty of the

10 /14

The whole duty of typography, *as with calligraphy,* is to communicate to the imagination, without loss by the way, the thought or image intended to be communicated by the author. And the whole duty of beautiful typography is not to substitute for the beauty or interest of the thing thought and intended to be conveyed by the symbol, a

12 /14

The whole duty of typography, *as with calligraphy,* is to communicate to the imagination, without loss by the way, the thought or image intended to be communicated by the author. And the whole duty of beautiful typography is not to substitute for the beauty or interest of the

12 /16

Stymie

abcdefghijklmnopqrstuvwxyz
ABCDEFGHIJKLMNOPQRSTUV
WXYZ$1234567890(.,'"-;:)!?&

Clarendon Regular

abcdefghijklmnopqrstuvwxyz
ABCDEFGHIJKLMNOPQRSTU
VWXYZ$1234567890(.,'"-;:)!?&

Clarendon Bold

abcdefghijklmnopqrstuvwxyz
ABCDEFGHIJKLMNOPQRSTU
VWXYZ$1234567890(.,'"-;:)!?&

ITC Century Book

abcdefghijklmnopqrstuvwxyz
ABCDEFGHIJKLMNOPQRSTUVWX
YZ$1234567890(.,'"-;:)!?&

ITC Century Bold

abcdefghijklmnopqrstuvwxyz
ABCDEFGHIJKLMNOPQRSTUVWX
YZ$1234567890(.,'"-;:)!?&

abcdefghijklmnopqrstuvwxyz
ABCDEFGHIJKLMNOPQRSTUV
WXYZ$1234567890(.,'"-;:)!?&

abcdefghijklmnopqrstuvwxyz
ABCDEFGHIJKLMNOPQRSTUV
WXYZ$1234567890(.,'"-;:)!?&

abcdefghijklmnopqrstuvwxyz
ABCDEFGHIJKLMNOPQRSTUV
WXYZ$1234567890(.,'"-;:)!?&

abcdefghijklmnopqrstuvwxyz
ABCDEFGHIJKLMNOPQRSTUVWXYZ
$1234567890(.,'"-;:)!?&

abcdefghijklmnopqrstuvwxyz
ABCDEFGHIJKLMNOPQRSTUVWXY
Z$1234567890(.,'"-;:)!?&

A.A. Abbreviation for "author's alteration," used to flag a mistake or correction by the author.

ABA form. Design principle of form interrelationships, involving repetition and contrast.

Accents. Small marks over, under, or through a letterform, indicating specific punctuation or changes in stress.

Agate. Vertical unit used to measure space in newspaper columns, originally five-and-one-half point type. Fourteen agate lines equal approximately one inch.

Alert box. A message box that appears on a computer screen with information for the user, for example, a "bomb message" when a computer crashes.

Alignment. Precise arrangement of letterforms upon an imaginary horizontal or vertical line.

Alphabet length. Horizontal measure of the lowercase alphabet in a type font, used to approximate the horizontal measure of type set in that font.

Ampersand. Typographic character (&) representing the word *and.*

Anti-aliasing. The blurring of a jagged line or edge on a screen or output device to give the appearance of a smooth line. Application program. Computer software used to create and modify documents.

Area composition. The organization of typographic and other graphic elements into their final positions by electronic means (keyboard, graphics tablets, and electronic pens, etc.), eliminating the need for hand assembly or pasteup.

Ascender. Stroke on a lowercase letter that rises above the mean-line.

ASCII code. Abbreviation for American Standard Code of Information Interchange. The numbers 0 through 127 represent the alphanumeric characters and functions on the keyboard.

Aspect ratio. The ratio of an image, screen, or other medium's height to its width. Images will become distorted if forced into a different aspect ratio during enlargement, reduction, or transfers.

Autoflow. A page-layout program setting for placing blocks of text from page to page without operator intervention.

Autopaging, Automatic pagination. A capability in computer typesetting for dividing text into pages. Advanced autopaging can add page numbers and running heads, and avoid awkward widows and orphans.

Auto-runaround, Automatic runaround. A page-layout program feature that flows text smoothly around graphics or headlines placed within the normal text area.

Base alignment. A typesetter or printer specification that the baseline for all letters should be horizontal, even in a line of mixed sizes or styles; also called baseline alignment.

Baseline. An imaginary horizontal line upon which the base of each capital letter rests.

Baud rate. The number of bits per second, often used as a measure of data transmission; for example, by a modem.

Bezier curves. A type of curve with nonuniform arcs, as opposed to curves with uniform curvature, which are called arcs. A Bezier curve is defined by specifying control points that set the shape of the curve, and are used to create letter shapes and other computer graphics.

Binary code. Number system using two digits: zero and one.

Bit. Contraction of binary digit, which is the smallest unit of information that a computer can hold. The value of a bit (1 or 0) represents a two-way choice, such as yes or no, on or off, positive or negative.

Bitmap. A computerized image made up of dots. These are "mapped" onto the screen directly from corresponding bits in memory (hence the name). Also referred to as paint format.

Bitmapped font. A font whose letters are composed of dots, such as fonts designed for dot-matrix printers. Compare *outline font* and *screen font.*

Body size. Depth of a piece of metal type, usually measured in points.

Body type. Text material, usually set in sizes from 6 to 12 points. Also called text type.

Boldface. Type with thicker, heavier strokes than the regular font. Indicated as "BF" in type specifications.

Boot. A computer's start-up procedures; coined from "pulling yourself up by your bootstraps."

Bounding box. In drawing or page-description languages, a bounding box is an imaginary box within which an image is located. It represents the rectangular area needed to create the image.

Byte. Unit of computer information. The number of bits used to represent a character. For personal computers, a byte is usually eight bits.

Backslant. Letterforms having a diagonal slant to the left.

C. and l.c. Used in marking copy, to instruct the typesetter to use capitals and lowercase.

C. and s.c. Used in marking copy, to instruct the typesetter to use capitals and small capitals.

Camera ready (or camera-ready copy). Copy and/or artwork that is ready to be photographed to make negatives, which are exposed to printing plates.

Cap height. Height of the capital letters, measured from the baseline to the capline.

Capline. Imaginary horizontal line defined by the height of the capital letters.

Capitals. Letters larger than – and often differing from – the corresponding lowercase letters. Also called uppercase.

Caps. See *Capitals.*

Caption. Title, explanation, or description accompanying an illustration or photograph.

Cascading style sheets. Web-site design software permitting the specification of type characteristics such as type size, letter-, and line-spacing.

Casting off. Determining the length of manuscript copy, enabling a calculation of the area that type will occupy when set in a given size and style of type.

Cathode ray tube (CRT). An electronic tube with a phosphorescent surface that produces a glowing image when activated by an electronic beam.

CD-ROM. An optical data storage device; initials for compact disk read-only memory.

Central processing unit (CPU). Computer component that controls all other parts, performs logical operations, and stores information.

Character. Symbol, sign, or mark in a language system. Character count. The number of characters in a block of text. In typography, spaces are counted but other nonprinting characters usually are not. In data processing, both printing and nonprinting characters are usually counted.

Chase. Heavy metal frame into which metal type is locked for proofing or printing.

Chip. A small piece of silicon impregnated with impurities that form miniaturized computer circuits.

Chooser. Software that tells a computer which output device and connection port to use.

Cicero. European typographic unit of measure, approximately equal to the American pica.

Clipboard. A computer's "holding place," a buffer area in memory for the last material to be cut or copied from a document. Information on the clipboard can be inserted (pasted) into documents.

Cold type. Type that is set by means other than casting molten metal. A term most frequently used to indicate strike-on composition rather than photo or digital typesetting.

Colophon. Inscription, frequently placed at the end of a book, that contains facts about its production.

Column guide. Nonprinting lines that define the location of columns of type.

Command. The generic name for an order or instruction to a computer.

Command character. The combination of a command key plus character(s) used to instruct a computer to take an action.

Comp. See *Comprehensive layout.*

Compensation. In visual organization, the counter-balancing of elements.

Composing stick. Adjustable handheld metal tray, used to hold handset type as it is being composed.

Composition. Alternate term for typesetting.

Compositor. Person who sets type.

Comprehensive layout. An accurate representation of a printed piece showing all type and pictures in their size and position. Comps are used to evaluate a design before producing final type and artwork.

Computer. Electronic device that performs predefined (programmed) high-speed mathematical or logical calculations.

Condensed. Letterforms whose horizontal width has been compressed.

Consonance. In design, harmonious interaction between elements.

Copyfitting. Calculating the area that will be occupied by a given manuscript when set in a specified size and style of type.

Counter. Space enclosed by the strokes of a letterform.

Counterform. "Negative" spatial areas defined and shaped by letterforms, including both interior counters and spaces between characters.

CPS. Characters per inch.

CPU. See *Central processing unit.*

CRT. See *Cathode ray tube.*

CSS. See Cascading style sheets.

Cursive. Type styles that imitate handwriting, often with letters that do not connect.

Cursor. Term for the pointer or insertion point on a computer screen.

Cut and paste. To move material from one location to another within a document, or from one document to another. This is a computer's electronic equivalent to clipping something with scissors, then using glue to paste the clipping in another location.

Cutoff rules. Rules used to separate pages into various units, such as advertisements or news stories.

Daisy wheel. Strike-on printing wheel containing relief characters on spokes, radiating from a central disk. As the wheel spins, a hammer impacts the characters against an inked ribbon.

Data. Information, particularly information upon which a computer program is based.

Data bank. Mass storage of large quantities of information, indexed for rapid retrieval.

Data processing. The storing and handling of information by a computer.

Data transmission. Rapid electronic transfer of coded data via telephone or other communication links.

Dazzle. Visual effect caused by extreme contrast in the strokes of letterforms.

Default. A value, action, or setting that a computer system assumes, unless the user gives an explicit instruction to the contrary; for example, a certain point size and typeface style will be used by a page-layout program unless the user selects another size and font.

Descender. Stroke on a lowercase letterform that falls below the baseline.

Desktop. Refers to the desktop metaphor depicted on the computer screen, with a menu bar across the top, icons for applications and disk drives, and other icons, such as a trash can used to throw away unwanted material.

Desktop publishing. The popular use of this term is incorrect, because publishing encompasses writing, editing, designing, printing, and distribution activities, not just makeup and production. See *Electronic page design.*

Dialog box. A box displayed on a computer screen requesting information or a decision by the user.

Digital type. Type stored electronically as digital dot or stroke patterns rather than as photographic images.

Digitizer. A computer peripheral device that converts images or sound into a digital signal.

Directory. The contents of a computer disk or folder. Directory contents can be arranged and displayed on a screen by name, icon, date created, size, or kind, etc.

Digital computer. A device that translates data into a discrete number system to facilitate electronic processing.

Disk. Thin, flat, circular plate with a magnetic surface upon which data may be stored. See *Floppy disk* and *Hard disk.* Also, a circular grid containing the master font in some typesetting systems.

Display Postscript. A technology by Adobe Systems that allows PostScript commands (for special graphic effects) to be displayed on the screen.

Display type. Type sizes 14 points and above, used primarily for headlines and titles.

Dissonance. In design, visual tension and contrast between typographic elements.

Dithering. A technique for alternating the value of adjacent dots or pixels to create the effect of an intermediate value.

When printing color images or displaying color on a computer screen, dithering refers to the technique of making different colors for adjacent dots or pixels to give the illusion of a third color; for example, a printed field of alternating cyan and yellow dots appears to be green. Dithering gives the effect of shades of gray on a black-and-white display or the effect of more colors on a color display.

Dot-matrix printer. A printer that forms characters out of a pattern of dots; many have pins that strike against an inked ribbon to transfer the pattern of dots making up each character onto paper.

Dots per inch (dpi). A measure of the resolution of a screen image or printed page. Dots are also known as pixels. Some computer screens display 72 dpi; many laser printers print 300 dpi; and imagesetters often print 1270 or 2540 dpi.

Downloadable font. A font can be downloaded into a printer or computerized typesetter, which means that tables telling how to construct the type characters are sent from the computer to the output device. By accepting additional character sets – downloadable fonts – an output device can print many typefaces. To be able to accept downloadable fonts, a printer or typesetter must have sufficient computer memory and processing power to receive and store the images.

Downloading. Transferring information from one computer and storing it on another one.

DRAM. Abbreviation for dynamic random access memory chip; *dynamic* refers to loss of data in memory when a computer is shut off.

Draw program. Computer applications for drawing graphics that are object-oriented; that is, it produces graphics from arc and line segments that are mathematically defined by points located on the horizontal and vertical axes on the screen. Compare *Paint program*.

Drop initial. Display letterform set into the text.

E.A. Abbreviation for "editor's alteration," used to flag errors or corrections made by the editor.

Editing terminal. Workstation consisting of a keyboard and visual display device, used to input and edit copy prior to typesetting.

Egyptian. Typefaces characterized by slablike serifs similar in weight to the main strokes.

Electronic page design. The layout and typesetting of complete pages using a computer with input and output devices.

Elite. Size of typewriter type approximately equal to 10-point typography.

Ellipses. Three dots used to indicate an omission in quoted material.

Em. The square of the body size of any type, used as a unit of measure. In some expanded or condensed faces, the em is also expanded or condensed from the square proportion.

Em dash. A dash one em long. Also called a long dash.

Em leader. Horizontal dots or dashes with one em between their centers.

Em space. A space equal to the width of an em quad.

En. One-half of an em (see *Em*).

En dash. A dash one en long. Also called a short dash.

En leader. Horizontal dots or dashes with one en between their centers.

En space. Space equal to the width of an en quad.

Encapsulated PostScript (ESP). A computer format for encoding pictures. These can be stored, edited, transferred, and output in the form of structured PostScript code.

EPS. See *Encapsulated PostScript*.

Exception dictionary. See *Hyphenation*.

Expanded. Letterforms whose horizontal width has been extended.

Export. To send text, graphics, or layouts created in one program from the computer memory in a form suitable for use with other programs.

Face. The part of metal type that is inked for printing. Also another word for *typeface*.

Family. See *Type family*.

FAX machine. An electronic device that scans documents and transmits them over telephone lines. Documents are received and output by another FAX machine.

Film font. A photographic film master used in some typesetting machines. Characters from a film font are exposed through lenses of different sizes onto paper or film. Unlike digital typesetting, typesetting systems using film fonts cannot set an entire page complete with graphics.

Finder. A computer program that generates the desktop and is used to access and manage files and disks. See *Multifinder*.

Firmware. Software that has been written into nonchangeable memory that does not need to be loaded into the system for each use. Most printers and output devices store their software in this form.

Fit. Refers to the spatial relationships between letters after they are set into words and lines.

Floppy disks. Portable, flexible disks housed in a 3.5-inch hard plastic case and inserted into a disk drive, which reads the information on the disk.

Flush left (or right). The even vertical alignment of lines of type at the left (or right) edge of a column.

Folio. Page number.

Font. A complete set of characters in one design, size, and style. In traditional metal type, a font meant a particular size and style; in digital typography a font can output multiple sizes and even altered styles of a typeface design.

Font/DA Mover. An application that allows a user to add and/or remove fonts and desk accessories from a file on a disk.

Font substitution. During output of a page, font substitution is the replacement of a requested but unavailable font by another (usually similar) available font.

Footer. An identifying line, such as a page number and/or a chapter title, appearing in the bottom margin of a document. Footers repeated throughout a document are called running footers or running feet.

Footprint. The amount of space a machine such as a computer takes up on a surface such as a desktop.

Format. The overall typographic and spatial schema established for a publication or any other application.

Formatting. In digital typesetting and phototypesetting, the process of issuing specific commands that establish the typographic format.

Foundry type. Metal type used in hand composition.

Furniture. Rectangular pieces of wood, metal, or plastic used to fill in excess space when locking up a form for letterpress printing.

Galley. A three-sided, shallow metal tray used to hold metal type forms before printing.

Galley proof. Originally, a type proof pulled from metal type assembled in a galley. Frequently used today to indicate any first proof, regardless of the type system.

GIF. See *Graphic Interface Format*.

Gigabyte (GB). A unit of data storage equal to 1,000 megabytes.

"Golf" ball. An interchangeable metal ball approximately one inch in diameter with raised characters on its surface, used as the printing element in some typewriters.

Graphic Interface Format (GIF). A graphic image format widely used in Web sites.

Greeking. Type set using random or Greek characters to simulate typeset text in a layout or comp.

Grayscale. An arbitrary scale of monochrome (black to white) intensity ranging from black and white, with a fixed number of intermediate shades of gray.

Grid. Underlying structure composed of a linear framework used by designers to organize typographic and pictorial elements. Also, a film or glass master font, containing characters in a predetermined configuration and used in phototypesetting.

Grotesque. Name for sans-serif typefaces.

Gutter. The interval separating two facing pages in a publication.

Gutter margin. Inner margin of a page in a publication.

Hairline. Thinnest strokes on a typeface having strokes of varying weight.

Hand composition. Method of setting type by placing individual pieces of metal type from a type case into a composing stick.

Hanging indent. In composition, a column format in which the first line of type is set to a full measure while all additional lines are indented.

Hanging punctuation. Punctuation set outside the column measure to achieve an optical alignment.

Hard copy. Computer output printed on paper.

Hard disks. Large rigid disks having large storage capacity, fast operating speed, and permanent installation within the computer or a separate case.

Hardware. The physical equipment of a computer system, such as the CPU, input/output devices, and peripherals.

Header. An identifying line at the top margin of a document. A header can appear on every page and can include text, pictures, page numbers, the date, and the time. Headers repeated throughout a document are called running headers or running heads.

Heading. Copy that is given emphasis over the body of text, through changes in size, weight, or spatial interval.

Headline. The most significant type in the visual hierarchy of a printed communication.

Hertz. One cycle per second. See *Megahertz.*

Hot type. Type produced by casting molten metal.

HTML. See *Hypertext markup language.*

Hypertext. Text on a computer screen that contains pointers enabling the user to jump to other text or pages by clicking a computer mouse on highlighted material.

Hypertext markup language. The basic computer-programming language used to design Web sites.

Hyphenation. The syllabic division of words used when they must be broken at the end of a line. In electronic typesetting, hyphenation can be determined by the operator or automatically by the computer.

I-beam pointer. The shape the pointer or cursor on a computer screen usually takes when working with text.

Icon. A pictorial representation. The elemental pictures on a computer screen used to represent disk drives, files, applications, and tools, etc., are called icons.

Import. To transfer text, graphics, or layouts into a program in a form suitable for its use.

Imposition. The arrangement of pages in a printed signature to achieve the proper sequencing after the sheets are folded and trimmed.

Incunabula. European books printed during the first half-century of typography, from Gutenberg's invention of movable type until the year 1500.

Indent. An interval of space at the beginning of a line to indicate a new paragraph.

Inferior characters. Small characters, usually slightly smaller than the x-height, positioned on or below the baseline and used for footnotes or fractions.

Initial. A large letter used at the beginning of a column; for example, at the beginning of a chapter.

Initialize. Electronically formatting a disk to prepare it to record data from a computer.

Input. Raw data, text, or commands entered into a computer memory from a peripheral device, such as a keyboard.

Insertion point. The location in a document where the next text or graphics will be placed, represented by a blinking vertical cursor. A user selects the insertion point by clicking where he or she wishes to work.

Interletter spacing. The spatial interval between letters, also called *letterspacing.*

Interline spacing. The spatial interval between lines, also called *leading.*

Interword spacing. The spatial interval between words, also called *wordspacing.*

Italic. Letterforms having a pronounced diagonal slant to the right.

Jaggies. The jagged "staircase" edges formed on raster-scan displays when displaying diagonal and curved lines. See *Anti-aliasing.*

JPEG. An acronym for Joint Photographic Experts Group. JPEG is a bitmap format used to transmit graphic images.

Justified setting. A column of type with even vertical edges on both the left and the right, achieved by adjusting interword spacing. Also called *flush left, flush right.*

Justified text. Copy in which all lines of a text – regardless of the words they contain – have been made exactly the same length, so that they align vertically at both the left and right margins.

K. Computer term for one thousand twenty-four bytes of memory.

Kerning. In typesetting, *kerning* refers to the process of subtracting space between specific pairs of characters so that the overall letterspacing appears to be even. Compare *Tracking.*

Keyboard. A device having keys or buttons used to enter data into typesetting and computer systems.

Laser. A concentrated light source that can be optically manipulated. Coined from "Light Amplification by Stimulated Emission of Radiation."

Laser printer. A computer printer that creates the image by drawing it on a metal drum with a laser. The latent image becomes visible after dry ink particles are electrostatically attracted to it.

Latin. Type style characterized by triangular, pointed serifs.

Leader. Typographic dots or periods that are repeated to connect other elements.

Lead-in. Introductory copy set in a contrasting typeface.

Leading. (Pronounced "LED-ing".) In early typesetting, strips of lead were placed between lines of type to increase the interline spacing, hence the term. See *Linespacing, Interline spacing.*

Letterpress. The process of printing from a raised inked surface.

Letterspacing. See *Interletter spacing.*

Ligature. A typographic character produced by combining two or more letters.

Line breaks. The relationships of line endings in a ragged-right or ragged-left setting. Rhythmic line breaks are achieved by adjusting the length of individual lines of type.

Line length. The measure of the length of a line of type, usually expressed in picas.

Linespacing. The vertical distance between two lines of type measured from baseline to baseline. For example, "10/12" indicates 10-point type with 12 points base-to-base (that is, with 2 points of leading). See *Leading, Interline spacing.*

Lining figures. Numerals identical in size to the capitals and aligned on the baseline: 1 2 3 4 5 6 7 8 9 10.

Linotype. A machine that casts an entire line of raised type on a single metal slug.

Local area network (LAN). A network of computers and peripherals, usually in the same office or building, connected by dedicated electrical cables rather than telephone lines.

Logotype. Two or more type characters that are combined as a sign or trademark.

Lowercase. The alphabet set of small letters, as opposed to capitals.

LPM. Lines per minute, a unit of measure expressing the speed of a typesetting system.

Ludlow. A typecasting machine that produces individual letters from hand-assembled matrices.

Machine composition. General term for the mechanical casting of metal type.

Majuscules. A term in calligraphy for letterforms analogous to uppercase letterforms, usually drawn between two parallel lines, the capline and the baseline. See *Minuscules.*

Makeup. The assembly of typographic matter into a page, or a sequence of pages, ready for printing.

Margin. The unprinted space surrounding type matter on a page.

Markup. The marking of typesetting specifications upon manuscript copy.

Marquee. A rectangular area, often surrounded by blinking dashed or dotted lines, used to select objects or regions in a application program.

Master page. In a page-layout program, a master page is a template providing standard columns, margins, and typographic elements that appear on a publication's individual pages.

Masthead. The visual identification of a magazine or newspaper, usually a logotype. Also a section placed near the front of a newspaper or periodical containing information such as names and titles of publishers and staff, along with addresses.

Matrix. In typesetting, the master image from which type is produced. The matrix is a brass mold in linecasting and a glass plate bearing the font negative in phototypesetting.

Meanline. An imaginary line marking the tops of lowercase letters, not including the ascenders.

Measure. See *Line length.*

Mechanical. A camera-ready pasteup of artwork including type, images showing position of color and halftone matter, line art, etc., all on one piece of artboard.

Megabyte (MB). A unit of measurement equal to 1024 kilobytes or 1,048,576 bytes.

Megahertz (MHz). A million cycles per second. Describes the speed of computer chips; used to measure of how rapidly a computer processes information.

Menu. A list of choices in a computer application, from which the user selects a desired action. In a computer's desktop interface, menus appear when you point to and click on menu titles in the menu bar. Dragging through a menu and releasing the mouse button while a command is highlighted chooses that command.

Menu bar. A horizontal band across the top of a computer screen that contains menu titles.

Message box. A box that appears on a computer screen to give the user information.

Microprocessor. A single silicon chip containing thousands of electronic components for processing information; the "brains" of a personal computer.

Minuscules. A term in calligraphy for letterforms analogous to lowercase letters and usually drawn between four parallel lines determining ascender height, x-height, baseline, and descender depth. See *Majuscules.*

Minus spacing. A reduction of interline spacing, resulting in a baseline-to-baseline measurement that is smaller than the point size of the type.

Mixing. The alignment of more than one type style or typeface on a single baseline.

Modem. Contraction of modulator/demodulator; a peripheral device to send data over telephone lines from a computer to other computers, service bureaus, and information services, etc.

Modern. Term used to describe typefaces designed at the end of the eighteenth century. Characteristics include vertical stress, hairline serifs, and pronounced contrasts between thick and thin strokes.

Monocase alphabet. A language alphabet, such as Hebrew and Indic scripts, having only capital-height letters and no lowercase letterforms.

Monochrome. Refers to material or a display consisting of a single color, typically black or white.

Monogram. Two or more letterforms interwoven, combined, or connected into a single glyph, typically used as abbreviations or initials.

Monoline. Used to describe a typeface or letterform with a uniform stroke thickness.

Monospacing. Spacing in a font with characters that all have the same set width or horizontal measure; often found in typewriter and screen fonts. See *Proportional spacing.*

Monotype. A trade name for a keyboard-operated typesetting machine that casts individual letters from matrices.

Mouse. A small computer device that controls an on-screen pointer or tool when the mouse is moved around on a flat surface by hand. The mouse-controlled pointer can select operations, move data, and draw images.

Multifinder. A computer program permitting several applications to be open at the same time, so that a designer can work back and forth between page-layout and drawing programs, for example, without having to repeatedly open and close programs.

Navigation. The act of manually moving a cursor through an on-screen page or series of pages.

Negative. The reversal of a positive photographic image.

Network. A system connecting multiple computers so they can share printers and information, etc.

Object-oriented. A method in drawing and other computer programs that produces graphics from arc and line segments that are mathematically defined by points located on the horizontal and vertical axes on the screen.

Oblique. A slanted roman character. Unlike many italics, oblique characters do not have cursive design properties.

Offset lithography. A printing method using flat photo-mechanical plates, in which the inked image is transferred or offset from the printing plate onto a rubber blanket, then onto the paper.

Old Style. Typeface styles derived from fifteenth- to eighteenth-century designs, and characterized by moderate thick-and-thin contrasts, bracketed serifs, and a handwriting influence.

Old Style figures. Numerals that exhibit a variation in size, including characters aligning with the lowercase x-height, and others with ascenders or descenders: 1 2 3 4 5 6 7 8 9 10.

Operating system. A computer program that controls a computer's operation, directing information to and from different components.

Optical adjustment. The precise visual alignment and spacing of typographic elements. In interletter spacing, the adjustment of individual characters to achieve consistent spacing.

Orphan. A single word on a line, left over at the end of a paragraph, sometimes appearing at the top of a column of text. See *Widow.*

Outline font. A font designed, not as a bitmap, but as outlines of the letter shapes that can be scaled to any size. Laser printers and imagesetters use outline fonts. See *Bitmapped font* and *Screen font.*

Outline type. Letterforms described by a contour line that encloses the entire character on all sides. The interior usually remains open.

Output. The product of a computer operation. In computerized typesetting, output is reproduction proofs of composition.

Page preview. A mode on many word-processing and page-layout programs that shows a full-page view of what the page will look like when printed, including added elements such as headers, footers, and margins.

Pagination. The sequential numbering of pages.

Paint program. A computer application that creates images as a series of bitmapped dots, which can be erased and manipulated by turning the pixels on and off. Compare *Draw program.*

Pantone Matching System (PMS). The trademarked name of a system for specifying colors and inks that is a standard in the printing industry.

Paragraph mark. Typographic elements that signal the beginning of a paragraph. For example, ¶.

Parallel construction. In typography, the use of similar typographic elements or arrangements to create a visual unity or to convey a relationship in content.

Paste. To place a copy of saved material into a computer-generated document or layout.

P.E. Abbreviation for "Printer's Error," used to flag a mistake made by the compositor rather than by the author.

Pen plotter. A printer that draws using ink-filled pens that are moved along a bar, which also moves back and forth. Many plotters have very high resolutions but have slow operation, poor text quality, and poor handling of raster images.

Peripheral. An electronic device that connects to a computer, such as a disk drive, scanner, or printer.

Photocomposition. The process of setting type by projecting light onto light-sensitive film or paper.

Photodisplay typesetting. The process of setting headline type on film or paper by photographic means.

Phototype. Type matter set on film or paper by photographic projection of type characters.

Photounit. Output component of a photocomposition system, which sets the type and exposes it to light-sensitive film or paper.

Pica. Typographic unit of measurement: 12 points equal 1 pica. 6 picas equal approximately one inch. Line lengths and column widths are measured in picas.

PICT. A computer format for encoding pictures. PICT data can be created, displayed on the screen, and printed, thus applications without graphics-processing routines can incorporate PICT data generated by other software.

Pixel. Stands for picture element; the smallest dot that can be displayed on a screen.

Point. A measure of size used principally in typesetting. One point is equal to 1/12 of a pica, or approximately 1/72 of an inch. It is most often used to indicated the size of type or amount of leading added between lines.

Pointer. A graphic form that moves on a computer screen and is controlled by a pointing device; usually a symbolic icon such as an arrow, I-beam, or clock.

Pointing device. A computer input device, such as a mouse, tablet, or joystick, used to indicate where an on-screen pointer or tool should be placed or moved.

Port. An electrical socket where cables are inserted to connect computers, peripheral devices, or networks. Ports are named for the type of signal they carry, such as printer port, serial port, or SCSI port.

PostScript.™ A page-description programming language created by Adobe Systems that handles text and graphics, placing them on the page with mathematical precision.

Preview. To view the final output on a computer screen before printing. Because most screens have lower resolution than an imagesetter or laser printer, fine details are often different from the final output.

Processor. In a computer system, the general term for any device capable of carrying out operations upon data. In phototypography, the unit that automatically develops the light-sensitive paper or film.

Program. A sequence of instructions that directs the operations of a computer to execute a given task.

Proof. Traditionally, an impression from metal type for examination and correction; now applies to initial output for examination and correction before final output.

Proportional spacing. Spacing in a font adjusted to give wide letters (M) a larger set width than narrow letters (I).

Quad. In metal type, pieces of type metal shorter than type-high, which are used as spacing matter to separate elements and fill out lines.

Quoins. Wedges use to lock up metal type in the chase. These devices are tightened and loosened by a quoin key.

Ragged. See *Unjustified type.*

RAM. Abbreviation for *random access memory,* the area of a computer's memory that temporarily stores applications and documents while they are being used.

RAM cache. An area of the computer's memory set aside to hold information from a disk until its needed again. It can be accessed much more quickly from a RAM cache than from a disk.

Raster display. A raster image is divided into scan lines, each consisting of a series of dots from a thin section of the final image. This dot pattern corresponds exactly to a bit pattern in the computer memory.

Raster image file format (RIFF). A file format for paint-style color graphics, developed by Letraset USA.

Raster image processor (RIP). A device or program that translates an image or page into the actual pattern of dots received by a printing or display system.

Raster scan. The generation of an image upon a cathode ray tube made by refreshing the display area line by line.

Recto. In publication design, the right-hand page. Page one (and all odd-numbered pages) always appears on a recto. The left-hand page is called the verso.

Resolution. The degree of detail and clarity of a display; usually specified in dots per inch (dpi). The higher the resolution, or the greater the number of dpi, the sharper the image.

Reverse. Type or image that is dropped out of a printed area, revealing the paper surface.

Reverse leading. A reduction in the amount of interline space, making it less than normal for the point size. For example, 12-point type set on an 11- point body size becomes reverse leading of 1 point.

Revival. A little-used historic typeface previously unavailable in current font formats, now released for contemporary technology.

RIFF. See *Raster Image File Format.*

River. In text type, a series of interword spaces that accidentally align vertically or diagonally, creating an objectionable flow of white space within the column.

ROM. Abbreviation for *read only memory,* which is permanently installed on a computer chip and can be read but cannot accept new or changed data; for example, some laser printers have basic fonts permanently installed in a ROM chip.

Roman. Upright letterforms, as distinguished from italics. More specifically, letters in an alphabet style based on the upright serifed letterforms of Roman inscriptions.

Rule. In handset metal type, a strip of metal that prints as a line. Generally, any line used as an element in typographic design, whether handset, photographic, digital, or hand-drawn.

Run-around. Type that is set with a shortened line measure to fit around a photograph, drawing, or other visual element inserted into the running text.

Run in. To set type without a paragraph indentation or other break. Also, to insert additional matter into the running text as part of an existing paragraph.

Running foot or running footer. A line of text that duplicates a line of text from another page but positioned at or near the bottom of a page.

Running head. Type at the head of sequential pages, providing a title or publication name.

Sans serif. Typefaces without serifs.

Saving. Transferring information – such as an electronic page design – from a computer's memory to a storage device.

Scanner. A computer peripheral device that scans pictures and converts them to digital form so they can be stored, manipulated, and output.

Scrapbook. A computer's "holding place" for permanent storage of images, text, etc.

Screen font. A bitmapped version of an outline font that is used to represent the outline font on a computer screen.

Script. Typefaces based on handwriting, usually having connecting strokes between the letters.

Scroll bar. A rectangular bar that may appear along the right or bottom of a window on a computer screen. By clicking or dragging on the scroll bar, the user can move through the document.

Scrolling. In typesetting and computer-assisted design, moving through a document to bring onto the screen portions of the document not currently displayed.

SCSI. Abbreviation for Small Computer System Interface; pronounced "scuzzy." SCSI is a computer-industry standard interface allowing very fast transfer of data.

Semantics. The science of meaning in linguistics; the study of the relationships between signs and symbols, and what they represent.

Serifs. Small elements added to the ends of the main strokes of a letterform in serifed type styles.

Set width. In metal type, the width of the body upon which a letter is cast. In phototype and digital type, the horizontal width of a letterform measured in units, including the normal space

before and after the character. This interletter space can be increased or decreased to control the tightness or looseness of the fit.

Shoulder. In metal type, the flat top of the type body that surrounds the raised printing surface of the letterform.

Sidebar. A narrow column of text, separated from the main text by a box or rule and containing a secondary article.

Side head. A title or other heading material placed to the side of a type column.

Slab serifs. Square or rectangular serifs that align horizontally and vertically to the baseline and are usually the same (or heavier) weight as the main strokes of the letterform.

Slug. A line of metal type cast on a linecasting machine, such as the Linotype. Also, strips of metal spacing material in thicknesses of 6 points or more.

Small capitals. A set of capital letters having the same height as the lowercase x-height, frequently used for cross reference and abbreviations. Also called small caps and abbreviated "s.c."

Smoothing. The electronic process of eliminating jaggies (the uneven staircase effect on diagonal or curved lines).

Software. Components of a computer system consisting of the programs or instructions that control the behavior of the computer hardware.

Solid. Lines of type that are set without additional interline space. Also called *set solid.*

Sorts. In metal type, material that is not part of a regular font, such as symbols, piece fractions, and spaces. Also, individual characters used to replace worn-out type in a font.

Stand-alone typesetting system. A typesetting system that is completely self-contained, including editing terminal, memory, and character generation.

Startup disk. The computer disk drive containing the system software used to operate the computer.

Stet. A proofreader's mark meaning that copy marked for correction should not be changed; rather, any instructions for changes should be ignored and the text should be left as originally set.

Storage. In computer typesetting, a device (such as a disk, drum, or tape) that can receive information and retain it for future use.

Straight matter. Text material set in continuous columns with limited deviation from the basic typographic specifications.

Stress. The gradual variation in the thickness of a curved character part or stroke; often used for any variation in the thickness of a character part or stroke.

Style sheets. In several word-processing and page-layout programs, style sheets are special files containing formatting instructions for creating standardized documents.

Subscript. A small character beneath (or adjacent to and slightly below) another character.

Superscript. A small character above (or adjacent to and slightly above) another character.

Swash letters. Letters ornamented with flourishes or flowing tails.

Syntax. In grammar, the way in which words or phrases are put together to form sentences. In design, the connecting or ordering of typographic elements into a visual unity.

System. A related group of interdependent design elements forming a whole. In computer science, a complete computing operation including software and hardware (Central Processing Unit, memory, input/output devices, and peripherals or devices required for the intended functions).

System software. Computer files containing the operating system program and its supporting programs needed to make the computer work, interface with peripherals, and run applications.

Tag Image File Format (TIFF). A computer format for encoding pictures as high-resolution bitmapped images, such as those created by scanners.

Telecommunications. Sending messages to distant locations; usually refers to communicating by telephone lines.

Terminal. See *Video display terminal.*

Text. The main body of written or printed material, as opposed to display matter, footnotes, appendices, etc.

Text type. See *Body type.*

Thumbnail. A miniature image of a page, either a small planning sketch made by a designer or a reduction in a page-layout program.

TIFF. See *Tag Image File Format.*

Tracking. The overall tightness or looseness of the spacing between all characters in a line or block of text. Sometimes used interchangeably with *kerning,* which more precisely is the reduction in spacing between a specific pair of letters.

Transitional. Classification of type styles combining aspects of both Old Style and Modern typefaces; for example, Baskerville.

Type family. The complete range of variations of a typeface design, including roman, italic, bold, expanded, condensed, and other versions.

Typeface. The design of alphabetical and numerical characters unified by consistent visual properties.

Type-high. The standard foot-to-face height of metal types; 0.9186 inches in English-speaking countries.

Typescript. Typewritten manuscript material used as copy for typesetting.

Typesetting. The composing of type by any method or process, also called *composition.*

Type specimen. A typeset sample produced to show the visual properties of a typeface.

Typo. See *Typographical error.*

Typographer. A firm specializing in typesetting. Sometimes used to denote a compositor or typesetter.

Typographical error. A mistake in typesetting, typing, or writing.

Typography. Originally the composition of printed matter from movable type. Now the art and process of typesetting by any system or method.

U. and l.c. Abbreviation for *uppercase and lowercase,* used to specify typesetting that combines capitals with lowercase letters.

Undo. A standard computer command that "undoes," or reverses, the last command or operation executed.

Uniform Resource Locator (URL). A location pointer name used to identify the location of a file on a server connected to the World Wide Web.

Unit. A subdivision of the em, used in measuring and counting characters in photo- and digital typesetting systems.

Unitization. The process of designing a typeface so that the individual character widths conform to a typesetter's unit system.

Unitized font. A font with character widths conforming to a typesetter's unit system.

Unit system. A counting system first developed for Monotype, used by most typesetting machines. The width of characters and spaces are measured in units. This data is used to control line breaks, justification, and interword and interletter spacing.

Unit value. The established width, in units, of a typographic character.

Unjustified type. Lines of type set with equal interword spacing, resulting in irregular line lengths. Also called *ragged.*

Uploading. Sending information from your computer to a distant computer. See *Downloading.*

Uppercase. See *Capitals.*

URL. See *Uniform Resource Locator.*

User interface. The way a computer system communicates with its user; the "look and feel" of the machine as experienced by the user.

Vector-based software. Software using computer instructions that specify shapes by defining linear elements by specifying starting and ending locations.

Verso. In publication design, the left-hand page. Page two (and all even-numbered pages) always appear on a verso. The right-hand page is called the recto.

Virus. A computer program that invades computers and modifies data, usually in a destructive manner.

Visual display terminal. A computer input/output device utilizing a cathode ray tube to display data on a screen. Information from memory, storage, or a keyboard can be displayed.

Web browser. A utility viewer used to display documents on the World Wide Web, which are usually written in HTML.

Web page. A document written in HTML, typically stored on a Web site and accessible through a Web browser.

Web site. A collection of files on a Web server computer system that are accessible to a Web browser or by Web TV.

Weight. The lightness or heaviness of a typeface, which is determined by ratio of the stroke thickness to character height.

White space. The "negative" area surrounding a letterform. See *Counter* and *Counterform.*

White-space reduction. A decrease in the amount of interletter space, achieved in typesetting by reducing the unit value of typeset characters. See *tracking.*

Widow. A very short line that appears at the end of a paragraph, column, or page, or at the top of a column or page. These awkward typographic configurations should be corrected editorially.

Width tables. Collections of information about how much horizontal room each character in a font should occupy, often accompanied by information about special kerning pairs or other exceptions.

Windows. An area of a computer screen in which a single document is displayed.

Woodtype. Hand-set types cut from wood by a mechanical router. Formerly used for large display sizes that were not practical for metal casting, woodtype has been virtually eliminated by display photographic typesetting.

Word. In computer systems, a logical unit of information, composed of a predetermined number of bits.

Word-processing program. A computer application used to type in text, then edit, correct, move, or remove it.

Wordspacing. The spatial interval between words. In setting justified body type, space is added between words to extend each line to achieve flush left and right edges. See *Interword spacing.*

World Wide Web. A global graphic media system used to exchange data between computer users.

WORM. Acronym for "Write Once Read Many," usually applied to storage media such as CD-ROMs, which can only be written once but read many times.

WYSIWYG. Abbreviation for "what you see is what you get;" pronounced Wizzywig. This means the image on the screen is identical to the image that will be produced as final output.

x-height. The height of lowercase letters in a font, excluding characters with ascenders and descenders. This is most easily measured on the lowercase *x.*

Copyfitting

Copyfitting is the process of converting a typewritten manuscript into text type that will accurately fit a typographic layout. Copyfitting often occurs at a computer workstation; however, designers are sometimes asked to copyfit manuscripts using these traditional procedures. Throughout this process, a designer should carefully consider legibility factors, visual characteristics, and spatial requirements. Understanding copyfitting enables the designer to control the details of typesetting, which can contribute to a typographic design of clarity and distinction. A suggested method for proper copyfitting follows.

1. Count all the characters in the typewritten manuscript.
The manuscript should be as clean and orderly as possible to increase accuracy while keeping costs to a minimum. Copy should be double-spaced in a single column. Although the size of manuscript type varies with different output devices, traditionally there are two sizes: elite, with twelve characters to an inch; and pica, with ten characters to an inch. To begin, determine the number of characters in an average line length of the author's manuscript by counting the number of characters in four typical lines (including all spaces and punctuation), adding the number of characters in these lines, and dividing this total by four. Then multiply this average by the number of lines in the whole manuscript to get the total number of characters.

When manuscript copy is provided on a computer disk, use the word-count feature of a word processor software program to determine the number of characters.

2. Fit the copy to the layout.
After choosing a specific typeface and size, refer to the layout and measure the line length in picas. Determine how many characters of the chosen typeface will fit on a line. This can easily be determined by referring to a characters-per-pica or characters-per-line table (Appendix B), often found in specimen books or provided by typographers. If a characters-per-pica figure is given, multiply the number of characters per pica by the number of picas in a line. if a characters-per-line table is

provided, simply find the line length that indicates the number of characters in the average typeset line. Divide the number of characters per line into the total number of characters in the typewritten manuscript to determine the total number of typeset lines. Compare the vertical column depth of this number of typeset lines to the vertical column depth on the layout. (Remember to consider the effect of paragraph indication, particularly if you are using additional interline space between paragraphs.) Will the depth of the typeset lines correspond to the depth of the area allowed on the layout? If the type-setting will run too long, or if it will be too short to fill the space, adjustments can be made. These adjustments might include changing the type size, interline spacing, or typeface.

3. Mark the manuscript.
After fitting the copy to the layout, it is important to clearly mark specifications for the typographer on the manuscript. Specifications should always include: type size and interline spacing (leading) in points; complete name of the typeface, including weight and width (Garamond Bold Condensed); line length in picas; line alignment (justified, flush left/ragged right, or centered); paragraph indication (indent one pica, or one line space between paragraphs); variations and special instructions (italics, underlining, changes in size, weight, or typeface).

Character count table for text type specimens

	1	10	12	14	16	18	20	22	24	26	28	30
8 point Baskerville	3.38	34	41	47	54	61	68	74	81	88	95	101
9 point Baskerville	2.97	30	36	42	48	53	59	65	71	77	83	89
10 point Baskerville	2.69	27	32	38	43	48	54	59	65	70	75	81
12 point Baskerville	2.24	22	27	31	36	40	45	49	54	58	63	67
8 point Bembo	3.39	34	41	47	54	61	68	74	81	88	95	101
9 point Bembo	3.03	30	36	42	48	55	61	67	72	79	85	91
10 point Bembo	2.71	27	33	38	43	49	54	60	65	70	76	81
12 point Bembo	2.26	23	27	32	36	41	45	50	54	59	63	68
8 point Bodoni	3.15	32	38	44	50	57	63	69	76	82	88	95
9 point Bodoni	2.76	28	33	39	44	50	55	61	66	72	77	83
10 point Bodoni	2.49	25	30	35	40	45	50	55	60	65	70	75
12 point Bodoni	2.08	21	25	29	33	37	42	46	50	54	58	62
8 point Caslon	3.43	34	41	48	55	62	69	75	82	89	96	103
9 point Caslon	3.00	30	36	42	48	54	60	66	72	78	84	90
10 point Caslon	2.67	27	32	37	43	48	53	59	64	69	75	80
12 point Caslon	2.29	23	27	32	37	41	46	50	55	60	64	69
8 point DIN	3.06	31	37	43	49	55	61	67	73	80	86	92
9 point DIN	2.76	28	33	39	44	50	55	61	66	72	77	83
10 point DIN	2.47	25	30	35	40	44	49	54	59	64	69	74
12 point DIN	2.08	21	25	29	33	37	42	46	50	54	58	62
8 point Futura	3.25	33	39	46	52	59	65	72	78	85	91	98
9 point Futura	2.89	29	35	40	46	52	58	64	69	75	81	87
10 point Futura	2.60	26	31	36	42	47	52	57	62	68	73	78
12 point Futura	2.17	22	26	30	35	39	43	48	52	56	61	65
8 point Galliard	3.15	32	38	44	50	57	63	69	76	82	88	95
9 point Galliard	2.81	28	34	39	45	51	56	62	67	73	79	84
10 point Galliard	2.36	24	28	33	38	42	47	52	57	61	66	71
12 point Galliard	2.00	20	24	28	32	36	40	44	48	52	56	60
8 point Garamond	3.90	39	47	55	62	70	78	86	94	101	109	117
9 point Garamond	3.38	34	41	47	54	61	68	74	81	88	95	101
10 point Garamond	2.78	28	33	39	44	50	56	61	67	72	78	83
12 point Garamond	2.29	23	27	32	37	41	46	50	55	60	64	69
8 point Helvetica	3.06	31	37	43	49	55	61	67	73	80	86	92
9 point Helvetica	2.69	27	32	38	43	48	54	59	65	70	75	81
10 point Helvetica	2.42	24	29	34	39	44	48	53	58	63	68	73
12 point Helvetica	2.03	20	24	28	37	37	41	45	49	53	57	61
8 point Meta	3.25	33	39	46	52	59	65	72	78	85	91	98
9 point Meta	2.89	29	35	40	46	52	58	64	69	75	81	87
10 point Meta	2.60	26	31	36	42	47	52	57	62	68	73	78
12 point Meta	2.17	22	26	30	35	39	43	48	52	56	61	65
8 point Minion	3.35	34	40	47	54	60	67	74	80	87	94	101
9 point Minion	2.97	30	36	42	48	54	59	65	71	77	83	89
10 point Minion	2.69	27	32	38	43	48	54	59	65	70	75	81
12 point Minion	2.21	22	27	31	35	40	44	49	53	57	62	66
8 point Palatino	2.97	30	36	42	48	53	59	65	71	77	83	89
9 point Palatino	2.64	26	32	37	42	48	53	58	63	69	74	79
10 point Palatino	2.36	24	28	33	38	42	47	52	57	61	66	71
12 point Palatino	2.00	20	24	28	32	36	40	44	48	52	56	60
8 point Univers 55	2.95	30	35	41	47	53	59	65	71	77	83	89
9 point Univers 55	2.62	26	31	37	42	47	52	58	63	68	73	79
10 point Univers 55	2.36	24	28	33	38	43	47	52	57	61	66	71
12 point Univers 55	1.98	20	24	28	32	36	40	44	48	52	55	59
8 point Myriad	3.19	32	38	45	51	57	64	70	77	83	89	96
9 point Myriad	2.78	28	33	39	44	50	56	61	67	72	78	83
10 point Myriad	2.51	25	30	35	40	45	50	55	60	65	70	75
12 point Myriad	2.09	21	25	29	33	38	42	46	50	54	59	63
8 point Serifa	2.81	28	34	39	45	51	56	62	67	73	79	84
9 point Serifa	2.49	25	30	35	40	45	50	55	60	65	70	75
10 point Serifa	2.24	22	27	31	36	40	45	49	54	58	63	67
12 point Serifa	1.88	19	23	26	30	34	38	41	45	49	53	56

Traditional working methods in typographic design

Display Typography

1. Carefully examine the copy. Consider its meaning and its relationship to other elements on the page. Study the visual aspects of display copy: word lengths, number of words, word structure (presence and location of ascenders and descenders), and interletter relationships (see Fig. **8**, "Syntax and Communication").

2. Select typefaces for exploration, considering their relationship to content, legibility factors, typesetting, and printing methods.

3. Begin a series of small preliminary sketches, exploring alternative design possibilities. Consider type size and weight, division of the copy into lines, line arrangements (justified, unjustified, centered), and overall spatial organization. If a grid is being used, each sketch should reflect its structure.

4. Evaluate the sketches, and select one or more for further development. Criteria should be based on an overview of visual syntax, message, and legibility.

5. Prepare actual-size rough sketches of the page, working freely. Once again, select a sketch or sketches for further development.

6. Study type specimens to select the exact style, size, and weight to be used. Often, designers make tracings of the specimens to explore subtle visual characteristics of the type and to determine the desired interletter, interword, and interline spacing.

7. After these design decisions are made, the final layout can be prepared. It becomes the basis for type specification, client approval, and preparation of reproduction art. The degree of refinement may vary from a rough sketch to a tight comprehensive with set type, depending on the nature of the project.

Text typography

1. In the small preliminary sketches, text areas should be treated as rectangles or other simple shapes.

2. An initial character count of the typewritten manuscript (see Appendices A and B) should be made to determine its length.

3. Select a type style, considering its appropriateness to content and its relationship to the display type. Carefully study the type specimens to evaluate legibility, texture, and tone.

4. Working on tracing paper or at a computer terminal, plan a specific format, establishing line length, vertical column depth, and margins.

5. Select the desired type size and interline spacing. Then, copyfitting, as described in Appendix A, should be used to determine the specific area occupied by the text type.

6. Adjustments are now made in the format or the type specifications if the copyfitting procedure indicates that the type will not fit the allocated space.

7. Attention should be given to details: paragraph indication, interletter and interword spacing, and treatment of headings, folios, captions, and other supporting text material.

8. The designer can now prepare final layouts and mark specifications on the manuscript with assurance that the set type will conform to this plan.

Reviewing type proofs.

After proofs are received from the typesetter, the designer should carefully examine them while the proofreader is checking for editorial accuracy.

1. Compare the set type with the layouts for proper fit. Determine what, if any, adjustments are necessary.

2. Check the type proofs to ensure that specifications were followed. Font selection, line lengths, and interline spacing should conform to the instructions.

3. Make sure that details were handled correctly. For example, did the typesetters overlook words set in italic or bold?

4. Use a T-square and triangle to check the horizontal and vertical alignment of columns.

5. Examine the interline and interword intervals, particularly in display type, to make sure that they conform to the specifications. Often designers make subtle optical adjustments by cutting apart the proofs.

6. Look for awkward text settings, such as rivers, widows, and undesirable line breaks in unjustified typography. The editor or writer may be able to make small editorial changes to correct these problems.

7. Inspect proof quality. Common problems include rounded terminals due to inaccurate exposure, poor image sharpness, uneven or gray tone from incorrect processing, "dancing" characters that don't align properly on the baseline, poor kerning between misfit letters, and inconsistent proof tone within a long text.

8. Standard proofreaders' marks, listed in Appendix D, should be used to specify corrections.

Proofreader's marks

Instruction	Notation in margin	Notation in type	Corrected type
Delete	*y*	the ~~type~~ font	the font
Insert	type	the font	the type font
Let it stand	*stet*	the ~~type~~ font	the type font
Reset in capitals	*cap*	the type font	THE TYPE FONT
Reset in lowercase	*lc*	THE TYPE FONT	the type font
Reset in italics	*ital*	the type font	the *type* font
Reset in small capitals	*sc*	See type font.	See TYPE FONT.
Reset in roman	*rom*	the *type* font	the type font
Reset in boldface	*bf*	the type font	**the type font**
Reset in lightface	*lf*	the type **font**	the type font
Transpose	*tr*	the font type	the type font
Close up space	◡	the ty pe	the type
Delete and close space	*y*	the type foont	the type font
Move left	[	the type font	the type font
Move right	]	the type font	the type font
Run in	*run in*	The type font is Univers. It is not Garamond.	The type font is Univers. It is not Garamond.
Align	‖	the type font the type font the type font	the type font the type font the type font
Spell out	*sp*	③ type fonts	Three type fonts
Insert space	#	the type font	the type font
Insert period	⊙	The type font	The type font.
Insert comma	⌄,	One two, three	One, two, three
Insert hyphen	⌒=⌒	Ten point type	Ten-point type
Insert colon	⊙:	Old Style types	Old Style types:
Insert semicolon	⌃;	Select the font spec the type.	Select the font; spec the type.
Insert apostrophe	⌄'	Baskervilles type	Baskerville's type
Insert quotation marks	⌄"/⌄"/	the word type	the word "type"
Insert parenthesis	(/)/	The word type is in parenthesis.	The word (type) is in parenthesis.
Insert en dash	⅟N	Flush left	Flush–left
Insert em dash	⅟M/⅟M/	Garamond an Old Style face is used today.	Garamond—an Old Style face—is used today.
Start paragraph	¶	The type font is Univers 55.	The type font is Univers 55.
No paragraph indent	*no* ¶	The type font is Univers 55.	The type font is Univers 55.

A chronology of typeface designs

The dates of design, production, and release of a typeface often differ, and additional fonts in a type family frequently follow later; therefore, many dates listed here are approximate.

[1] Revivals of many typefaces are often named after early designers or authors. These faces were not so named during their epoch; however, their contemporary names are used here for identification purposes.

c. 1450: First Textura-style type, Johann Gutenberg
1467: First Roman-style type, Sweynheym and Pannartz
1470: Jenson,[1] Nicolas Jenson
1495: Bembo, Francesco Griffo
1499: Poliphilus, Francesco Griffo
1501: First italic type, Francesco Griffo
1514: Fraktur, Hans Schoensperger
1532: Garamond, Claude Garamond
1557: Civilité, Robert Granjon
c. 1570: Plantin, Anonymous
c. 1570: Canon d'Espagne, the Plantin Office
c. 1582: Flemish bold Roman, the Plantin Office
1616: Typi Academiae, Jean Jannon
c. 1670: Fell Roman, Peter Walpergen
1690: Janson, Nicholas Kis
1702: Romain du Roi, Philippe Grandjean
1722: Caslon Old Style, William Caslon
c. 1743: Early transitional types, Pierre Simon Fournier le Jeune
c. 1746: Fournier decorated letters, Pierre Simon Fournier le Jeune
1757: Baskerville, John Baskerville
c. 1764: Italique Moderne and Ancienne, Pierre Simon Fournier le Jeune
1768: Fry's Baskerville, Isaac Moore
c. 1780: Bodoni, Giambattista Bodoni
1784: Didot, Firmin Didot
c. 1795: Bulmer, William Martin
1796: Fry's Ornamented, Richard Austin
c. 1800: Walbaum, J. E. Walbaum
c. 1810: Scotch Roman, Richard Austin
1815: Two Lines Pica, Antique (first Egyptian style), Vincent Figgins
1815: Five Lines Pica, In Shade (first perspective font), Vincent Figgins
1816: Two-line English Egyptian (first sans serif), William Caslon IV
1820: Lettres Ornees, Fonds de Gille
1828: Roman, Darius Wells
1830: Two-line great primer sans serif, Vincent Figgins
1832: Grotesque, William Thorowgood
1838: Sans serryphs ornamented, Blake and Stephenson
1844: Ionic, Henry Caslon
1845: Clarendon, Robert Besley and Company

1845: Rustic, V. and J. Figgins
1845: Zig-Zag, V. and J. Figgins
1850: Scroll, Henry Caslon
1859: Antique Tuscan Outlined, William Page
1856: National, Philadelphia Type Foundry
c. 1860: P. T. Barnum, Barnhart Brothers and Spindler
c. 1865: French Antique (later called Playbill), Miller and Richard
c. 1865: Old Style Antique (called Bookman in the U.S.), Miller and Richard
c. 1869: Runic, Reed and Fox
c. 1870: Figgins Condensed No. 2, Stevens Shanks
c. 1870: Bank Gothic, Bardhart Brothers and Spindler
1878: Circlet, Barnhart Brothers and Spindler
1878: Glyphic, MacKellar, Smiths and Jordan
c. 1885: Geometric, Central Type Foundry
c. 1890: Ringlet, Marr Typefounding
c. 1890: Gothic Outline No. 61, American Typefounders
c. 1890: Rubens, Marr Typefounding
c. 1890: Karnac, Marr Typefounding
1890: Century, L. B. Benton
1890: Golden, William Morris
1892: Troy, William Morris
1893: Chaucer, William Morris
1894: Bradley, Will Bradley
1895: Merrymount Type, Bertram Goodhue
1895: Century Roman, Theodore Low DeVinne and L. B. Benton
1896: Cheltenham, Bertram Goodhue
1896: Vale Type, Charles Ricketts
1898: Grasset, Eugene Grasset
c. 1898: Paris Metro Lettering, Hector Guimard
1898–1906: Akzidenz Grotesque (Standard), Berthold Foundry
1900: Eckmann-Schrift, Otto Eckmann
1900: Century Expanded, Morris F. Benton
1900: Doves Roman, T. J. Cobden-Sanderson and Emery Walker
1901: Endeavor, Charles R. Ashbee
1901: Copperplate Gothic, Frederic W. Goudy
1901–4: Auriol, Georges Auriol
1902: Behrens-Schrift, Peter Behrens
1902: Subiaco, C. H. St. John Hornby
1903: Brook Type, Lucien Pissarro
1904: Korinna, H. Berthold

1904: Franklin Gothic, Morris F. Benton
1904: Arnold Böcklin, O. Weisert
1904: Linoscript, Morris F. Benton
1907: Behrens-Kursiv, Peter Behrens
1907: Clearface Bold, Morris F. Benton
1907–13: Venus, Bauer Foundry
1908: Behrens-Antiqua, Peter Behrens
1908: News Gothic, Morris F. Benton
1909: Aurora, Wagner and Schmidt Foundry
1910: Kochschrift, Rudolf Koch
1910–15: Hobo, Morris F. Benton
1911: Kennerly Old Style, Frederic W. Goudy
1912: Nicolas Cochin, G. Peignot
1913: Belwe, Georg Belwe
1914: Souvenir, Morris F. Benton
1914: Cloister Old Style, Morris F. Benton
1915: Century Schoolbook, Morris F. Benton
1915–16: Goudy Old Style, Frederic W. Goudy
1916: Centaur, Bruce Rogers
1916: Johnston's Railway Type, Edward Johnston
1919–24: Cooper Old Style, Oswald Cooper
1921: Cooper Black, Oswald Cooper
1922: Locarno (Eve), Rudolf Koch
1923: Windsor, Stephenson Blake Foundry
1923: Tiemann, Walter Tiemann
1923: Neuland, Rudolf Koch
1925: Perpetua, Eric Gill
1926: Weiss Roman, E. R. Weiss
1926: Bauer Bodoni, Bauer typefoundry
1927–29: Futura, Paul Renner
1927–29: Kabel, Rudolf Koch
1928: Ultra Bodoni, Morris F. Benton
1928–30: Gill Sans, Eric Gill
1928: Modernique, Morris F. Benton
1929: Zeppelin, Rudolf Koch
1929: Golden Cockerel, Eric Gill
1929–30: Metro, William A. Dwiggins
1929: Bernhard Fashion, Lucien Bernhard
1929: Bifur, A. M. Cassandre
1929: Broadway, Morris F. Benton
1929: Novel Gothic, H. Becker
1929: Bembo, Monotype Corporation
1929: Lux, Josef Erbar
1929: Memphis, Rudolf Weiss
1929–30: Perpetua, Eric Gill
1929–34: Corvinus, Imre Reiner

1930: City, Georg Trump

1930: Joanna, Eric Gill

1930: Dynamo, Ludwig and
Mayer Foundry

1930: Metro, William A. Dwiggins

1931: Prisma, Rudolf Koch

1931: Times New Roman, Stanley
Morison and Victor Lardent

1931: Stymie, Morris F. Benton

1931–36: Beton, Heinrich Jost

1932–40: Albertus, Berthold Wolpe

1933: Agency Gothic,
Morris F. Benton

1933: Atlas, K. H. Schaefer

1934: Rockwell, H. F. Pierpont

1935: Electra, William A. Dwiggins

1935: Huxley Vertical,
Walter Huxley

1936: Acier Noir, A. M. Cassandre

1937: Peignot, A. M. Cassandre

1937: Stencil, Robert H. Middleton

1937: Onyx, Gerry Powell

1938: Caledonia,
William A. Dwiggins

1938: Libra, S. H. De Roos

1938: Lydian, Warren Chappell

1938: Empire, American
Typefounders

1939: Chisel, Stephenson Blake
Foundry

1940: Trajanus, Warren Chappell

1940: Tempo, Robert H. Middleton

1945: Stradivarius, Imre Reiner

1945: Courier, Bud Kettler

1946: Profil, Eugen and Max Lenz

1948: Trade Gothic, Mergenthaler
Linotype

c. 1950: Brush, Harold Brodersen

1950: Michelangelo, Hermann Zapf

1950: Palatino, Hermann Zapf

1951: Sistina, Hermann Zapf

1952: Horizon, K. F. Bauer and
Walter Baum

1952: Melior, Hermann Zapf

1952: Microgramma, A. Butti

1953: Mistral, Roger Excoffon

1954: Trump Mediaeval,
Georg Trump

1955: Columna, Max Caflisch

1955: Egizio, Aldo Novarese

1955–56: Egyptienne,
Adrian Frutiger

1956: Craw Clarendon,
Freeman Craw

1956: Murry Hill, E. J. Klumpp

1957: Meridien, Adrian Frutiger

1957: Univers, Adrian Frutiger

c. 1957: Helvetica, Max Miedinger

1960: Aurora, Jackson Burke

1961: Octavian, Will Carter and
David Kindersley

1962: Eurostile, Aldo Novarese

1962–66: Antique Olive,
Roger Excoffon

1964: Sabon, Jan Tschichold

1965: Americana, Richard Isbell

1965: Snell Roundhand,
Matthew Carter

1965: Friz Quadrata, Ernest Friz

1966: Egyptian 505, André Gürtler

1966: Vladimir, Vladimir Andrich

1966: Sabon, Jan Tschichold

1967: Serifa, Adrian Frutiger

1967: Americana, Richard Isbell

1967: Cartier, Carl Dair

1967: Avant Garde Gothic, Herb
Lubalin and Tom Carnase

1967: Poppl-Antiqua, Friedrich
Poppl

1968: Syntax, Hans E. Meier

1969: Aachen, Colin Brignall

1970: Olympian, Matthew Carter

1970: Machine, Tom Carnase
and Ron Bonder

1970: ITC Souvenir,
Edward Benguiat

1972: Iridium, Adrian Frutiger

1972: Times Europa, Walter Tracy

1972: University, Mike Daines

1974: American Typewriter,
Joel Kadan

1974: ITC Tiffany, Edward Benguiat

1974: Newtext, Ray Baker

1974: Korinna, Ed Benguiat
and Vic Caruso

1974: American Typewriter, Joel
Kaden and Tony Stan

1974: Serif Gothic, Herb Lubalin
and Tony DiSpigna

1974: Lubalin Graph, Herb Lubalin,
Tony DiSpigna, and Joe
Sundwall

1975: ITC Bauhaus, based on
Bayer's universal alphabet

1975: ITC Bookman, Ed Benguiat

1975: ITC Century, Tony Stan

1975: ITC Cheltenham, Tony Stan

1975: Concorde Nova, Gunter
Gerhard Lange

1975: ITC Garamond, Tony Stan

1975: Marconi, Hermann Zapf

1976: Eras, Albert Hollenstein and
Albert Boton

1976: Poppl-Pontiflex,
Friedrich Poppl

1976: Zapf Book, Hermann Zapf

1976: Frutiger, Adrian Frutiger

1977: Quorum, Ray Baker

1977: Korinna Kursiv,
Edward Benguiat

1977: Italia, Colin Brignall

1977: Benguiat, Edward Benguiat

1977: Zapf International,
Hermann Zapf

1977: Fenice, Also Novarese

1978: Basilia, André Gürtler

1978: Bell Centennial,
Matthew Carter

1978: Galliard, Matthew Carter

1979: Benguiat Gothic,
Edward Benguiat

1979: Glypha, Adrian Frutiger

1979: Zapf Chancery,
Hermann Zapf

1980: Fenice, Aldo Novarese

1980: Novarese, Aldo Novarese

1980: Icone, Adrian Frutiger

1980: Marconi, Hermann Zapf

1980: Edison, Hermann Zapf

1981: Adroit, Phil Martin

1981: Barcelona, Edward Benguiat

1981: Isbell, Dick Isbell
and Jerry Campbell

1982: Cushing, Vincent Pacella

1983: ITC Berkeley Old Style,
Tony Stan

1983: Weidemann, Kurt
Weidemann and Kurt
Strecker

1983: Neue Helvetica,
Linotype (Stempel)
staff designers

1984: Macintosh screen fonts,
Susan Kare

1984: Osiris, Gustav Jaeger

1984: Usherwood, Les Usherwood

1984: Veljovic, Jovica Veljovic

1985: Aurelia, Hermann Zapf

1985: Elan, Albert Boton

1985: Emigre, Zuzana Licko

1985: Kis-Janson, Autologic
staff designers

1985: Lucida, Charles Bigelow
and Kris Holmes

1985: Mixage, Aldo Novarese

1985: Oakland, Zuzana Licko

1986: Linotype Centennial,
Matthew Carter

1986: Matrix, Zuzana Licko

1986: Centennial, Adrian Frutiger

1987: Amerigo, Gerard Unger

1987: Charter, Matthew Carter

1987: Gerstner Original,
Karl Gerstner

1987: Glyphia, Adrian Frutiger

1987: Neufont, David Weinz

1987: Stone Informal, Sans
and Serif, Sumner Stone

1987: Charlemagne, Carol Twombly

1987: Belizio, David Berlow

1987: Zapf Renaissance,
Hermann Zapf

1988: Visigoth, Arthur Baker

1988: Avenir, Adrian Frutiger

c. 1989: FF Meta, Erik Spiekermann

1989: Adobe Garamond,
Robert Slimbach

1989: Giovanni, Robert Slimbach

1989: Helicon, David Quay

1989: Lithos, Carol Twombly

1989: Rotis, Otl Aicher

1989: Trajan, Carol Twombly

1989: Keedy Sans, Jeffery Keedy

1989: Phaistos, David Berlow

1989: Commerce, Greg Thompson
and Rick Valicenti

1989–90: Bronzo, Rick Valicenti

1990: Bodega Sans,
Greg Thompson

1990: Journal, Zuzana Licko

1990: Adobe Caslon,
Carol Twombly

1990: Quay, David Quay

1990: Tekton, David Siegel

1990: Template Gothic, Barry Deck

1990: Dead History, Scott Makela

1990: Myriad, Robert Slimbach
and Carol Twombly

1990: Minion, Robert Slimbach

1990: Arcadia, Industria, and
Insignia, Neville Brody

1991: Print, Sumner Stone

1991: Exocet, Jonathan Barnbrook

1991: Adobe Caslon,
Carol Twombly

1991: Remedy, Frank Heine

1992: EndsMeansMends,
Sumner Stone

1992: Syndor, Hans Edward Meier

1992: Mason: Jonathan Barnbrook

1992: Poetica, Robert Slimbach

1992: Commerce, Rick Valicenti
and Greg Thompson

1993: Mantinia and Sofia,
Matthew Carter

1993: Agenda, Greg Thompson

1994: Barcode, Brian Lucid

1994: Dogma, Zuzana Licko

1994: Big Caslon CC,
Matthew Carter

1994: Ultrabronzo, Rick Valicenti
and Mouli Marur

1995: Not Caslon, Mark Andresen

1995: Walker, Matthew Carter

1995: Shogun, Richard Lipton

1996: FB Reactor,
Tobias Frere-Jones

1996: Filosofia, Zuzana Licko

1996: Mrs Eaves, Zuzano Licko

1997: Vendetta, John Downer

1997–2000: Poynter Old Style,
Tobias Frere-Jones

1999: Council, John Downer

1999: Spira, Andy Stockley

1999: Champion Gothic,
Jonathan Hoefler

1999: Gestalt, Jonathan Hoefler

1999: Fetish No. 338,
Jonathan Hoefler

1999: Ziggurat, Jonathan Hoefler

1999: Acropolis, Jonathan Hoefler

1999: Leviathan, Jonathan Hoefler

1999: Dispatch, Cyrus Highsmith

2000: Verdana, Matthew Carter

2000: Georgia, Matthew Carter

Bibliography

Aicher, Otl. *Typographie.* Berlin: Ernst & Sohn, 1988.

Anderson, Donald M. *A Renaissance Alphabet.* Madison, WI: University of Wisconsin Press, 1971.

—————. *The Art of Written Forms.* New York: Holt, Reinhart and Winston, 1969.

Arnheim, Rudolf. *The Power of the Center: A Study of Composition in the Visual Arts.* Berkeley, CA: University of California Press, 1982.

Bauermeister, Benjamin. *A Manual of Comparative Typography,*

Bigelow, Charles, Duensing, Paul Hayden, and Gentry, Linnea. *Fine Print on Type: The Best of Fine Print on Type and Typography.* San Francisco: Fine Print/Bedford Arts, 1988.

Binns, Betty. *Better Type.* New York: Watson-Guptill, 1989.

Blackwell, Lewis. *20th Century Type.* New York: Rizzoli, 1992.

Bojko, Szymon. *New Graphic Design in Revolutionary Russia.* New York: Praeger, 1972.

Bringhurst, Robert. *The Elements of Typographic Style.* Port Roberts, WA: Hartley and Marks, 1992.

Brody, Neville, and Blackwell, Lewis. *G3: New Dimensions in Graphic Design.* New York: Rizzoli, 1996.

Burns, Aaron. *Typography.* New York: Van Nostrand Reinhold, 1961.

Bruckner, D. J. R. *Frederic Goudy.* New York: Harry Abrams, 1990.

Carter, Rob. *American Typography Today.* New York: Van Nostrand Reinhold, 1989.

—————. *Working with Computer Type,* Volumes 1–5, London: Rotovision; and New York: Watson Guptill, 1995–99.

Carter, Sebastian. *Twentieth Century Type Designers.* New York: W. W. Norton & Co., 1995.

Chang, Amos I. *The Tao of Architecture.* Princeton, NJ: Princeton University Press, 1981.

Dair, Carl. *Design with Type.* Toronto: University of Toronto Press, 1967.

Damase, Jacque. *Revolution Typographique.* Geneva: Galerie Mott, 1966.

Doczi, Gregory. *The Power of Limits: Proportional Harmonies in Nature, Art and Architecture.* Boulder, CO: Shambhala Publications, 1981.

Dowding, Geoffrey. *Fine Points in the Spacing and Arrangement of Type.* Point Roberts, WA: Hartley and Marks, 1993.

Drogin, Marc. *Medieval Calligraphy: Its History and Technique.* Montclair, NJ: Allanheld and Schram, 1980.

Dwiggins, William Addison. *Layout in Advertising.* New York: Harper and Brothers, 1948.

Elam, Kimberly. *Expressive Typography: The Word as Image.* New York: Van Nostrand Reinhold, 1990.

Friedl, Fiedrich, Ott, Nicolaus, and Stein, Bernard. *Typography: An Encyclopedic Survey.* New York: Black Dog, 1998.

Friedman, Mildred, ed. *De Stijl: 1917–1931, Visions of Utopia.* New York: Abbeville Press, 1982.

Frutiger, Adrian. *Type, Sign, Symbol.* Zurich: ABC Verlag, 1980.

—————. *Signs & Symbols: Their Design & Meaning.* New York: Van Nostrand Reinhold, 1989.

Gardner, William. *Alphabet at Work.* New York: St. Martins Press, 1982.

Gerstner, Karl. *Compendium for Literates: A System for Writing.* Translated by Dennis Q. Stephenson. Cambridge, MA: MIT Press, 1974.

Gill, Eric. *An Essay on Typography.* Boston: David R. Godine, 1988.

Goines, David Lance. *A Constructed Roman Alphabet.* Boston: David R. Godine, 1981.

Gottschall, Edward. *Typographic Communications Today.* Cambridge, MA: MIT Press.

Goudy, Frederic W. *The Alphabet and Elements of Lettering.* New York: Dover, 1963.

—————. *Typologia: Studies in Type Design and Type-making.* Berkeley, CA: University of California Press, 1940.

Gray, Nicolete. *Nineteenth Century Ornamented Typefaces.* Berkeley, CA: University of California Press, 1977.

—————. *A History of Lettering: Creative Experiment and Letter Identity.* Boston: David R. Godine, 1986.

Harlan, Calvin. *Vision and Invention: A Course in Art Fundamentals.* New York: Prentiss Hall, 1969.

Harper, Laurel. *Radical Graphics/Graphic Radicals.* San Francisco: Chronicle Books, 1999.

Heller, Steven, and Anderson, Gail. *American Type Play.* Glen Cove, NY: PBC International, 1994.

Heller, Steven, and Meggs, Philip B. eds. *Texts on Type: Critical Writings on Typography.* New York: Allworth, 2001.

Hiebert, Kenneth J. *Graphic Design Processes: Universal to Unique.* New York: Van Nostrand Reinhold, 1992.

Hinrichs, Kit. *Typewise.* Cincinnati: North Light, 1990.

Hoffman, Armin. *Graphic Design Manual: Principles and Practice.* New York: Van Nostrand Reinhold, 1992.

—————. *His Work, Quest, and Philosophy.* Basel: Burkhäuser Verlag, 1989.

Jaspert, W. Pincus, Berry, W. Turner, Jaspert, W. P., and Johnson, A. F. *The Encyclopaedia of Typefaces.* New York: Blandford Press, 1986.

Kelly, Rob Roy. *American Wood Type 1828–1900.* New York: Van Nostrand Reinhold, 1969.

Kepes, Gyorgy. *Sign, Symbol, Image.* New York: George Braziller, 1966.

Kinross, Robin. *Modern Typography: An Essay in Critical History.* London: Hyphen Press, 1992.

Knobler, Nathan. *The Visual Dialogue.* New York: Holt, Reinhart and Winston, 1967.

Lawson, Alexander. *Anatomy of a Typeface.* Boston: Godine, 1990.

Lewis, John. *Anatomy of Printing: The Influence of Art and History on Its Design.* New York: Watson-Guptill, 1970.

Lobell, Frank. *Between Silence and Light: Spirit in the Architecture of Louis I. Kahn.* Boulder, CO: Shambhala Publications, 1979.

McGrew, Mac. *American Metal Typefaces of the Twentieth Century.* New Castle, DE: Oak Knoll Books, 1993.

McLean, Ruari. *The Thames and Hudson Manual of Typography.* London: Thames and Hudson, 1980.

————. *Jan Tschichold: Typographer.* Boston: David R. Godine, 1975.

————. *Jan Tschichold: A Life in Typography.* New York: Princeton Architectural Press, 1997.

Meggs, Philip, and Carter, Rob. *Typographic Specimens: The Great Typefaces.* New York: John Wiley & Sons, 1993.

Meggs, Philip B. *Type and Image: The Language of Graphic Design.* New York: John Wiley & Sons, 1989.

————. *A History of Graphic Design, 3rd Edition.* New York: John Wiley & Sons, 1998.

Morison, Stanley. *First Principles of Typography.* Cambridge, England: Cambridge University Press, 1936.

————, and Day, Kenneth. *The Typographic Book: 1450–1935.* Chicago: University of Chicago Press, 1964.

Müller-Brockmann, Josef. *Grid Systems in Graphic Design: A Visual Communications Manual.* Niederteufen, Switzerland: Arthur Niggli Ltd., 1981.

Nesbitt, Alexander. *The History and Technique of Lettering.* New York: Dover, 1950.

Rehe, Rolf F. *Typography: How to Make It Most Legible.* Carmel, CA: Design Research Publications, 1974.

Richardson, Margaret. *Type Graphics: The Power of Type in Graphic Design.* Gloucester, MA: Rockport, 2000.

Roberts, Raymond. *Typographic Design: Handbooks to Printing.* London: Ernest Bend Limited, 1966.

Rogers, Bruce. *Paragraphs on Printing.* New York: Dover, 1980.

Ruder, Emil. *Typography: A Manual of Design.* Switzerland: Verlag Arthur Niggli, 1967.

Ruegg, Ruedi. *Basic Typography: Design with Letters.* New York: Van Nostrand Reinhold, 1989.

Schmidt, Helmut. *Typography Today.* Tokyo: Seibundo Shinkosha, 1980.

Scott, Robert Gilliam. *Design Fundamentals.* New York: McGraw-Hill, 1951.

Solt, Mary Ellen. *Concrete Poetry.* Bloomington, IN: University of Indiana Press, 1971.

Spencer, Herbert. *Pioneers of Modern Typography.* Londonn: Lund Humphries, 1969, and Cambridge, MA: MIT Press, 1983.

————. *The Visible Word.* New York: Hastings House, 1969.

————, Editor. *The Liberated Page.* San Francisco: Bedford, 1987.

Spiekermann, Erik, and Ginger, E. M. *Stop Stealing Sheep and Find Out How Type Works.* Mountain View, CA: Adobe Press, 1993.

Stone, Summer. *On Stone.* San Francisco: Bedford Arts, 1991.

Sutnar, Ladislav. *Visual Design in Action – Principles, Purposes.* New York: Hastings House, 1961.

Swann, Cal. *Techniques of Typography.* New York: Watson-Guptill, 1969.

Tschichold, Jan. Translator, Ruari McLean. *The New Typography.* Berkeley, CA: University of California Press, 1998.

Updike, Daniel. *Printing Types: Their History, Form, and Use.* New York: Dover, 1980.

VanderLans, Rudy, Licko, Zuzana, and Gray, Mary E. *Emigre: Graphic Design in the Digital Realm.* New York: Van Nostrand Reinhold, 1993.

Wallis, Lawrence W. *Modern Encyclopedia of Typefaces: 1960–90.* New York: Van Nostrand Reinhold, 1990.

Weingart, Wolfgang. *Typography.* Baden: Switzerland: Lars Müller, 2000.

(Frontispiece) *Saint. Barbara,* 15th-Century German or French polychromed walnut sculpture. (50"H x 23"W x 13"D) 127.0 cm x 58.4 cm x 33.0 cm. The Virginia Museum of Fine Arts, Richmond. The Williams Fund, 1968.

Chapter One.

1. Impressed tablet from Godin Tepe, Iran. West Asian Department, Royal Ontario Museum, Toronto.

2. Facsimile of the cuneiform impression on a clay tablet, after Hansard.

3. The Pyramids at Giza, from *The Iconographic Encyclopaedia of Science, Literature, and Art* by Johann Georg Heck, 1851.

4. Egyptian Old Kingdom *False Door Stele,* limestone. The Virginia Museum of Fine Arts, Richmond. Museum Purchase: The Williams Fund.

5. Cuneiform tablet. Sumero-Akkadian. The Metropolitan Museum of Art, New York. Acquired by exchange with J. Pierpont Morgan Library, 1911.

6. Photograph of Stonehenge; courtesy of the British Tourist Authority.

7. Egyptian Polychromed Wood Sculpture, XVIII–XIX Dynasty. Ushabti. The Virginia Museum of Fine Arts, Richmond. Museum Purchase: The Williams Fund, 1955.

8. *The Book of the Dead of Tuthmosis III.* Museum of Fine Arts, Boston. Gift of Horace L. Meyer.

10. Phoenician inscription. The Metropolitan Museum of Art, New York. The Cesnola Collection. Purchased by subscription, 1874–76.

12. Photograph of the Parthenon; courtesy of the Greek National Tourist Office.

13. Photograph of Greek record of sale; Agora Excavations, American School of Classical Studies, Athens.

15. Photograph of a wall in Pompeii, by James Mosley.

17. Photographer anonymous; c. 1895. Private collection.

18. *Funerary inscription of Lollia Genialis.* Marble. The Metropolitan Museum of Art, New York.

19. Photograher anonymous; c. 1895. Private collection.

20. Photograph; courtesy of the Italian Government Travel Office.

24. Detail, "Christ attended by angels," from *The Book of Kells,* fol. 32v; photograph; courtesy of the Irish Tourist Board.

25 and 26. Photographs; courtesy of the Irish Tourist Board.

28. Photograph; courtesy of the French Government Tourist Office.

30. Bronze and copper *Crucifix.* The Virginia Museum of Fine Art, Richmond. Museum Purchase: The Williams Fund, 1968.

32. *Madonna and Child on a Curved Throne.* Wood, 0.815 x 0.490m (32 1/8 x 19 3/8 in.) National Gallery of Art, Washington. Andrew W. Mellon Collection, 1937.

34. Lippo Memmi; Sienese, active 1317–47. *Saint John the Baptist.* Wood, 0.95 x 0.46m (37 1/4 x 18 in.). National Gallery of Art, Washington. Samuel H. Kress Collection, 1939.

35. Photograph courtesy of the Italian Government Tourist Office.

37. Fra Filippo Lippi; Florentine c. 1406–69. *Madonna and Child.* Wood, 0.80 x 0.51m (31 3/8 x 20 1/8 in.). National Gallery of Art, Washington. Samuel H. Kress Collection, 1939.

38. The Rosenwald Collection; The Library of Congress, Washington, DC.

39. Woodcut illustration from *Standebuch* by Jost Amman, 1568.

40. Photographer anonymous; c. 1895. Private collection.

42. Typography from *Lactantu . . . .* Printed by Sweynheym and Pannartz; Rome, 1468. The Library of Congress Rare Book and Special Collections Division, Washington, DC.

43. From *De evangelica praeparatione* by Eusebius Pamphilii. Printed by Nicolas Jenson; Venice, 1470.

44. From *The Recuyell of the Historyes of Troye* by Raoul Le Fevre. Printed by William Caxton and Colard Mansion; Burges, c. 1475.

45. Filippino Lippi; *Portrait of a Youth.* Wood, 0.510 x 0.355 m (20 x 13 7/8 in.). National Gallery of Art, Washington, DC. Andrew Mellon Collection, 1937.

46. Erhard Ratdolt, earliest extant type specimen sheet. Published April 1, 1486, in Augsburg, Germany. Bayerische Staatsbibliothek, Munich.

47. Woodcut portrait of Aldus Manutius. Published by Antoine Lafrery; Rome, 16th century.

48. From *De aetna* by Pietro Bembo. Published by Aldus Manutius, Venice, 1495.

49. Page from *Virgil.* Published by Aldus Manutius; Venice, 1501.

50. Photograph by Rommler and Jonas; 1892. Private collection.

53. From *Underweisung der Messung* by Albrecht Durer; Nuremburg, 1525.

54. From *Champ Fleury* by Geoffroy Tory; Paris, 1529.

55. Photograph; courtesy of the French Government Tourist Office.

57. Titian; Venetian c. 1477–1565. *Cardinal Pietro Bembo.* Canvas, 0.945 x 0.765m (37 1/8 x 30 1/8 in.). National Gallery of Art, Washington, DC. Samuel H. Kress Collection, 1952.

58. Title page for *Elementary Geometry* by Oronce Fine. Printed by Simone de Colines; Paris, I544.

59. From *Hypnerotomachia Poliphili* by Fra Francesco Colonna. Printed by Jacque Kerver; Paris, 1546.

60. El Greco; Spanish 1541–1614. *Saint Martin and the Beggar.* Canvas, 1.935 x 1.030m (76 1/8 x 40 1/2 in.). National Gallery of Art, Washington, DC. Widener Collection, 1942.

61. From *Nejw Kunstliches Alphabet* by Johann Theodor de Bry; Germany, 1595.

62. Photographer anonymous; c. 1895. Private collection.

63. Detail, typographic specimens of Jean Jannon; Sedan, 1621.

64. Page from *Stamperia Vaticana Specimen;* Rome, 1628.

65. Photograph; courtesy of the Government of India Tourist Office.

66. Sir Anthony van Dyck; Flemish, 1599–1641. *Henri II de Lorraine, Duc de Guise.* Canvas, 2.046 x 1.238m (80 5/8 x 48 5/8 in.). National Gallery of Art, Washington, DC. Gift of Cornelius Vanderbilt Whitney, 1947.

67. Jan Vermeer; Dutch 1632–75. *Woman Holding a Balance,* c. 1664. Canvas, 0.425 x 0.380m (16 3/4 x 15 in.). National Gallery of Art, Washington, DC. Widener Collection, 1942.

69. Photograph; courtesy of the British Tourist Authority.

71. Photographer anonymous; 1896. Private collection.

72. From the 1764 specimen book of W. Caslon and Son, London.

73. Photograph; courtesy of the Irish Tourist Board.

74. Title page for *Cato Major, or His Discourse on Old Age* by M. T. Cicero. Printed by Benjamin Franklin; Philadelphia, 1744.

75. Francois Boucher; French 1703–70. *The Love Letter,* 1750. Canvas, 0.813 x 0.741m (32 x 29 1/8 in.). National Gallery of Art, Washington, DC. Timken Collection, I959.

76. Anonymous; engraved portrait of John Baskerville.

77. From the specimen book of Thomas Cottrell, English typefounder; London, c. 1765.

78. Detail, title page of *Historie de Louis de Bourbon . . . ,* using types and ornaments designed by Pierre Simon Fournier le Jeune. Published by Lottin; Paris, 1768.

79. Johann David Steingruber, 1702–1787. Engraved letter *A* from *Architectonishes Alphabet,* Schwabach, 1773. The Metropolitan Museum of Art. The Elisha Whittelsey Collection, 1955. The Elisha Whittelsey Fund.

80. Photograph; courtesy of the Library of Congress, Washington, DC.

82. Detail, title page using type designed by Bodoni. Dante's *Divine Comedy;* Pisa, 1804.

83. From Thorowgood's *New Specimen of Printing Types, late R. Thorne's, No. 2;* London, 1821.

84. Jacques-Louis David; French 1748–1825. *Napoleon in his Study,* 1812. Canvas, 2.039 x 1.251m (80 1/4 x 49 1/4 in.). National Gallery of Art, Washington, DC. Samuel H. Kress Collection, 1961.

85–6. From *Specimen of Printing Types* by Vincent Figgins; London, 1815.

87. From *Specimen of Printing Types* by William Caslon IV; London, 1816.

88. From *Manuale Typographico.* Published by Signora Bodoni and Luigi Orsi; Parma, Italy, 1818.

89. From Thorowgood's *New Specimen of Printing Types, late R. Thorne's, No. 2;* London, 1821.

90. Photograph; courtesy of the Virginia State Travel Service.

91. From *Bower, Bacon & Bower's Specimen of Printing Types;* Sheffield, c. 1825.

92. Wood engraving of Darius Wells, from *The Inland Printer;* Chicago, July 1888.

93. From *Specimen of Printing Types* by Vincent Figgins; London, 1833.

94. Poster by the Davy & Berry Printing Office; Albion, England, 1836.

95. From *Specimen of Printing Types by V. & J. Figgins, successors to Vincent Figgins, Letter-Founder;* London, 1836.

96. Courtesy of the Library of Congress Rare Book and Special Collections Division, Washington, DC.

97. Photograph; courtesy of the British Tourist Authority.

98. From *The Specimen Book of Types Cast at the Austin Foundry by Wood & Sharwoods;* London, c. 1841.

99. From *A General Specimen of Printing Types.* Published by W. Thorowgood and Company; London, 1848.

100. Photograph; The Library of Congress Rare Book and Special Collections Division, Washington, DC.

101. Photograph; The Library of Congress Rare Book and Special Collections Division, Washington, DC.

102. From the wood type specimen book of William H. Page & Company; Greenville, Connecticut, 1859.

103. Private collection.

104. Honoré Daumier; French 1808–79. *The Third-Class Carriage.* Oil on canvas, 65.4 x 90.2m (25 3/4 x 35 1/2 in.). The Metropolitan Museum of Art, New York. Bequest of Mrs. H. O. Havemeyer, 1929. The H. O. Havemeyer Collection.

105. Private collection.

106. Private collection.

107. Courtesy of The New York Convention and Visitors Bureau.

108. Private collection.

109. Private collection.

110. Wood engraving from *The Inland Printer;* Chicago, December, 1889.

112. Courtesy of the French Government Tourist Office.

113. Photograph; courtesy of the Archives: The Coca-Cola Company.

114. Paul Gauguin; French 1848–1903. *Fatata Te Miti (By the Sea),* 1892. Canvas, 0.679 x 0.915m (26 3/4 x 36 in.). National Gallery of Art, Washington, DC. The Chester Dale Collection, 1962.

117. William Morris. *News from Nowhere.* Published by Kelmscott Press; London, 1892.

118. Title page from *Van nu en Straks.* Designed by Henri van de Velde, 1893.

119. Title page from *Limbes de Lumieres* by Gustave Kahn; Brussels, 1897.

120. From *The Inland Printer;* Chicago, June, 1900.

121. Title page from *A Lady of Quality* by Francis Hodgson Burnett. Published by Charles Scribner's Sons; New York, 1897.

122. Cover for Vienna Secession Catalog No. 5; Vienna, 1899.

123. Photograph; courtesy of the French Government Tourist Office.

124. Dedication page from *Feste des Lebens und der Kunst: Ein Betrachtung des Theaters als hochsten Kultursymbols (Celebrations of Life and Art: A Consideration of the Theater as the Highest Cultural Symbol)* by Peter Behrens; Darmstadt, 1900.

125. Filippo Marinetti, Futurist poem, S.T.F., 1914.

126. Cover, *Delikatessen Haus Erich Fromm, Haupt-List 2;* Cologne, c. 1910.

127. Wassily Kandinsky. *Improvisation 31 (Sea Battle),* 1913. National Gallery of Art, Washington, DC. Ailsa Mellon Bruce Fund.

128. War Bond Fund Drive poster for the British government by Bert Thomas, c. 1916.

129. Advertisement for the *Kleine Grosz Mappe (Small Grosz Portfolio)* from *Die Neue Jugend.* Designed by John Heartfield. Published by Der Malik-Verlag, Berlin, June 1917.

130. First cover for *De Stijl,* the journal of the de Stijl movement. Designed by Vilmos Huszar. Published/edited by Theo van Doesburg, The Netherlands; October 1917.

131. Raoul Hausmann. *Poeme Phonetique,* 1919.

132. Piet Mondrian; Dutch 1872–1944. *Diamond Painting in Red, Yellow, and Blue.* Oil on canvas, 40 x 40 in. National Gallery of Art, Washington, DC. Gift of Herbert and Nannette Rothschild, 1971.

133. Poster announcing availability of books, by Alexander Rodchenko; Moscow, c. 1923. Private collection.

134. Illustration by Mike Fanizza.

135. Title page from *Die Kunstismen* by El Lissitzky and Hans Arp. Published by Eugen Rentsch Verlag; Zurich, 1925.

136. Proposed universal alphabet. Designed by Herbert Bayer as a student at the Bauhaus.

137. Constantin Brancusi; Romanian 1876–1957. *Bird in Space.* Marble, stone, and wood, hgt. 3.446m (136 1/2 in.). National Gallery of Art, Washington, DC. Gift of Eugene and Agnes Meyer, 1967.

138. Title page for special insert, "Elementare Typographie" from *Typographische Mitteilungen;* Leipzig, October 1925.

139–40. Advertisements by Piet Zwart; courtesy of N. V. Nederlandsche Kabelfabriek, Delft.

141. Trial setting using Futura. Designed by Paul Renner. Published by Bauersche Giesserei; Frankfurt am Main, 1930.

142. Photograph; courtesy of New York Convention and Visitors Bureau.

143. Max Bill. Poster for an exhibition of African Art at the Kunstgewerbemuseum, Zurich.

144. Alexey Brodovitch. Poster for an industrial design exhibition at the Philadelphia Museum of Art.

145. Walker Evans. Photograph, "Fields family, sharecroppers," Hale County, Alabama. The Library of Congress, Washington, DC.

146. Jean Carlu. Advertisement for Container Corporation of America, December 21, 1942.

147. Max Bill. Poster for an exhibition of Art Concrete at the Kunsthalle, Basle.

148. Paul Rand. Title page for *On My Way* by Hans Arp. Published by Wittenborn, Schultz Inc.; New York, 1948.

149. Willem de Kooning. *Painting,* 1948. Enamel and oil on canvas, 42 5/8 x 56 1/8 in. Collection; Museum of Modern Art, New York. Purchase.

150. Ladislav Sutnar. Cover for *Catalog Design Progress* by K. Lonberg-Holm and Ladislav Sutnar. Published by Sweet's Catalog Service; New York, 1950.

151. Illustration by Stephen Chovanec.

152. Henri Matisse; French 1869–1954. *Woman with Amphora and Pomegranates.* Paper on canvas (collage), 2.436 x 0.963m (96 x 37 7/8 in.). National Gallery of Art, Washington, DC. Ailsa Mellon Bruce Fund, I973.

153. Josef Müller-Brockmann. Poster for a musical concert; Zurich, January 1955.

154. Saul Bass. Advertisement from the Great Ideas of Western Man series, Container Corporation of America.

155. Willem Sandberg. Back and front covers for *Experimenta Typographica.* Published by Verlag Galerie der Spiegel; Cologne, 1956.

156. Saul Bass, designer. Film title for *Anatomy of a Murder.* Produced and directed by Otto Preminger, 1959.

157. Photograph; courtesy of the New York Convention and Visitors Bureau.

158. Carlo L. Vivarelli. Cover for *Neue Grafik.* Published by Verlag Otto Walter AG; Olten, Switzerland, 1959.

159. Henry Wolf. Cover for *Harper's Bazaar* magazine, December 1959.

160. Gerald Holton. Symbol for the Campaign for Nuclear Disarmament; Great Britain, c. 1959.

161. Otto Storch. Typography from *McCall's* magazine; July 1959.

162. Karl Gerstner. Poster for the newspaper *National Zeitung;* Zurich, 1960.

163. Herb Lubalin. Advertisement for Sudler and Hennessey Advertising Inc.; New York.

164. George Lois. Advertisement for A. H. Robins Company Incorporated.

165. Photograph; courtesy of the Virginia State Travel Service.

166. Seymour Chwast and Milton Glaser, Push Pin Studios Inc. Poster for the Lincoln Center for the Performing Arts, New York.

167. George Lois. Cover for *Esquire* magazine, October 1966.

168. Seymour Chwast and Milton Glaser, Push Pin Studios Inc. Poster for Filmsense, New York.

169. Photograph; courtesy of the Public Relations Department, City of Montreal, Canada.

170. Designer not known. Symbol widely used in the environmental movement.

171. Photograph; courtesy of the National Aeronautics and Space Administration.

172. Wolfgang Weingart. Experimental interpretation of a poem by Elsbeth Bornoz; Basle, Switzerland.

173. Herb Lubalin. Volume 1, Number 1, of *U&lc.* Published by the International Typeface Corporation, New York.

174. Cook and Shanosky, commissioned by the American Institute of Graphic Arts under contract to the U.S. Department of Transportation. From *Symbol Signs,* a series of thirty-four passenger-oriented symbols for use in transportation facilities.

175. Bruce Blackburn, then of Chermayeff and Geismar Associates. Symbol for the U.S. Bicentennial Commission and stamp for the U.S. Postal Service, first released in 1971.

176. Photograph; courtesy of the French Government Tourist Office.

177. Trademark reproduced by permission of Frederic Ryder Company; Chicago, Illinois.

178. Willi Kuntz. Poster for an exhibition of photographs by Fredrich Cantor, FOTO Gallery, New York.

179. Title film for *All That Jazz,* Twentieth Century-Fox. Director/designer Richard Greenberg, R/Greenberg Associates Inc., New York.

180. MTV logo courtesy of Pat Gorman, Manhattan Design, New York.

181. Photograph; courtesy of the Office of the Mayor, Portland, Oregon.

182. Warren Lehrer, designer. Published by ear/say, Purchase, NY, and Visual Studies Workshop, Rochester, NY.

183. Emperor 8, 10, 15 & 19 designed by Zuzana Licko in 1985. Courtesy of Emigre Inc., Sacramento, CA.

184. David Carson, designer; Art Brewer, photographer. *Beach Culture* next issue page, 1990.

185. Ted Mader and Tom Draper, designers. Ted Mader + Associates, Seattle, WA. Published by Peachpit Press Inc., Berkeley, CA.

186. Template Gothic designed by Barry Deck in 1990. Courtesy of Emigre Inc., Sacramento, CA.

187. Exocet Heavy designed by Jonathan Barnbrook in 1991. Courtesy of Emigre Inc., Sacramento, CA.

188. Fetish typeface designed by Jonathan Hoefler. Copyright 1994, The Hoefler Type Foundry Inc.

189. Meta typeface designed by Erik Spiekerman and released by FontShop, c. 1991.

190. Robert Slimbach and Carol Twombly, designers. Myriad Multiple Master typeface designed by courtesy of Adobe Systems Inc., San Jose, CA.

191. Ron Kellum, designer. Courtesy of Kellum McClain, Inc., New York.

192. James Victore, designer. Racism poster, 1993.

193. Registered logo of Netscape, used by permission of America Online Inc.

194. Matthew Carter, designer. Walker typefaces, 1994.

195. Landor Associates, designers. Courtesy of Xerox/The Document Company.

196. Frank Gehry, architect. Guggenheim Museum in Bilbao, Spain, 1997. Photograph courtesy of the Tourist Office of Spain, New York.

197. Paula Scher and Keith Daigle, designers. Courtesy of Pentagram Design Inc., New York.

198. Robert Slimbach, designer. Adobe Garamond, 1989. Courtesy of Adobe Systems Inc., San Jose, CA.

199. Janice Fishman, Holly Goldsmith, Jim Parkinson, and Sumner Stone, designers. ITC Bodoni, 1994–95.

200. Mrs Eaves Roman designed by Zuzana Licko in 1996. Courtesy of Emigre Inc., Sacramento, CA.

201. Neville Brody, designer. Fuse 98: Beyond Typography poster, 1998.

202. Jennifer Sterling, designer. Fox River Paper Company calendar, 2001.

Chapter Three

3. Designed by Frank Armstrong, Armstrong Design Consultants, New Canaan, CT.

4. Willi Kunz. Poster; 14 x 16 1/2 in.

6. Designed by Frank Armstrong, Armstrong Design Consultants, New Canaan, CT.

30. Designed by Frank Armstrong, Armstrong Design Consultants, New Canaan, CT. Photograph by Sally Anderson-Bruce.

32. Designer: Philip Meggs.

35. Designer: Ben Day.

54. Designed by Frank Armstrong, Armstrong Design Consultants, New Canaan, CT.

62. Designer: Ben Day.

75–77. Designed by Keith Jones.

78. Eugen Gomringer. "ping pong," from *Concrete Poetry: A World View.* Edited by Mary Ellen Solt, Indiana University Press, 1970.

92. Designer: Herb Lubalin; courtesy of *Reader's Digest.*

97. Photograph; courtesy of Olivetti.

102. Gerrit Rietveld. Red/blue chair, 1918. Collection Stedelijk Museum, Amsterdam.

103. Masthead for *eye, The International Review of Graphic Design.*

104. Berkey Belser, designer.

105. Jean Beniot-Lévy, designer.

106. J. Abbott Miller, James Hicks, Paul Carlos, and Scott Davendorf, designers.

107. John Stratiou, designer.

108. John Malinoski, designer.

109. Rob Carter, designer

110. Mirko Ilic, designer.

Chapter Four

23. Bradbury Thompson, designer.

30. Rob Carter, designer.

32–35. Matt Woolman, designer.

36. Matthew Carter, designer. Copyright Microsoft.

37. Matthew Carter, photographer.

38. Emperor 8, 10, 15 & 19 designed by Zuzana Licko in 1985. Courtesy of Emigre Inc., Sacramento, CA.

39. Lois Kim, designer.

Chapter Five

4, 5, and 6. Photographs; courtesy of Mergenthaler Linotype Company.

9. George Nan, photographer.

18. Courtesy of Autologic Inc., Newbury Park, CA.

26. Photograph; courtesy of Mergenthaler Linotype Company.

34. Microphotographs courtesy of Mike Cody, Virginia Commonwealth University, Richmond, VA.

Chapter Seven

1–7. Courtesy of Jean Beniot-Lévy, designer.

8–11. Courtesy of United States National Park Service.

13–20. Courtesy of *Interiors* magazine.

21–25. Courtesy of Richard Greenberg, designer.

26–38. Courtesy of Sussman/Prejza, designers.

39–50. Courtesy of Meta Design/San Francisco.

51–60. Courtesy of Maureen Kringen, Kringenmedia, Sebastopol, CA.

61–69. Courtesy of Frankfurt, Gips, Balkind, New York.

Chapter Eight

5. From *American Advertising Posters of the Nineteenth Century* by Mary Black; courtesy of Dover Publications Inc., New York.

Sources for specimen quotations

Pages i, 180–185, 212–217, 224–225, 232–233, and 240–241. From *The Book Beautiful* by Thomas James Cobden-Sanderson. Hammersmith: Hammersmith Publishing Society, 1902.

Pages 111, 252–255. From *The Alphabet and Elements of Lettering* by Frederic W. Goudy, courtesy of Dover Publications Inc., New York.

Type Specimen Index

Printing:	R.R. Donnelley and Sons, Roanoke, Virginia
Binding:	R.R. Donnelley and Sons, Roanoke, Virginia
Cover printing:	Brady Palmer Printing Co., Carmel, New York
Typography:	9/11 Univers 55 text with 7/11 Univers 55 captions and 9/11 Univers 65 headings
Design:	First edition: Rob Carter, Stephen Chovanec, Ben Day, and Philip Meggs; Second edition: Rob Carter and Philip Meggs; Third edition: Rob Carter, Philip Meggs, and Sandra Wheeler
Design Assistance:	First edition: Tina Brubaker Chovanec, Justin Deister, John Demao, Akira Ouchi, Tim Priddy, Anne Riker, Joel Sadagursky, and Jennifer Mugford Weiland; Second edition: Linda Johnson, Jeff Price, and Brenda Zaczek
Photography and digital imaging:	First and second edition: George Nan; Third edition: Rob Carter, Philip Meggs, George Nan, North Market Street Graphics, and Sandra Wheeler

The authors wish to thank the following people for their contributions to this book. At John Wiley and Sons, Architecture and Design Editor Margaret Cummins, Senior Managing Editor Diana Cisek, Associate Managing Editor David Sassian, and Manufacturing Manager Tom Hyland guided this book through the editorial and production phases. Libby Phillips Meggs contributed ongoing consultation and advice. Jerry Bates, Margaret Bates, Tina Brubaker Chovanec, Diana Lively, and Harriet Turner have provided logistical support. At Virginia Commonwealth University, John Demao and Dr. Richard Toscan offered encouragement.